Politics from Anarchy to Democracy

Rational Choice in Political Science

Edited by IRWIN L. MORRIS,

JOE A. OPPENHEIMER, *and*

KAROL EDWARD SOLTAN

Stanford University Press

Stanford, California

2004

Stanford University Press
Stanford, California
www.sup.org

Library of Congress Cataloging-in-Publication Data

Politics from anarchy to democracy : rational choice in political science /
edited by Irwin L. Morris, Joe A. Oppenheimer, and Karol Edward Soltan.
    p. cm.
    Includes bibliographical references and index.
    ISBN 0-8047-4583-8 (alk. paper)—ISBN 0-8047-4584-6 (pbk : alk. paper)
    1. Political science—Methodology.   2. Political science—Decision mak-
ing.   3. Rational choice theory.   I. Morris, Irwin L. (Irwin Lester), 1967–
II. Oppenheimer, Joe A.   III. Soltan, Karol Edward, 1950–
JA71.P642 2004
320'.01'156—dc22   2003023240

Printed in the United States of America on acid-free, archival-quality
paper.

Original printing 2004

Last figure below indicates year of this printing:

13   12   11   10   09   08   07   06   05   04

Designed and typeset at Stanford University Press in 10.5/12 Bembo.

Contents

Figures

Tables

Preface

EDITED VOLUMES are obviously collective endeavors. At the very least, you have an editor and several authors. In our case, there are three editors (who also wrote chapters) and a dozen authors. For their participation in this volume—and the lecture series that preceded it—we want to thank all of the contributors. Clearly, this volume would not exist without them. We also want to thank several organizations that played an important and very supportive role in the development of this volume: the Collective Choice Center, the Department of Government and Politics, and the College of Behavioral and Social Sciences, all at the University of Maryland. Finally, we would like to thank a number of our colleagues who were particularly supportive during the lecture series out of which this volume grew and during the development and production of the volume itself: David Lalman, Mark Lichbach, Peter Coughlin, Thomas Schelling, and John Wallis.

1

Rational Choice and Politics

Introduction

People have been analyzing politics and political institutions for a long time, at least since the time of the ancient Greeks. The prominence of politics in human history is certainly a partial cause of its fascination. Aristotle tried to understand the implications of governmental type and form for the lives of citizens. Other questions have similar classical roots because our political institutions have set the parameters for our social lives, and they have done so since ancient times. They determine much of our freedoms, our prohibitions, our obligations, and our privileges. In sum, politics plays and has always played a large part in determining who we are or who we can be. It should come as no surprise then that politics has occupied our intellects for well over two thousand years.

And many of the central questions that interested the earliest political scientists still remain on our agendas. We still wonder about the origins of governments, their proper scope and authority, and their conditions for stability. Although we continue to grapple with some of these age-old questions, we are fortunate to live and work in a time when new and powerful tools are being developed to explore these fundamental questions. These intellectual tools include a set which has come to be broadly characterized as "rational choice theory." This body of theory provides new leverage for identifying answers to age-old questions, answers that can be tested and corrected.[1] Although rational choice theory has a long lineage—going back at least as far as Thomas Hobbes—it has undergone a transformation in the past few decades, and its promise and potential as a tool for understanding politics has become clearer to many in the discipline.

With this volume, we illustrate this promise and potential, and we provide examples of some of the very best and most interesting current work in the rational choice research program. The essays have been written in a fashion that requires little prior knowledge of the theory or its methods; as such, the volume is self-contained. The essays represent several research frontiers but may also serve as an introduction that may motivate the reader to further investigate rational choice theory by fostering an appreciation of the power of the theory among those interested in a rigorous analytical study of politics.

But the volume also has a substantive bent. It is a book concerning foundational political issues: What is the state and what should it do? Where did it come from? How should the state be structured? The essays provide an intellectual bridge between the basic principles of rational choice theory and their current applications to these central questions of politics.

To highlight the way rational choice theory addresses traditionally important topics, we have divided the volume into an introduction and three substantive sections. The chapters in each section focus on particular aspects of three specific fundamental questions:

1. Why do humans establish governments?
2. How can we design better political institutions?
3. What is needed to establish democracy?

And the essays do not stop at asking the questions; they formulate testable answers using rational choice theory. For example, Chapters 2 and 5 grapple with how social trust can be established "to stabilize valued institutions." Chapters 3 and 4 address the question "what is the proper role of the state and what are its alternatives?" Chapter 7 analyzes "what it takes to establish a democracy," as well as what can be expected from it once it is established. Chapter 6 identifies how to design institutions so that the information they give out will be trusted, while Chapter 8 considers the properties that can lead to an independent judiciary. These are the questions that occupy the chapters to come. But we have gotten ahead of ourselves. We have already referred to rational choice theory several times, but we have yet to properly introduce it.

Although there are numerous formulations of the concept of "rational choice," for the purposes at hand, individuals are said to make "rational choices" when they make a decision or choose a strategy instrumentally so as to achieve some value. Traditionally the definition has been that rational choice is choice that maximizes the attainment of the self-determined value. (This has also been known as "optimizing" behavior.) However, certain more modern theoretical formulations (especially those related to evolutionary game theory, as in the chapter by Bendor and Swistak in this volume, but also see Simon 1986 and Bendor 1995) do not restrict rational choice to optimizing behavior. In these cases, making a decision that generates a predetermined level of a certain value—though not necessarily the maximum level of that value—also fits under the rubric of rational choice. In contrast to optimizing, this type of behavior is often referred to as "satisficing" (Simon 1986).

Regardless of the specific definition chosen for rational choice, rational choice theories are designed to explain individuals' choices using their values and the environment in which they must make their choices. These models have elements in common: decision makers with specifiable alternatives and goals, an institutional context, a relationship (or set of rules) which maps the choices into outcomes, and some criteria (e.g., Paretian optimality as described below) by which we can evaluate performance of the institution. In the models, the environment therefore consists mainly of the other individuals in the situation and the social institutions that determine each of the individuals' rights, endowments, and powers. In the jargon of these theories, we say that the outcome resulting from the situation depends upon the set of feasible outcomes, individuals' preferences, and the rules of the institutions. The institutions determine both the acts available to the individuals and the consequences that result from any pattern of acts taken by them. In sum, the acts of the individuals, and hence the outcomes which arise from these acts, depend upon both the choices of the individuals and the institutions which define the processes.

Analyzing what to expect from individuals in different contexts tells us neither which change is desirable nor which is not. To do that, one needs values. For example, we need content for the evaluative words *better* and *optimal*. In any case, these types of problems, relating individual decisions to collective decisions and outcomes for a group, are at the heart of both politics and institutional design. How our institutions relate these individual decisions to group choices determines the extent to which we are able to achieve both our own individual and collective goals. Given the centrality of the relation between the individual and the group to politics, political scientists need to understand the effect of the institutions in the translation of individual behaviors (say, votes) into social outcomes (say, choice of political leaders). As will be clear, rational choice theory is well suited for analyzing these interrelated phenomena.

In this essay, our main objective is to present applications and expansions of the central findings of the theory in accessible and nontechnical ways. In doing this, we hope to introduce enough of the basic tools of the theory for the unschooled reader to follow the arguments that come later. Hence, although we do not attempt to provide a textbooklike presentation of the "basics" of rational choice theory, we do present a somewhat more intuitive pedagogical introduction. Our intended audience is students and professional scholars with an interest in politics and public policy and a curiosity regarding the applicability of rational choice to their own interests. We do not presume prior knowledge of rational choice theory. Of course, in such an introduction we must also introduce and explain a variety of rational choice concepts and terms, but that is not our main objective.

CLASSIC ILLUSTRATION I: TWO-PERSON AND N-PERSON PRISONERS' DILEMMAS

Suppose you and a partner have just robbed a bank. While you had time to hide the money stolen from the vault, you and your partner were unsuccessful in your efforts to evade the police. Once caught, you were immediately separated. You are now in the interrogation room. You assume that your friend is in some other interrogation room somewhere in the police station, but you have no way of knowing for sure. The detective who has been questioning you has just returned with a mug of coffee, and as he gets comfortable, he details your situation. You can either admit to the crime or not, but the penalty you receive if you confess (or not) depends upon the choice made by your partner (who is given exactly the same choice). If you both confess, you both receive ten years in jail. If neither you nor your partner confesses, you both receive three years in jail (some circumstantial evidence links both you and your partner to the crime). If either you or your partner confesses and the other keeps silent, the silent partner receives twenty years in jail (you stole a lot of money), and the confessor goes free. What do you do?

Thus begins the standard motivation of the prisoners' dilemma game. The game is but one simple model in a complex theory of how an individual goes about calculating what to do when achieving goals requires taking into account the behavior of others. Here is another depiction of the same sort of model, a prisoners' dilemma game, but this time with a larger number of actors.

You are a member of Congress and must decide whether to request federal funding for a local public works project (a levee for a river in your district, for example). You know that the project is expensive and that the local benefit is significantly less than its overall cost (the river rarely floods), but it would be popular with your constituents (who would bear only a tiny portion—$1/435$th—of the cost but would enjoy the entire benefit). You worry that many of your colleagues want to make similar requests. And your next electoral opponent certainly won't let your constituents forget about the projects their tax dollars funded in other places and the opportunity you wasted if they don't get their levee. What do you do? Are you fiscally responsible or politically savvy?

In both of these scenarios, you face a choice, and that choice has serious consequences that are a function of the choices made by one or more other

TABLE 1.1

A Two-Person Prisoners' Dilemma Game

	Your partner doesn't confess.	Your partner confesses.
You don't confess.	-3, -3	-20, 0
You confess.	0, -20	-10, -10

NOTE: The first number in each box represents the penalty (years in prison) to you, and the second to your partner.

people. In the first scenario, the classic prisoners' dilemma, your freedom is at stake. In the second, an explicitly political scenario that occurs all too frequently, your career is at stake. Given the circumstances, you want to make the best choice. The question, of course, is, *what is the best choice?* And the answer is, it depends on how your choice aggregates with those of others to generate an outcome.

As you can see from Table 1.1, in the first situation, regardless of your partner's choice, you are better off if you confess.[2] That is, confessing *always* yields a better outcome; one says that confessing *dominates* the alternative choices or strategies.[3] This is so even though the most obvious best response for both of you *collectively* is to keep silent. Collectively, total jail time is minimized if both players keep their mouths shut. Unfortunately, *individually*, for *both* parties, the best response is to confess. Collectively, of course, this behavior on both your parts produces a suboptimal outcome (you would both get ten-year sentences) and you could have both done better (three-year sentences).

The same dynamic plays out in the legislative pork barrel scenario. The collectively optimal choice is for no one to receive funding for a project in which the overall costs exceed the overall benefits (see Table 1.2). But in the current scenario, the group is not deciding whether to disallow all such inefficient projects. Rather, the group is deciding upon one more or one less project. If any individual legislator chooses not to request a pork barrel project for her district, that legislator receives nothing for her district *and* her district pays its share of the costs of *all* of the other pork barrel projects received by other districts—clearly a politically inferior outcome. In both cases, the individual has a dominant strategy. Further, individually optimal behavior generates a collectively suboptimal outcome. (See the extended discussion of optimality and suboptimality below.)

Given the structure of both of these situations, optimizing behavior induces worse outcomes than the participants would want. And better outcomes are clearly obtainable. Naturally, this suggests the (policy) question

TABLE 1.2

Voting for a Public Works Bill: An n-Person Prisoners' Dilemma Game

	Each of the 434 others requests a project.	None of the 434 others requests a project.
You don't request a project.	$0 - 434C_i/435 < 0$	0
You request a project.	$B_i - 435C_i/435 < 0$	$B_i - C_i/435 > 0$

NOTE : In each table cell, the number represents the net benefit to you (benefit minus cost).
The benefit to District i of a project in the district $= B_i$.
The benefit to District i of a project in any other district $= 0$.
The cost of each project $= C$.
The cost of each project to any one district, i: $C_i = C/435$.
$C > B > C/435$.

"How can we obtain the better outcomes?" For example, in the first scenario, what if you and your partner were both members of a criminal syndicate, a syndicate that had a known policy of severely punishing confessors (in or out of prison)? Would knowing this lead you to make a different choice? If you faced a severe punishment for ratting on your accomplice—death, let's say—then might that not so increase the costs associated with ratting that you would keep your mouth shut regardless of the deal offered by the authorities? If your partner had a similar understanding of the situation, neither of you would rat on the other, and both of you would receive the lighter prison sentences.

In the pork barrel case, would you make a different choice about your district's project if you knew it would be difficult (if not impossible) for other legislators to win projects for their districts (because of some formal institutional constraint or rule)? In those altered situations, the incentives shift, and with them, so do the preferences, so you might just change your mind. If others find it difficult to win pork barrel projects for their districts, you might find efforts to win a pork barrel project for your own district equally unprofitable. Following the logic of the same theory permits one both to analyze behavior within the context of alternative hypothetical institutions and to think about changing the institutions to alter the outcomes.

CLASSIC ILLUSTRATION 2: THE ROLE OF THE STATE

What ought to be the role of the state in the life of the citizen? Many an argument has hinged on this issue. In the seventeenth century, Thomas Hobbes wrestled with the question of the necessity of the state. He saw coercive institutions as requisite for the development of any of the creature comforts of civilization; indeed, he argued that coercive institutions were a necessary precursor to civilization itself. With the advent of game theory and the extension of economic reasoning to the problems of collective action, the picture has clarified. Rather than a single monochromatic story, as Hobbes told it, we now have a multiplicity of possibilities of cooperation based on incentive structures other than mere coercion.[4] In a simple one-shot prisoners' dilemma game, as in Table 1.1 or 1.2, coercive solutions seem quite natural. But, as we point out below, there are numerous other possibilities to support human cooperation.

And beyond the basic structure of the state lie other questions. What should be its responsibilities and functions? Socialists and capitalists have argued the point for centuries. How are we to judge the answers? Can we even discern what are the implications and consequences of the different conceptions of the state's proper role? Certainly, much has been learned in economics of the power of markets: how, under a certain set of assumptions, they produce efficient collective outcomes by giving individuals with diverse values a set of incentives to guide their own highly decentralized choices.[5]

Unfortunately, the set of assumptions required to generate efficient outcomes in market settings is quite restrictive. In many real-world settings, markets fail to satisfy the admittedly restrictive assumptions that the efficient market outcomes demand. In some cases competition is imperfect. In others, goods are not private or there is no informational symmetry between buyer and seller. The traditional prescription for market failures was state intervention. But since at least the early 1960s, a school of thought within the rational choice tradition commonly referred to as public choice theory has critiqued state-oriented responses to market failures. For example, Ronald Coase (1960) argued that the solution to market failures did not require political intervention. Other students of public choice—James Buchanan and Gordon Tullock in particular—argued that state intervention designed to prevent market failures might actually generate worse outcomes than those associated with the original market failure. In response to this literature, game theorists Varouj A. Aivazian and Jeffrey Lawrence Callen (1981; Aivazian, Callen, and Lipnowski 1987) showed that under a set of conditions it is impossible to arrive at an adequate solution without governmental intervention. More specifically, they demonstrated that there were conditions under which the parties to "market failure" could not be expected to negotiate a stable, socially optimal agreement among themselves. At about the same time, Thomas Schwartz (1981) made similar discoveries regarding the role of state-assured property rights to stabilize market transactions.[6] As our understanding of organizations other than markets developed, the comparative evaluation of the relative costs and benefits of the two sorts of institutional failures (market and governmental) could be analyzed and compared. Rational choice theory had provided a set of conceptual tools to make just these sorts of crucial comparative evaluations.

Rational choice theory has improved our understanding of the relationship between institutional designs and the implications they generate. We can now hope to further improve our design of institutions to reconcile individual behaviors with group needs without requiring oppressively strong governments or massive and continual intervention. Thus, we may be on the cusp of being able to design the overall and specific institutional structure of government so as to help ensure that it can deliver the social benefits citizens might choose.

We offer these classic illustrations to suggest the theoretical power of the rational choice perspective. In short, rational choice theory has important things to say about the fundamental questions that fascinate political scientists. Let us now consider, in somewhat more detail, the foundations—or building blocks, if you will—of rational choice theory itself.

Rational Choice Theory: Its Premises and Methods

There are at least three major aspects to the study and understanding of the theory illustrated above. First, we must understand the underbelly of choice, its structure, motivation, or *psychology*. Second, we must come to understand the aggregation problem, how the choices of many individuals relate to what becomes understood as a group choice. Both the structure of choice and the aggregation problem are mediated by *social institutions*. Finally, there is a need for *performance criteria*, measuring rods by which we can decide whether one choice or another might be more advantageous.

Much of the leverage in social science theory in understanding these aspects of politics has come from the applications of particular assumptions about human behavior to particular social institutions. Rational choice theory is a conglomeration of "models of choice" made up of a family of psychological premises applied to behavior in a variety of institutions. The models are put together by a methodology of logical inference from a set of premises. The premises stem from the "rational choice theory" and a stylized approach to the description of institutions, one that synergistically weaves a deductive story from the psychological premises. The result has been a family of models with wide acceptance in economics and a broad influence and role in the other social sciences, including political science. They consist of three elements: a psychology, a style of institutional description, and a method of careful logic.

THE PSYCHOLOGICAL PREMISES OF RATIONAL CHOICE THEORY

Rational choice is choice with purpose, goal seeking, even maximizing. As such, it presumes goals and is not itself an argument about how goals are identified, nor how the underlying values are acquired. Rather, it allows the theorist to begin analysis assuming a set of goals. It follows, immediately, that rational choice theory is about choosers. This often (but not necessarily) gives it an *individualistic* focus and starting point.[7]

Theorists conjecture that the behavior of groups, or institutions, may best be understood as the outcome of the aggregation of individual decisions. Hence, generally one must analyze the behavior of the constituting decision makers and their aggregation. This does not mean, however, that group memberships and group interactions are unimportant determinants of human behavior. It simply means that the making of decisions is a starting point.

The trick (or difficulty, depending upon your perspective) is the development of arguments that show how characteristics of group behavior can be understood to stem from individualistic premises. These arguments usually take the form of combining the psychology of the individuals and their endowments (or resources) with the structure of the institutions within which the decisions are made. This structure is specified as that which determines the rights and powers of individuals—more specifically, the acts available to players and the consequences which result from any pattern of acts taken by the set of players.[8] Thus the social choice from among the feasible alternatives depends upon both the choices of the individuals and the institutions which define the process. In the jargon of game theory, the outcome results from the set of feasible outcomes, the individuals' preferences, and the rules of the situation (see Plott 1978, 207).

Psychological Elements

As indicated above, rational choice theory has to do with goal seeking, purposive behavior. The traditional starting point is the assumption that the actors have well-defined, stable, and ordered preferences. The idea is that all decision makers can make sensible decisions; they can make the necessary comparisons between the alternatives they face, and can and will choose the best available alternative. In facing choices, this leads them to have identifiable *preferences* among the alternatives they face. The theory is built upon two substantial assumptions that permit the theorist to assume that the individuals' choices are consistent with these preferences. This permits the theory to be used to generate interesting results.

The first assumption is simply that the individual can always make sensible judgments between alternatives. Substantively this means that someone (call her Iris, whom we might note with the subscript i) can choose which of any two alternatives is preferable or whether they are equally attractive. Thus, in comparing x and y, Iris can say whether she prefers x to y (written as xP_iy) or y to x (yP_ix) or whether they are equally good and she is indifferent (xI_iy). This assumption, that all items are comparable, is known as *completeness*. It is technically coupled with the notion that something is equally good as itself, which is known as *reflexivity*.

The second assumption is that individuals' preferences show consistency across pairs. This allows the decision maker to order alternatives from "best to worst" and permits a sensible choice of "best" alternatives. To ensure this, it is assumed that the preferences are *transitive*. Transitivity with respect to preference means that if x is preferred to (or as good as) y, and y is preferred to (or as good as) z, then x is preferred to (or as good as) z. This can be written as follows: if xP_iy and yP_iz, then xP_iz. Taken together with reflexivity, this means that Iris's preferences generate an "ordering" of her options such that she can say which is best, or "at the top," which is worst, or "at the bottom," and which is to be placed at each position in between.

Combine this with the notion that Iris chooses on the basis of her preferences, and these assumptions imply that when given the chance to choose, she is going to choose the best available option, or maximize. Mix a little substance with these formalities (that the individual has some private interests or values which she wants to achieve) and we have a sufficient brew to create the menu of models developed above, plus many others, including those in the chapters that follow.

Some Criticisms

The perspective of rational choice has not been without serious detractors. Over the last twenty-five years or so, psychologists have developed a number of tests and critiques of this model.[9] Most of these results have focused on two sorts of limitations of the rational choice theories. First, critics of rational choice theory have questioned the stability of the values or goals held by individuals in their making of choices. Goals of individuals were found to be a function of the framing of the decision, rather than independent of framing, as the theory required. Second, individuals were discovered to have severe limitations in their ability to handle probability calculations in a consistent manner.

These empirical questions certainly have come to define the deep research frontiers of rational choice modeling. Indeed, rational choice theorists themselves are the researchers who have been among the most involved in trying to understand the shifting foundations of their theories. But one can make too much of such threats. Similar research problems sit in every scientific discipline. As Karl Popper (1959, 111) has said:

The empirical basis of objective science has thus nothing "absolute" about it. Science does not rest upon rock-bottom. The bold structure of its theories rises, as it were, above a swamp. It is like a building erected on piles. The piles are driven down from above into the swamp, but not down to any natural or "given" base; and when we cease our attempts to drive our piles into a deeper layer, it is not because we have reached firm ground. We simply stop when we are satisfied that they are firm enough to carry the structure, at least for the time being.

The questions raised of the foundations seem not to threaten the edifice itself. Rather, recent developments in evolutionary game theory which show its relations to the more traditional modes of analysis have made the work of rational choice theorists more stable and less dependent upon highly stylized definitions. For example, the results in the evolutionary game theory literature (see Chapter 2) don't require what might be called full rationality. Rather those theories require only a psychology that generates choices that improve one's situation.[10] What then are some of the other characteristics of this edifice? And then, what is the mortar that holds the pieces together?

METHOD

To this point, we have mentioned a few elements that characterize the analysis referred to as rational choice theory. We began by developing, in the preceding section, the psychological premises. But we will need more. We must furnish other necessary elements such as a template to sketch institutions so as to generate "analytic results" and some way of incorporating our need for performance criteria to judge the outcomes of institutions and processes. We will focus on these concerns below. Now we turn to consider the characteristic "method" of analysis associated with the theory. Of course, we implicitly gave examples of the method of analysis when we gave our prisoners' dilemma examples, but here we will sketch out its elements in a bit more detail.

Knowledge Claims

Let us take a step back from our exercise for a moment. The theories, and its models, extend our knowledge by making "knowledge claims." But how, precisely, do the models facilitate this? Indeed, what is a "knowledge claim"? And for that matter, what is "knowledge"? To understand knowledge, one ought to juxtapose it against something weaker, say, "belief." One can believe that the world is flat, but it isn't. And how would we deal with someone who says, "I know it is flat!" We might say, "You are wrong," for we do not easily count as knowledge something that is believed but cannot be justified. Knowledge is usually referred to as "justified true belief."[11]

But what in the world is justified true belief? In the fields of science and social science, truth of a statement (i.e., a theory, a conjecture, a belief) is usually understood best in terms of whether the statement corresponds to "reality."[12] This definition of truth permits one a relatively straightforward understanding of the standard testing of hypotheses and models as they occur in our discipline.

A knowledge claim is then merely a "justified" claim or a "justified" conjecture that the world is as described in a particular statement or set of statements. But what does it mean to be "justified"? To justify a statement is to show why it is to be accepted. The strongest form of justification is what we have already alluded to, the careful exercise of logic to show that it can be implied from some other, better-known facts or conjectures. This exercise of logic is to generate a relation between the premises of an argument and its conclusion, a relation of deduction.[13]

What is deduction? Deduction is a method of generating conclusions from premises such that the conclusions are true if the premises are true. Conversely, deduction requires that if the conclusions are false, the premises can't be true. But this assertion is insufficient to fully describe what is going on in a rational choice argument.

Rational Choice Theory and Deductive Modeling

Rational choice theory is equally known for its methods as for its substantive conclusions. The methods are to carefully deduce from the premises of institutional and psychological elements as described above. The bold step is to see that a political phenomenon, such as a legislative struggle, can be covered by, or understood as, a "rational choice system." (See Giere 1984 for a description of this step in the role of scientific understanding.)

This is the radical, inductive leap, one that says, "I think this thing over here actually works like this system that we already know." To show this, one must develop the deductive steps which show that the psychological and institutional premises actually lead to the conclusions one wants to explain (as in the median voter model below). And this requires the careful steps of logic.

So the models exhibit deductive reasoning. And this is often formulated as mathematical reasoning. Why is this? The core assumptions of purposive behavior are often consistent with the properties of maximization (see above). Maximization of a function is a particular mathematical operation, and this has permitted the arguments of rational choice to be developed with mathematical rigor.[14] Mathematics has made it easier for rational choice theory to be developed in a fundamentally deductive fashion. The use of logical and mathematical methods of argument is precisely what makes the models generate easily testable "knowledge claims."

On the other hand, just because the premises *lend themselves to mathematical expression* doesn't mean they require it. Though often presented symbolically, rational choice theory is not *inherently* symbolic or mathematical in character. While rational choice theories are often presented in nonverbal form (either through a series of equations or geometric diagrams), the nature of deduction does not always require the use of such symbols. Rational choice theory can be, and often is, presented verbally. Examples abound— from the realm of normative theory, Hobbes's *Leviathan* is clearly a rational choice theory presented completely in prose. Much more recently, David Mayhew's pathbreaking *The Electoral Connection* is an argument presented verbally (or in prose) based on rational choice.

Whether or not deductive models are highly *mathematized*, their value depends upon the extent to which they illuminate real-world political dynamics. But how are these deductive models to be applied to the world of politics? After all, for most of us, the aim of our study is not to test a theory, but rather to explain real events and the functioning of real institutions. The rational choice models are used to generate results that can be redefined as bold hypotheses which apply the core premises to specific sets of social events or political phenomena. This is done by identifying the relevant actors, the institutional structure and rules of the situation, and the characterized plausible set of individuals' preferences to see if one can develop explanations for the sorts of outcomes as a result of these elements. (An illustration was the legislator's request for an inefficient project for her district given above).

As such, the empirical application of rational choice theory is a difficult combination of deductive and inductive endeavor. One must take general models and apply them to specific situations that have been conjectured (inductively) to conform to the patterns of the theory. Each study not only investigates the particular facts using the model at hand but also becomes a small element in the discussion of the utility and accuracy of the overall theory. An example is a model of a the committee system in our state's legislature. Is it useful? Would its accuracy (or inaccuracy) affect how we judge the theory? To demonstrate how rational choice models are built and then used to develop testable implications, we describe a prominent strain of rational choice theory in the next section—the spatial model perspective.

Modeling Institutions

An institution structures outcomes. Defined as the rules of the game, those which tell us how the behaviors of the individuals aggregate to group outcomes, institutions must be described in a fashion which allows them to be "modeled by the theory," so the theory can be used to help us clarify the underlying process. To identify *how* this is done, we begin with models generating a rational choice analysis of some aspects of democracy, starting with the simplest and moving to more complex ones so that the reader can understand the importance of the details.

SIMPLE DEMOCRATIC MAJORITY VOTING INSTITUTIONS

As an example of a simple democratic majority voting institution, take a simple case of voting in a one-street village. After a damaging fire in a nearby neighborhood, everyone has agreed to install a fire hydrant on the street. Indeed, each person, fearful of the consequences of a bad blaze, would like the fireplug as near as possible to his own address. This permits us to develop what we might call a traditional one-dimensional *spatial* voting model in which it can be shown there is a simple way to predict the outcome of the vote.[15]

Predictions

As in most of these models there will be assumptions regarding preferences and the choice environment (i.e., the rules of decision making and the set of alternatives). The preference assumption generating the analysis is that each voter has an ideal point "along a line" such that the farther the collective choice is from the voter's ideal point, the worse off the voter is.[16] In this case, that implies that the farther the fireplug is from the house, the less happy the voter is about the outcome. The major result of the analysis is that the median voter's position will be the final winner under most implementations of majority rule.[17]

A typical sketch of a proof of what to expect concludes that there is a predicted outcome that will be "in equilibrium" (see below for a discussion of equilibria) that we can identify as follows:

Begin by noting that x_i is the ith individual's ideal point and x_{med} is the median individual's ideal point. The median position, x_{med}, with respect to the set of voter ideal points, $\{x_i\}$, means that the number of points at or to the left, N_L, and at or to the right, N_R, of x_{med} are equal, and both are less than $N/2$.[18] (See Figure 1.1.)

The proof then proceeds as follows:

Consider x_{med}, and some other voter's ideal point, x_j, to the left of x_{med}. Now all ideal points at or to the right of x_{med} are closer to x_{med} than they are to x_j. By definition of x_{med}, there are more points at and to the right of x_{med} than to the left of x_{med}. Therefore more voters would prefer x_{med} than would prefer x_j. Hence, if voters "vote their preferences," they would defeat any $x_j \neq x_{med}$. Note that no majority could form which could *guarantee* itself outcomes better than that of the ideal point of the median voter. Hence, once x_{med} was reached, it would be "in equilibrium."

Performance

How well does such a system perform? One answer stems from the geometry of the situation. The result in the above example is not in some

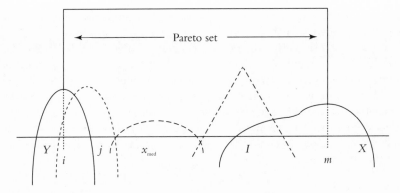

FIGURE 1.1 Simple majority rule in one dimension

"outlying" area of the street, but rather in the neighborhood of the people. Thus, in some very rough sense, the system "hits the target." Further, it also delivers the hydrant not to the *edge* of the neighborhood, but in front of the median location: toward a central location. Of course, this is not the same as conforming with some other desirable characteristic—such as minimizing the average distance from the hydrant to the homes (that would require placement at the geographic mean of the ideal points). Nevertheless, by choosing a median outcome, this system of choice does move the group decision in the direction of moderation.

Another answer would be to see if the system satisfies a performance criterion. In this case we will consider whether it satisfies the notion of optimality. The traditional notion of optimality is called Pareto optimality, after Vilfredo Pareto. Pareto, an Italian economist of the late nineteenth and early twentieth centuries, invented the concept. What is Pareto optimality? It is a condition of a situation that is desirable, and it is best to introduce it by first describing its failure. When a situation is *not* optimal, or is *suboptimal*, at least some of the individuals could be made better off without hurting anyone. That means if a situation is optimal, to make someone still better off will require redistribution; some in the group must be hurt. The Pareto set would be the set of situations that are Pareto optimal. Again, look at Figure 1.1. Consider two points, X and Y, which are not part of the Pareto set. To show this, we need to show that everyone can agree to move from either of them to some point between i and m. Then we would need to show that all the points between i and m are in the Pareto set.

The proof of this is straightforward. Consider first the argument that Y is not Paretian. Note that Y is to the left of the leftmost house on the street, that of individual i. Imagine that someone suggests another point for the hydrant, call it Z, between Y and i. This would mean that everyone in the group would find Z closer to their house, and hence better, than Y. They would therefore prefer Z to Y, and thus Y is not in the Pareto set.

We must still show that the points between i and m are in the Pareto set. Consider a k somewhere between i and m. Does there exist some other point, call it q, which everyone would prefer? Consider a q slightly to the left of k. Then those at k or to the right of k prefer k to q. And what if q is to the right of k? Then those at or to the left of k prefer k.

So majority rule, when all voters have their best points along a single line, and all prefer being closer to their best points than farther, delivers Paretian, or optimal, results.

Extensions

There are numerous complex models constructed much like tinker toy structures by putting together the elements of the above simple institutional structure. To illustrate, imagine a legislature using a simple majority rule and considering a change of a law. The relevant parameters might be the placement of the status quo, the distribution of the preferences of the legislators, and some other structural issues. We would need to know the mechanisms of bill writing in the legislature. Let us assume that specialized committees undertake the initial task of writing the proposed bill and that such a committee reaches its decisions by majority rule. Further, assume that the voters' loss of value is symmetric around their ideal preference points.

We can now use the above spatial voting model to see if there is an equilibrium outcome and, if so, use it to predict the outcome. As an example, consider the committee's strategy. In Figure 1.2, the committee members' preferences (shown by the short line near the top of the diagram) are distributed to the right of both the preference of the legislature's median member (marked as L_{med}) and the status quo (see the bottom line). Note that normally we might predict that the median voter on the committee (C_{med}) would win the day, and that would be the bill reported out of the committee. But C_{med} is further from the median in the legislature than is the status quo. And the committee's members obviously would like to move to the right of the status quo as far as possible, certainly at least to the median voter of the legislature. But an outcome as far to the right as C_{med} will not beat the status quo. For all at and to the left of the L_{med} would find themselves closer to the status quo than to C_{med}. So those voters, if faced with the status quo and C_{med}, will vote for the status quo. So the committee can agree to put forward a bill that appeals to the majority without mirroring its own median. To do this, committee members will select a proposal that is almost as far to the right from the median as the status quo is to the left of it. This would mean that all those at the median and those to the right of the median would find themselves closer to the proposal than they are to the status

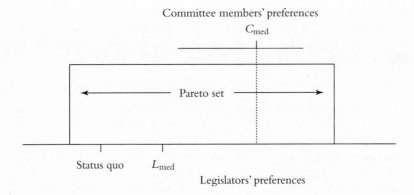

FIGURE 1.2 Modeling a legislative committee's strategy for writing a bill

quo. Hence, they would prefer it to the status quo. And they constitute a majority. So that is the best that the median voter on the committee can achieve.

Let us consider the performance of such a system. Obviously, the status quo can end up being altered, but not in a manner so simple, and intuitively "benign" as we found above. Here the result is not necessarily a significantly better outcome than the status quo, but rather a move that could be considered a manipulation of the system for the special interests represented on the committee.

Similar models are used to explain why governmental bureaus may be overfunded, how school boards negotiate for bond issues, and the like (see Eavey and Miller 1984; as well as Romer and Rosenthal 1978). Many other models of similar multistage negotiations and votes (often discussed as "structure-induced equilibria," a phrase introduced by Kenneth Shepsle and Barry Weingast [1981]) have been developed to explain other phenomena which reflect the above reasoning. Multiple institutions can generate equilibria, much as the legislature and its committee structure can. Numerous models have been developed to analyze the nature of American national legislative and presidential structures (for a particularly good example, see Miller and Hammond 1987, 1990), as well as that of other institutions such as the Federal Reserve Bank (see Morris 2000).

And what happens when there is more than one dimension along which all ideal points regarding the policy outcomes can be located? We will go into such extensions of the analysis of majority rule in the next section. But note that none of the nice properties which we have identified (the existence of, and central tendency for, the location of the equilibrium, Paretian outcomes) carry over to this more general case. That is, moving from the single dimension to a more generalized, or less restricted, conception of allowable preferences leaves us with very difficult normative problems, and the analytic literature of these cases is extraordinarily rich. The interested reader might well seek a more elaborate discussion in a good textbook.[19]

MORE COMPLEX POLITICAL SITUATIONS AND INSTITUTIONS

Models of problems in real democracies, of course, often cannot be restricted to "single issues" which have the characteristic that each voter has an ideal preference point along a line and preferences which fall off as the distances from the ideal increase. We have many options to describe what happens when we depart from the simple model above. Easiest in exposition, probably, is the expansion of the model to multiple dimensions. Institutions must still aggregate the decisions of many voters across many issues. The few problems that we identify here, looking at a simple expansion from one to two dimensions, will help us understand many of the other difficulties which are endemic to democratic decision making.

To help in the analysis, consider Figure 1.3. There we show the decision problem facing three individuals (A, B, and C) who are to decide a two-dimensional issue. Such an issue, to draw a parallel with the simpler case, might be where to put commonly held fire-fighting equipment on a prairie to protect each of the voters' homes. We might consider an outcome inside and toward the center of the triangle (say at Y) as a useful benchmark, a good compromise. As before, assume that all voters wish the equipment to be as close as possible to their own house. That would mean that each individual would prefer (and vote for) points closer to her corner of the triangle than Y.

The analysis follows directly from the observation that in this case each individual would prefer to Y any point inside that circle which is centered at their house and which has Y as a point on its edge (these circles are shaded in Figure 3.1). What can we predict to be the outcome of a simple majority rule decision? Note the circles drawn in Figure 1.3, each going through Y, with a center at the "ideal point" of each of the individuals. We can see that the circles intersect to make three "lenses" which stretch from Y to a point outside of each of the three sides of the triangle (X is an example of such a point). Take, as an example, any point inside the lens XY. Both A and C would vote for such an alternative, as it is closer to both of their houses. In other words, movement from Y to a point in any one of those lenses permits *a majority* (two) of the voters to be better off. Thus, Y is not a stable outcome. For at Y any of three two-person coalitions can form to improve the position of their coalition members. And an analysis shows that there is *no* point that can't be improved upon for a majority. Indeed, majorities can even swing the choice outside the triangle![20]

And what happens when we analyze this using our previously discussed

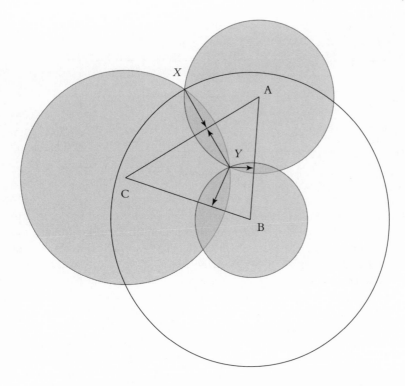

FIGURE 1.3 Majority rule when preferences are single-peaked in two dimensions

notion of optimality? Examination of the problem will lead you to see that if we begin outside the triangle, we can find points which all can agree to as an improvement. Thus, from X, A and C would prefer movement inside the lens going from X back toward Y, and B would also.[21] Once in, or on, the triangle, no further movement improves the position for all three individuals. So the triangle is the Pareto set, and the set of points outside is suboptimal. But no point in the triangle is in equilibrium.

Similar discouragement is found if we seek stability of majoritarian decisions on such questions as redistributive policies, vote trading, and more generally for virtually all democratic procedures when analyzed from this perspective.[22] But we can still say a number of things beyond the discussion of structure-induced equilibria.

In much of the analysis, a specific form of equilibrium will be considered. It is a notion of equilibrium that arises "endogenously" from the situation itself. The idea is that the actors' choices are in equilibrium with each other when no single party has an incentive to change his choice, given the

TABLE 1.3

A Chicken Game

	Player B swerves.	Player B continues head-on.
Player A swerves.	0, 0	*-5, 10*
Player A continues head-on.	*10, -5*	-100, -100

NOTE: The Nash equilibria are indicated in *italic*.

choices of the others. In a simple two-person interaction, or game, as in the simple case of the prisoners' dilemma sketched in this introduction, the simplest solution concept—the *Nash equilibrium*—is reached when neither player has an incentive to unilaterally deviate from the strategy she has played. Hence, when a Nash equilibrium is reached, neither player changes her strategy, and the outcome is stable. Reexamining Table 1.1 should satisfy the reader that this is a quality implied by all players choosing their dominant strategies as in the prisoners' dilemma. But it turns out that all games, regardless of whether they have dominant strategies, have Nash equilibria. So, for example, consider the simple "chicken" game depicted in Table 1.3. In this game neither player has a dominant strategy, and yet there are two Nash equilibria.

Of course, the fact that no one actor has a unilateral incentive to change her choice, does not mean that the equilibrium might not be upset. So, for example, players could come together in groups and reach an understanding as to what might be a better "joint" or "cooperative" strategy. But if the understanding was to adopt an outcome that was not a Nash equilibrium, then some incentive might be required to stabilize the agreement. Such an incentive required to make the agreement binding often requires some mechanism or institution that may not be an inherent part of the situation. In the simple case of the prisoners' dilemma, this was illustrated by the notion of a criminal syndicate that coerces the preferred outcome.

The Nash equilibrium is a very useful solution concept, especially when all the elements that may be needed to support a cooperative outcome are not available. But Nash has some limitations. The most severe limitation, for our purposes, is its application to some situations that are repeated, or continuous and structured over time. When modeled as games, these situations are usually referred to as "multistage games." In such games, the problem is that some choices that are Nash equilibria are "unreasonable." This is relatively easy to illustrate. For example, consider the chicken game in Table 1.3.

TABLE 1.4

A Chicken Game Over Time

	Player B always swerves.	Player B always continues head-on.	Player B matches Player A's move.	Player B does the opposite of Player A (dominant strategy).
Player A swerves.	0, 0	*-5, 10*	0, 0	-5, 10
Player A continues head-on.	*10, -5*	-100, -100	-100, -100	*10, -5*

NOTE: The Nash equilibria are indicated in *italic*.

There we showed the game as it is normally considered, a simultaneous move game, where the actor doesn't know the choice of her opponent prior to making her own choice.

But what happens if we stretch the game over a bit of history? Now let player A move first, and let us assume that player B observes the play and then chooses her response. We can analyze this new situation quite directly; player A still has the same two possibilities, but player B now has four ways of responding (see Table 1.4). She can choose (1) always to refuse to swerve (clearly not a good idea if her opponent has done likewise), or (2) always to swerve (not the best again because it is too inflexible; what if the row player has swerved?), or (3) to match player A's move (swerve for swerve, head on for head on; this is clearly the worst choice), or (4) to play the opposite of her opponent (her dominant strategy).

Examining the depiction of this in table form, we find that there are an embarrassing number of Nash equilibria—three, rather than just the one associated with the dominant strategy. The two that are associated with the dominated strategies wouldn't normally be reached; player B would play her rational (dominant) strategy. In games of this type, the Nash solution concept fails to identify a unique outcome, which means that the concept will not let us predict a determinate outcome. In this case, we can "explain away some of these Nash points," for they are misleading. To do so we need a different way to analyze the problem of choice structured by time—the use of a "game tree," which depicts the moves of each player, given the choices which have been made to that point in the game. This is referred to as the extensive form of the game. To show how to analyze this, we show the game tree for the chicken game in Figure 1.4.

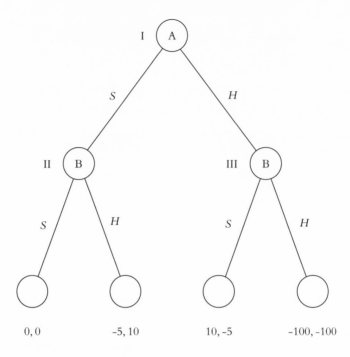

0, 0   –5, 10   10, –5   –100, –100

FIGURE 1.4 Game tree for the game of chicken

In any game tree the following are depicted:

1. Decision points (or moves) of the players (called nodes). The nodes are usually depicted as circles with the label of the player in the circle. One of these is
the (single) starting node; others are the end nodes, one of which would be
reached by some pattern of play. Other end points would require other moves.

2. At each node, the options from which the choice will be selected are depicted as "branches" from the node to successor nodes.

3. Now the whole tree depicts the two-move chicken game. But after the
player A moves, to begin the game, player B finds herself in the tree with part
of the game left. Note that any section of the tree can be thought of as a game
beginning from a node and continuing with all the branches from that point
down the tree. When the players can identify where they are in the tree, such
subsets of the game are referred to as "subgames." Thus, the simple tree has
three subgames, one starting from the top (labeled "I," and the other two starting from each of player B's decision points, labeled "II" and "III").

Putting the game in this form gives us a simple and intuitive form of "solving" the game called *backward induction*.[23] For example, the first player, A,

looks to the *end* of the game, the last choices being made by the last player to choose. Consider Figure 1.4. The first player can ask, what would happen, at the last move, if the last player were on the right-hand branch of the tree, subgame III (i.e., Player A played head on, or *H*)? At this point, player B could choose *H* or *S*. Choosing *H* would lead to a payoff of -100, and *S* would lead to -5. Clearly, player B is better off choosing *S* and hence can be expected to choose *S*. Similar analysis of subgame II would lead A to conclude that A would be better off choosing *H* (gaining 10, rather than nothing) and she can therefore be expected to choose *H*. This being the case, A can now readily predict the outcomes of his two strategies: choosing *H* will lead to B swerving, and A will get 10; his choice of *S* would lead to B going head on and A getting -5. So A chooses *H*.

We are now ready to discuss those three Nash equilibria in the chicken game "stretched" over time. They show up as each understandable in one of the three subgames of the game. To see this, let us consider each of the three subgames separately. Were player B considering how to play the game in subgame II, after player A chooses to swerve, she would find that a strategy of always going head on would be in equilibrium (and equivalent to "opposite" for the subgame she was in). Similarly, were player B considering how to play in subgame III, after player A chooses to move head on, she would find that a strategy of always swerving would be in equilibrium (and equivalent to "opposite" for subgame III). Of course, thinking about the game as a whole, that is, from the point of view of subgame I, the first player might not always swerve (indeed, given the dominant fourth strategy, she won't), and the rational response is to play "opposite." Thus, only the Nash equilibrium associated with the dominant strategy is sensible for the entire game (subgame I). If a Nash equilibrium holds for the entire game, and its implied rules are a Nash equilibrium in each of the subgames, then it is called a *subgame perfect Nash equilibrium*.

It is this last sense of equilibrium that will be important in a number of the chapters in this volume, and the reason is relatively easy to understand. When a game is played over time, players may adopt "threats" to convince their opponents to adopt specific strategies in the future. Consider the above chicken game. Perhaps player A can't be fully committed to the "head on" play with which she seems to open. Perhaps she can be dissuaded by a threat that player B will always continue head on. Indeed, were that threat communicated, and believed, the equilibrium first move would be to swerve. Of course, a careful analysis of the situation by player A could lead her to the belief that such a threat by player B would not be credible. The *subgame perfect equilibrium* (*Nash* is often dropped) would then tell us what to expect upon the rejection of the noncredible threats. Hence, in games of this type an outcome based solely on one player's threat to behave irrationally may satisfy the Nash criteria, but we would consider this an unlikely or unreasonable solution since it could sometimes depend upon blatantly irrational behavior.

To avoid these problems with the Nash equilibrium, analysts often use the more restrictive solution concept—subgame perfect equilibrium. Obviously, although all subgame perfect equilibria are Nash equilibria, the converse is not true, and the concept eliminates those Nash equilibria that are based on threats of irrational behavior. Because of the nature of the situations being analyzed by the authors of some of the chapters in this volume, subgame perfect equilibria play a prominent role. Especially in those situations where there is no institution or outside mechanism to help enable cooperation, analysts try to predict those strategies that can stabilize an agreement. Here we would explore the ways behaviors can "play out" so as to induce the parties to honor an agreement, a notion strongly related to the subgame perfect equilibrium concept. Chapter 5 gives a good exposition of an application of the concept, as does Chapter 7.

A Collective Action Illustration

Perhaps surprisingly, the simple set of assumptions behind rational choice can also generate quite powerful conclusions without any assumptions about institutional contexts. Individuals maximizing their payoffs create problems for the achievement of shared goals among members of groups. This is the famous insight behind what is often called the "logic of collective action" (Olson 1965) and is the problem we illustrated with the pork barrel example above (see page 6). To see this, consider the case of Iris in a group of some size (say ten persons) made up of like-minded individuals. Let them share a costly goal, and assume the "institutional" structure of the group is rudimentary; individuals voluntarily contribute to the obtaining of the goal. Consider then the following simple case.

Let each individual have some endowment of "private" resources. So Iris might start with ten dollars. Consider a case where the goal can be partially achieved, and to the degree that it is, it rebounds in value symmetrically to each member. So, we might say any one dollar spent on the attainment of the goal generates twenty-five cents of value to each individual. Then each individual, say Iris, might note that for her it is not worth her while to invest in the group goal. For every dollar she spends out of her endowment, she loses seventy-five cents (she, like each of the others, gets twenty-five cents' worth of value from the dollar's worth of partial attainment of the group's objective). We can put her situation in perspective by specifying her options more carefully, as depicted in Table 1.5.[24]

In Table 1.5, Iris, as the typical member of the ten-person group, con-

TABLE 1.5

The Value of Donating, Given the Behaviors of Others

Iris's (Typical Person's) Strategy	Number of Others Who Donate					
	9	8	. . .	2	1	0
Contribute.	$11.50	$11.25	. . .	$9.75	$9.50	$9.25
Don't contribute.	$12.25	$12.00	. . .	$10.50	$10.25	$10.00

templates giving one dollar or nothing toward the achievement of the goal. That is, Iris chooses between the two rows of the table. In keeping with our substantive understanding of the premises of rationality theory, Iris will examine her options and choose the one that she prefers. Assuming that the financial calculations properly capture her values, how ought she to choose what to do? Iris can't select the column with which she "is faced." Rather, this is determined by the choices of others. But she can note that regardless of which situation she is faced with (i.e., which column represents the outcome), the second row yields preferred outcomes to the first row (it is seventy-five cents better).

But recall that though each dollar's partial achievement of the group's goal generates only a return of a quarter of a dollar, it does so for every member of the group as they all share the partial achievement of the goal of the group. Thus, each dollar given generates a total benefit of two dollars and fifty cents if we add up the difference it makes for each person (ten persons at twenty-five cents each). In other words, each individual following his own incentives leads to a situation that is not very good, certainly not *optimal*. Specifically, if all follow their incentives, the group could agree *unanimously* that it would have been better had they all contributed.

Consider the implications. Iris would be substantially better off were she and everyone else forced to contribute. Then each of them would have an outcome worth eleven dollars and fifty cents, rather than ten dollars.

1. Iris and all others find that it pays them not to contribute.
2. Iris and all others in the group would prefer that they did contribute.
3. The group is saddled with a suboptimal outcome.

Some would argue that the situation sketched here, properly generalized of course, underlies many of the dilemmas of politics. To understand the links between individual choice and more general notions of collective action and group patterns of behavior, we might begin with a simple observation: individuals will usually not find it worthwhile to help achieve shared interests;

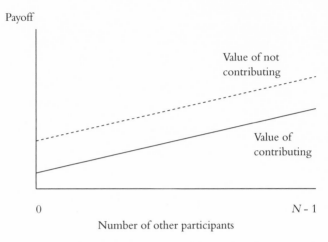

FIGURE 1.5 Value of contributing or not, given others' behaviors in
a prisoners' dilemma

they will find it useful to shirk their responsibilities. Why does this happen?
One of the major contributions of the theory of rational choice is that it
gives a relatively simple account of this.[25] Each contribution to a group or
collective project yields benefits for all members of the group, but costs accrue only to the individual who makes the effort. For the group and all its
members, it is not difficult to see that it would be best if all contributed (see
Figure 1.5, which is based on work by T. Schelling [1973]). In the diagram,
giving is worth less (the lower line) than not giving (the upper line), regardless of how many others give (depicted on the horizontal axis). But if all
give, one gets more by giving than by not giving when all don't give; the
right-hand end of the bottom line is above the left-hand intercept of the upper line. If the individually accruing benefits don't fully compensate for the
individual's costs, the incentives lead to noncooperation. Thus the group
goal would not be easily achieved until the members of the group worked
out a more complex institution. With this depiction, the general situation
can often be analyzed as an *n-person prisoners' dilemma game*. In such a game,
the group optimum is not achieved because each of the group members is in
equilibrium (i.e., group members can't do better by unilaterally changing their
choice) when they decide to not contribute or to shirk their responsibilities.

   The theoretical predictions of such simple models don't generalize or often don't predict well. People *do* contribute to collective efforts, so the theory appears false. But the modeling of collective action doesn't stop with the
single-shot prisoners' dilemma analysis. Other models of the problem have
been developed.[26]

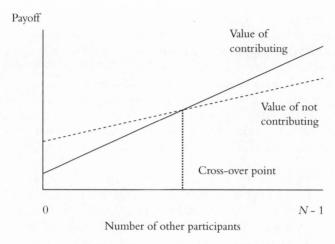

Payoff

Value of
contributing

Value of not
contributing

Cross-over point

0   N - 1

Number of other participants

FIGURE 1.6 Value of contributing or not, given others' behaviors in
an assurance game

SOME ELABORATIONS

Of course, not all situations lead to such bad outcomes, and we might
wonder why. There are a number of possibilities. First, not all games need be
prisoners' dilemmas. Much has been made of the possibility that some collective action games are actually assurance games and not prisoners' dilemmas. In assurance games, the lines showing the value of contributing or not
cross each other at some point (see Figure 1.6). If enough persons come together to solve a problem, it becomes worth the individual's while to join
the project rather than to shirk. A number of studies have shown that the
leadership of the American civil rights movement transformed the situation
into an assurance game and thereby greatly improved the chances for success
(see, for example, Chong 1991 and Dixit and Skeath 1999).

Another complicating factor is the possibility that these are not one-shot
games but rather are repeated. When interactions similar to the one developed above are repeated, the incentives are altered. This is especially clear if
we restrict the discussion to two-person situations. Then things improve if
each person can make choices contingent upon the choices of the other
person. A repeated event, often referred to as a *repeated game*, requires the depiction of possible ways of choosing throughout the repetitions, called a *strategy*. For example, Iris might start to contribute and continue to do so if Jerry
also contributes. If he doesn't, then Iris will stop contributing until such time
as Jerry contributes again. Such a strategy is referred to as "tit for tat."

One form of analysis has been especially useful in understanding repeated events—the idea that people observe the payoffs of others and the "norms" they follow. Individuals then change their strategies or norms when they find others with better payoffs. Such a perspective is called *evolutionary* because it mimics quite accurately notions of evolution in biology (see Chapter 2). With an evolutionary perspective, one can radically weaken the psychological assumptions and still come up with interesting and testable results. Indeed, one of the surprising discoveries is that the evolutionary analysis of a situation yields, in equilibrium, what can be seen as an equilibrium in the more traditional mode of analysis (see Dixit and Skeath 1999, 347).

CITIZENS

Rational choice theory is also useful in understanding the characteristics of the behavior of the citizens of democratic systems. Normative theorists have often argued that the democratic citizen ought to be vigilant, attentive to the public and to the government which she helped elect. But an extension of the logic of collective action leads one to believe that the average citizen is highly *un*likely to be well informed. Rather, the individual's rational choice is to take into account the great likelihood that she is not going to affect the outcome, and then calibrate her effort at information acquisition accordingly.

The conclusion is that we can expect citizens to remain "rationally ignorant" (a conclusion first developed by Anthony Downs [1957]). The normative implications of this are severe. For just as one can argue that the voters ought to be informed, to note that the rational voter won't be is also, in part, to excuse the voter from the responsibility of being informed (see Oppenheimer 1985). Certainly all that the law requires for excuse from responsibility is reasonable care. Since this excuses the citizenry from the responsibility of exercising control over the government (the defense of the "good German"—"I didn't know what was going on"—comes to mind), concern has been developed about two aspects of expectable ignorance.

But, of course, the first concern is that of governmental performance. All the discussion above regarding democratic governmental performance assumed that the government *knew* the preferences of the citizenry. But if the citizens don't know the activities of the government and do not have an incentive to communicate their preferences to the government, what can we expect of governmental performance? A number of models and experimental studies have shown that we can expect substantially better governmental performance than we might intuitively believe (see Collier, Ordeshook, and Williams 1989; Lupia and McCubbins 1998; and Popkin 1991). More recently, analysts have begun to consider how institutions might be better designed to ensure adequate information flows and absorption by citizens (see Chapter 6).

Rational Choice's Attractiveness

So we can see that rational choice theory is a useful tool for answering many fundamental and other questions. It is useful because it provides a means for predicting behavior and identifying the gap between predicted behavior and optimal performance (depending upon one's standard of optimality). Thus, rational choice theory can tell us what we can reasonably expect in the way of performance and how we ought to change institutions to improve performance. In any particular institutional setting and social environment, one can also usually measure the gap between the predicted and the actual behaviors. Thus rational choice theory can be tested and improved. For these reasons, rational choice theory is attractive to individuals interested in solving real-world problems.

Description of This Volume

The volume is divided into three substantive sections within which the chapters are organized. The first section, "From Anarchy to Society," deals with the formation and underlying social conditions for the development of political societies and states. The second section, "Institutional Design," deals with the workings of the modern state. And finally, the last section, "Toward Democracy," deals with issues of political development. An introductory essay precedes each of the three sections, and Karol Soltan concludes with some thoughts on rational choice and theoretical history. A subject index follows the conclusion.

The two chapters in part 1, "From Anarchy to Society," focus on the conditions in society needed to support any sort of cooperation, and the original organization of the state. Jonathan Bendor and Piotr Swistak develop a rational choice model of the evolution of the social norms and informal institutions that are needed as a foundation for cooperation. In doing so, they provide an individualistic foundation for the types of social characteristics that are often presumed to precede the formation of states. One of the most interesting aspects of their analysis is the manner in which they "measure" the extent to which a particular norm is manifest in social behavior. Once they develop a technology for evaluating the ubiquity of a norm, they analyze the preconditions that lead to the widespread diffusion of these norms. And they demonstrate that certain important norms can gain a foothold in a society without being imposed authoritatively from the top. These results have implications for our understanding of the role of government (or the need for government) in generating certain social outcomes.

Robert Bates, Avner Greif, and Smita Singh join economics and politics to explain what economic circumstances lead to the development of what has come to be described as minimal states by the free market libertarians. They show that privately supplied coercive defensive patterns to protect investment and property grow up naturally within traditional societies. By focusing on kinship relationships (and their development), they demonstrate the existence of rational "escape routes" from the anarchy of life and the state of nature. This work has implications for our understanding of both the potential for economic development in stateless societies and the relationship between economic development and political development. The model of Bates et al. derives a relationship that poses the alternative starkly either as poverty and no coercive protection of property or as coercion and a possible escape from want. Bates finds that economic and political development are necessarily linked, though not in the manner often thought. Bates's model implies that economic development precedes (is, in fact, a precondition for) the development of the precursors to the state. And hence, the state is shown to be but one set of equilibrium outcomes which can solve the problems of anarchistic predation of concern to Hobbes. In other words, Bates identifies a slightly different environment, with a radically different path of solutions for the problems of Hobbes. But even more impressive, the essay shows how a different state solution can be implied from a Hobbesian set of premises, something that we political scientists have long thought possible but have not achieved. It does this by identifying private protection to be a subgame perfect equilibrium. As is often true, the logic of the model is intuitive after the fact. Its achievement suggests a rethinking of the more conventional perspective toward the relationship between political and economic development. Bates puts the findings in greater perspective, one that shows the potential economic gains from a modern state.

Part 2, "Institutional Design," contains three essays. In this case the authors deal with two normative elements in politics: trust (Gary Miller and Dino Falaschetti) and responsiveness to citizen welfare (Russell Hardin) and a property which is in part normative, the dispersal of credible information (Arthur Lupia). Hardin discusses the prevalence of rational choice principles in political philosophy—at least since Hobbes—and argues against the characterization of rational choice as an *alternative* rather than as a *foundation* for moral behavior. He then goes on to argue that the necessary lack of available and collectively held information and knowledge at the center leads to a necessary prescription for a limited governmental structure. Miller and Falaschetti's chapter on institutions deals with the central problem of organizational design: how does one structure an organization to achieve collective goals with individually self-interested members? The authors demonstrate that trust is the central element which must be addressed and show that no final, general solution to this problem exists. Rather the problem has to be broken into responses to specific contexts, and they then identify several potential responses for particular contexts. Finally, Lupia develops the conditions under which information is likely to be believed. He shows that there needs to be knowledge of the incentives that the dispenser of the information faces for the dispensed information to be accepted. He then presents an experimental study of individual decision making and information acquisition that corroborates his model's implications. Lupia shows that institutional structures may have a significant impact on the substantive transmission of information, and he demonstrates how a sophisticated understanding of the psychology of choice can be used to design better democratic institutions which could generate better-informed citizens.

The third and final section, "Toward Democracy," consists of two chapters investigating the development and internal political dynamics of institutions in democracies. Barry Weingast is concerned with the establishment of democracy, how it is possible. He notes that the problem is one of agreements among the elite, or the power brokers. His concern is the conditions under which any such agreement is forthcoming and stable. Finally, Jack Knight and Lee Epstein discuss the use of rational choice theory to understand the politics and the development of an independent judiciary, especially one empowered to review the practice of government to preserve constitutional rules and agreements.

These chapters, individually and in their collective methodological and substantive overlap, highlight the characteristics of the best current work in the rational choice paradigm and demonstrate why rational choice theory is such a powerful tool for understanding politics. Rational choice theory often generates counterintuitive implications, results that can suggest that our unsophisticated understandings may be incomplete or misguided. For example, Lupia shows how identical communications can have very different informational content depending upon the institutional structure within which the communications are transmitted. Similarly, rational choice theory frequently highlights the importance of variables that had been underexamined or completely ignored. In several essays (Chapters 2, 3, 5, 7, and 8), time—or more specifically *time horizons*—play a particularly important role in determining the extent to which desirable outcomes can be achieved.

The practitioners of rational choice theory have spent considerable effort at testing and at trying to improve the theory to take into account the empirical problems these tests have uncovered. Further, the theory itself often can be folded back on itself to show potential difficulties with models that have been put forward. This effort to improve the analysis is certainly part of what is going on in Chapter 5, as well as Chapter 2.

These chapters also highlight two important aspects of much of current rational choice theory that have not always been true of work in this paradigm. First, rational choice theory and sophisticated empirical analysis are complementary endeavors that are extremely productive when melded effectively. Several of the chapters in this volume explicitly connect the implications of formal models with specific empirical phenomena (see Chapters 6 and 7 for two very different enterprises ranging from experimental results to case studies).

On the other hand, the essays in this volume also suggest that rational choice theory—as it is currently understood—is inadequate to the task of providing a general theory of sociopolitical relations. Some authors (such as Knight and Epstein, Lupia, and Miller and Falaschetti) deal directly with the limitations of conventional rational choice theorizing. Others emphasize the importance of factors or variables (such as leadership and *fortuna* in Weingast) for which rational choice has yet to provide a compelling description and explanation. For all of these reasons, we expect rational choice theory to play a major supportive role in the future development of our understanding of political phenomena. We hope that these essays (and our comments about them) will foster a similar appreciation of the theory among our readers.

Notes

1. We clarify what is meant by *leverage* when the discussion turns to knowledge claims and methods (see p. 11).

2. In the table, "you" get to choose the *row* (*not* the outcome); your partner chooses the column. Together, the pair of choices determines the outcome (cell, or box) you end up in. The first number in each box represents the payoff to you, and the second to your partner were you to end up in that box. Note that you are best off in row 2, regardless of which column you are caught in by the choice of your partner.

3. The way to see this is that the payoffs for confessing are bigger for the row player regardless of which column the player ends up in.

4. Chapter 3 clarifies precisely what trade-offs are involved in the granting of coercive power to the governing authorities of the society.

5. Chapter 4 tackles this question by considering how the distribution of information affects the degree to which governmental institutions can satisfy people's basic goals.

6. Weingast's view of the stabilization of inherently unstable political agreements parallels the problem of markets in politics.

7. This is referred to as "methodological individualism" in the philosophical literature surrounding questions of behaviorism in the social sciences. In principle, any agent "with purposes" will do, whether it be an individual or a bureau or a state. However, one of the principle findings of the theoretical efforts has been that only rarely can we expect collective decision makers (e.g., governments) to behave in the same fashion as purposive individuals (Arrow 1963). On the other hand, models of rational choice have been applied to other actors making choices, nation states included.

8. Of course the institutions can be thought of as creating the endowments through the giving of suffrage or property rights. Then endowments would be folded in to the institutional aspects of the analysis. But often the institutions we analyze are not those that create the endowment rights, and hence we must explicitly identify these as part of our analysis.

9. Good summaries of this literature abound. The reader might look at Quattrone and Tversky 1988, Osherson 1995, and Tversky and Kahneman 1986.

10. See Bendor 1995, which has a useful catalog of possible reformulations of the psychology. On the other hand, Kreps 1990 and Dixit and Skeath 1999 give interesting introductions to the theory of noncooperative games and its less demanding foundations.

11. A useful introductory treatment of this can be found in Giere 1984, but almost any standard treatment of epistemology in philosophy will give the same perspective and definition.

12. Again, almost any introductory work on truth will do as a serious starting point, but we recommend the very fine short book by Alan White (1970), or his even shorter essay (1967).

13. It is surprising how many persons do not know that logic is a set of rules— indeed, that logic is *the* set of rules that preserves truth in argument. Any introductory text is useful, but an especially useful one is Jeffrey 1981.

14. The relation between mathematics and logic is a bit complicated, but let it be said that much (but not all) of mathematics can be shown to be a subset of logic. Again, many texts suffice to show this, but Jeffrey 1981 is particularly clear.

15. Good introductory descriptions of these models can be found in Mueller 1989 and Enelow and Hinich 1984. The major elements of the theory were worked out by Duncan Black in the 1940s and are reported in Black 1958.

16. Many variations are possible. Specifically, for example, the analysis can be done even if the preferences fall off on a nonsymmetric basis to the left and right.

17. The designation "final winner" requires a notion of equilibrium; once the final winner is reached, we expect that no voters will be effective in changing the group choice from it to another outcome.

18. Here note that in a more rigorous proof we need to deal in a more detailed fashion with cases where more than one voter shares having the median ideal point, and so on.

19. See, for example, the discussion of Arrow and multidimensional voting in a standard text such as Mueller 1989.

20. Recall that any point in the lens will beat the midpoint Y, and all three lenses have a portion outside the triangle.

21. To illustrate, we have drawn a circle through X, B's indifference curve. B would prefer any point inside that circle to X.

22. See note 15 above for some basic references.

23. This technique of solving games works on all games with "perfect and complete" information, and only some of the others. For a fuller discussion of this, see Dixit and Skeath 1999, 48–52.

24. This model reflects the perspective taken in Hardin 1971. Other ways of

modeling the problem involve either no game theory (e.g., Olson 1965) or other forms of games (see Frohlich and Oppenheimer 1970 and below, page 27, for alternatives).

25. This is not the place to give a comprehensive account of the theory of collective action. The reader is referred to numerous volumes and articles on this. Any list would have to begin with the work of the late Mancur Olson (1965), but Hardin 1971 shows that the relationship could sometimes be considered a prisoners' dilemma game. Ledyard 1995 reviews the experimental studies of the subject.

26. Green and Shapiro also criticize the plethora of models by saying that such a surfeit means that the theory is not falsifiable. But this is too simple. The different models are for different conditions, and the issue is which conditions, or institutional designs, lead to group goals being achieved and which do not. For example, Olson's perspective was *not* game theoretic, and certainly some contexts don't lend themselves to Hardin's game theoretic interpretation (see Dixit and Skeath 1999, chap. 2). But beyond this, if the collective goals are not "continuously" differentiable, or, in other words, are "step functions" or "lumpy," then other forms of analysis are required (see Frohlich and Oppenheimer 1970, 1978). Still other forms of analysis are required if there is repetition of the interactions, and so on (see Dixit and Skeath 1999, chaps. 8, 10, and 11).

References

Aivazian, V. A., and Jeffrey L. Callen. 1981. "The Coase Theorem and the Empty Core." *Journal of Law and Economics* 24: 175–81.

Aivazian, V. A., J. L. Callen, and I. Lipnowski. 1987. "The Coase Theorem and Coalitional Stability." *Economica* 54: 517–20.

Arrow, Kenneth J. 1963. *Social Choice and Individual Values*, 2nd ed. New Haven, Conn.: Yale University Press.

Bendor, Jonathan. 1995. "A Model of Muddling Through." *American Political Science Review* 89, no. 4 (December): 819–40.

Black, Duncan. 1958. *The Theory of Committees and Elections*. Cambridge: Cambridge University Press.

Brandl, John E. 1998a. *Money and Good Intentions Are Not Enough, or Why a Liberal Democrat Thinks States Need Both Competition and Community*. Washington, D.C.: Brookings Institution Press.

———. 1998b. "Governance and Educational Quality." In *Learning from School Choice*, ed. Paul Peterson and Bryan C. Hassel, 55–82. Washington, D.C.: Brookings Institution Press.

Buchanan, James M., and Gordon Tullock. 1962. *The Calculus of Consent: Logical Foundation of Constitutional Democracy*. Ann Arbor: University of Michigan Press.

Chong, Dennis. 1991. *Collective Action and the Civil Rights Movement*. Chicago: University of Chicago Press.

Coase, R. 1960. "The Problem of Social Cost." *Journal of Law and Economics* 3: 1–44.

Collier, Kenneth, Peter C. Ordeshook, and Kenneth C. Williams. 1989. "The Rationally Uninformed Electorate: Some Experimental Evidence." *Public Choice* 60: 3–29.

Dixit, Avinash, and Susan Skeath. 1999. *Games of Strategy*. New York: Norton.

Downs, Anthony. 1957. *An Economic Theory of Democracy*. New York: Harper & Row.

Eavey, C., and G. Miller. 1984. "Bureaucratic Agenda Control: Imposition or Bargaining?" *American Political Science Review* 78 (September): 719–33.

Enelow, J., and M. Hinich. 1984. *The Spatial Theory of Voting*. Cambridge: Cambridge University Press.

Friedman, Jeffrey, ed. 1995. *The Rational Choice Controversy: Economic Models of Politics Reconsidered*. New Haven, Conn.: Yale University Press.

Frohlich, Norman, and Joe A. Oppenheimer. 1970. "I Get By with a Little Help from My Friends." *World Politics* 11 (October): 104–21.

———. 1978. *Modern Political Economy*. Englewood Cliffs, N.J.: Prentice-Hall.

Giere, Ronald N. 1984. *Understanding Scientific Reasoning*, 2nd ed. Chicago: Holt, Rinehart and Winston.

Green, Donald P., and Ian Shapiro. 1994. *Pathologies of Rational Choice Theory: A Critique of Applications in Political Science*. New Haven, Conn.: Yale University Press.

Grossman, Philip, and Catherine C. Eckel. 1996. "Altruism in Anonymous Dictator Games." *Games and Economic Behavior* 16 (October): 181–91.

Hardin, R. 1971. "Collective Action as an Agreeable N-Prisoners' Dilemma." *Behavioral Science* 16, no. 5: 472–79.

Hempel, Carl G. 1966. *The Philosophy of the Natural Sciences*. Englewood Cliffs, N.J.: Prentice-Hall.

Hoffman, Elizabeth, Kevin McCabe, and Vernon L. Smith. 1996. "Social Distance and Other-Regarding Behavior in Dictator Games." *American Economic Review* 86, no. 3 (June): 653–60.

Jeffrey, Richard. 1981. *Formal Logic: Its Scope and Limits*, 2nd ed. New York: McGraw-Hill.

Kreps, David M. 1990. *Game Theory and Economic Modelling*. Clarendon Lectures in Economics. Oxford: Oxford University Press.

Landa, Janet. 1986. "The Political Economy of Swarming in Honeybees: Voting with the Wings, Decision-Making Costs, and the Unanimity Rule." *Public Choice* 51, no. 1: 25–38.

Ledyard, John O. 1995. "Public Goods: A Survey of Experimental Research." In *The Handbook of Experimental Economics*, ed. John H. Kagel and Alvin E. Roth, 111–94. Princeton, N.J.: Princeton University Press.

Lupia, Arthur, and Mathew D. McCubbins. 1998. *The Democratic Dilemma: Can Citizens Learn What They Need to Know?* New York: Cambridge University Press.

Miller, Gary J., and T. H. Hammond. 1987. "The Core of the Constitution." *American Political Science Review* 81: 1156–74.

———. 1990. "Committees and the Core of the Constitution." *Public Choice* 66, no. 3: 201–28.

Moe, Terry. 1984. "The New Economics of Organization." *American Journal of Political Science* 28 (November): 739–77.

Morris, Irwin L. 2000. *Congress, the President, and the Federal Reserve: The Politics of American Monetary Policymaking*. Ann Arbor: University of Michigan Press.

Mueller, Dennis C. 1989. *Public Choice II*. Cambridge: Cambridge University Press.

Olson, Mancur. 1965. *The Logic of Collective Action*. Cambridge: Harvard University Press.

Oppenheimer, Joe A. 1985. "Public Choice and Three Ethical Properties of Politics." *Public Choice* 45: 241–55.

Osherson, Daniel N. 1995. "Probability Judgement." In *An Invitation to Cognitive Science: Thinking*, vol. 3, 2nd ed., 35–76. Cambridge: MIT Press.

Plott, Charles R. 1978. "Rawls's Theory of Justice: An Impossibility Result." In *Decision Theory and Social Ethics: Issues in Social Choice*, ed. Hans W. Gottinger and Werner Leinfellner. Dordrecht, Holland: Reidel.

Popkin, Samuel L. 1991. *The Reasoning Voter: Communication and Persuasion in Presidential Campaigns*. Chicago: University of Chicago Press.

Popper, Karl. 1959. *The Logic of Scientific Discovery*. New York: Harper & Row.

Quattrone, George A., and Amos Tversky. 1988. "Contrasting Rational and Psychological Analyses of Political Choice." *American Political Science Review* 82, no. 3 (September): 719–36.

Romer, Thomas, and Howard Rosenthal. 1978. "Political Resource Allocation, Controlled Agendas, and the Status Quo." *Public Choice* 33(4): 27–43.

Schelling, Thomas C. 1973. "Hockey Helmets, Concealed Weapons, and Daylight Savings: A Study of Binary Choices with Externalities." *Journal of Conflict Resolution* 17, no. 3 (September): 381–428.

Schwartz, T. 1981. "The Universal Instability Theorem." *Public Choice* 37(3): 487–502.

Sen, A. K. 1977. "Rational Fools: A Critique of the Behavioral Foundations of Economic Theory." *Philosophy and Public Affairs* 6, no. 4 (summer): 317–44. Reprinted in *Beyond Self-Interest*, ed. Jane J. Mansbridge, 25–43. Chicago: University of Chicago Press, 1990.

Shepsle, K., and Barry Weingast. 1981. "Structure Induced Equilibrium and Legislative Choice." *Public Choice* 37(3): 503–20.

Simon, Herbert A. 1986. "Rationality in Psychology and Economics." *Journal of Business* 59(4, part 2): S209–S224.

Tversky, Amos, and Daniel Kahneman. 1986. "Rational Choice and the Framing of Decisions." *Journal of Business* 59(4): pt. 2, s251–78. Reprinted in *The Limits of Rationality*, ed. Karen Schweers Cook and Margaret Levi, 90–131. Chicago: University of Chicago Press, 1990.

White, Alan R. 1967. "Coherence Theory of Truth." In *Encyclopedia of Philosophy*, vol. 2. New York: Macmillan, 130–32.

———. 1970. *Truth*. Garden City, N.Y.: Doubleday Anchor.

PART I

From Anarchy to Society

THERE ARE MANY forms of the chicken and egg problem. For example, what came first, the individual human or the social unit that could foster her development? Clearly, as a mammal with a long period of dependency, a human individual requires a nurturing social environment to survive. Hobbes would have us believe that without strong, coercive, political arrangements there can be no society. But that appears too strong. Social arrangements without formal coercive political structures must be possible. Indeed, to set up political structures, we humans must be able to develop social norms that support cooperation prior to the existence of such structures.

The essays in this section deal with the world without central coercive political structures, the world of anarchy, and how politics, and hence society as we think of it, might have begun. It has been a while since students of political science took up the issue of anarchy. But libertarians calling for free market minimalist states (see Nozick 1974, for example) and our increased understanding of behavior regarding public goods has made this a compelling subject for fresh consideration. Of course, considering free markets leads one to consider the problems of market failures. Beyond the relatively early musings of Ronald Coase (1960) that perhaps we don't need any social decision process (i.e., government) to get efficient solutions to some typical market failures, lie the more sophisticated analyses that his and related studies spawned. They deal with both empirical and theoretical problems (Ostrom 1994; Ostrom, Walker, and Gardner 1992; and Ledyard 1995 give solid overviews of the field based and experimental findings; see also Aivazian and Callen 1981; Aivazian, Callen, and Lipkowski 1987; and Mueller 1989).

And most relevant among these theories is our advances in our understanding of the nature of collective action (see the discussion in the Introduction). With the modern theory of collective action (based on what in Samuelson 1954 was called public goods), we now have a relatively good understanding of the likely outcome of groups of individuals without central decision institutions making allocations of resources to solve public problems. Indeed, such societies have been found among the tribes in Africa and have been studied by cultural anthropologists (for an example, see Schapera 1956).[1]

The result of both empirical and theoretical investigation has been found not to be the dreaded "war of all against all" presumed by that earliest rational choice theorist of social institutions, Thomas Hobbes. Hobbes set the stage for much of modern inquiry. But in his famous *Leviathan* Hobbes had little more than reason to guide him in the understanding of the properties of the state of nature. Further, without the tools of either modern rational choice theory or economics, he could not comprehend the development of a social fabric which could be held together without an authoritarian sovereign. But by now we have considerable empirical experience with our models and have come to understand the possible varied paths to, and role of, governments.

Chapters 2 and 3 continue the Hobbesian argument. Using an up-to-date understanding of rationality, they generate an implicit modern dialogue with Hobbes on these issues. Hence, they begin with a similar notion, that choice is at the center of the political problem. And they develop answers to two questions at the heart of Hobbes's enterprise: Jonathan Bendor and Piotr Swistak ask how purely selfish individuals can cooperate prior to the existence of the state so as to establish social and governing institutions. And Robert Bates, Avner Greif, and Smita Singh wonder what we can expect to be gained by the establishment of a coercive authority in primitive kinship societies and what this tells us about the conditions for its development.

In Chapter 3, Bates, Greif, and Singh identify the logic of the trade-offs that have to be made between economic development and the existence of a central coercive authority as one considers the possibilities of anarchy rather than government. When property is protected purely privately, as in some of both the minimal state proposals and African tribes, private violence is employed to engage in, and to defend against, predation. This may work if there is little to steal. And privatized property protection services may even be necessary if the wealth is very unequally distributed so that only the properties of a few are targeted. But as the stakes grow and are more widely distributed, the collective efforts that can be justified to prevent the possible thefts grow proportionately. In other words, wealth accumulation generates a demand for defense of property. Predation results at best in mere redistribution; being destructive, it more often results in a loss of social welfare. When organized, however, coercion can have socially productive consequences. Employed to defend property rights, coercion can thereby strengthen incentives to engage in productive activity. Rephrasing Hobbes, it can be used to develop social overhead capital.[2] Of course, that same coercive force can be used for other things, such as overcoming the tendency of groups to undersupply themselves with public goods via taxation, and so on. So even without the apocalyptic perspective of Hobbes, Bates, Greif, and Singh show that there are good reasons and reasonable paths to get beyond the anarchic life of the state of nature.

The authors do this by considering the equilibrium conditions of a pair of families with agricultural interests. The resulting repeated noncooperative game of defense and predation has a number of plausible equilibria, which they then explore. Rather than the severity of the corner solution that Hobbes thought necessary (absolute fealty to an outside coercive force), Bates, Greif, and Singh argue that there are endogenously occurring equilibria. That is, one needn't have the deus ex machina of an outside force to subdue violence. Violence may be reined in by a balanced investment between defense, offense, and production. In the kinship societies, individuals will have to allocate scarce resources between defense and production.

Yet the reorganization of violence is needed to protect the income stream from long-term investments and as such renders coercion productive and lays the foundations for the state. This permits movement from stateless societies where people's rights to the product of their labor are secure only if they possess coercive capabilities.

Others have argued similarly that the state is needed for any but rudimentary development because of the need to defend property. For example, Mancur Olson (1993) also argued that the state is needed to secure property rights once there is enough to support a profession of thieving. His notion is that the state grows naturally out of the entrepreneurial profit motivation of the "bandits" who find that it is worthwhile to stop roving for prey. Olson's story is a clear common pool resource story. Imagine m equal, competing, professional gangs of thieves who have a number of targets. Now let one gang consider a targeted community from which it can steal everything or leave enough so that the community is able to produce a surplus again in the next period. If the gang leaves enough for regrowth, it has only a $1/m$ chance to harvest this surplus during the next season. So the rational gang will raze the community to the ground; it will take everything. This insight led Olson to conclude that the profit-seeking bandit will prefer to be the sole thief in his villages, and if he can establish the monopoly, the villagers are better off.[3]

But in Bates's broad sketch of the political economy of kinship societies, the authors consider other aspects of political economy beyond the need to secure one's property from predation. By drawing out the implications of decreasing marginal productivity to the exploitation of land, they show important lessons for kinship structures. This allows them to analyze the difficulties in securing intergenerational cooperation within extended family structures in the process of establishing long-term family equilibria and social community. They show that society, without technological innovation, can be a very dynamic, changing structure, which can lead to frictions and difficulties.

But with only minimal structure, precisely how could we get to cooperation among purely self-interested individuals? Some form of cooperation is surely needed if the solution of government is not to be imposed from above. Hobbes's dark vision of humanity requires that we develop a covenant of absolute fealty to the ruler. But in modern terms, this is a rather thankless choice. Jonathan Bendor and Piotr Swistak put forward a plausible route for the evolution of cooperation in a group even prior to the establishment of institutions. They begin with a sketch of the general world of people as a somewhat underdefined mixed motive game, a game in which there are both competitive and cooperative elements. Then Bendor and Swistak show how social norms—norms that induce us to reward or punish people not only for what they did to us but for what they did to other members of one's group—can be deductively derived as likely behaviors.[4] Other norms, like envy and discrimination, can be explained in a similar fashion.

Bendor and Swistak's analysis is built on an understanding of how to analyze repeated social interactions as a stage game. The idea is that people observe the behavior and payoffs of others and consider the adoption of "norms of behavior" that are more successful than their current norms of interaction. In this scenario, individuals learn, and even more important, change their strategies or norms when they find others with better payoffs. Such a perspective is called "evolutionary" because at its heart is a "replicator dynamic" which mimics notions of evolution in biology. With an evolutionary perspective, one can radically weaken the psychological assumptions used by traditional analysts such as Hobbes and still come up with interesting and testable results.

Development of evolutionary game theory regarding political behavior stems from the work of Robert Axelrod (1984). But Axelrod's analysis and the ensuing literature were plagued by an obvious limitation. They were built upon an assumption that all social relations were dyadic, that involved no more than two persons. Any larger social fabric was to be understood as a weaving of these binary relations. For relevance to the "real world," some means of generalizing beyond this limitation is necessary. Standard evolutionary theory of games has another problem, that the solutions are not easily "stabilized," or that the conditions for "equilibrium" are not robust. Bendor and Swistak propose an elegant solution to most of the substance in these objections, through which they demonstrate how selfish behavior can evolve to group-oriented behavior. Only with this or a substitute solution can one actually support the theoretical moves made by Bates (or Olson 1993) and others.

Notes

1. Empirical examinations of many of these arrangements in other social settings have been cataloged, and analyzed, by Elinor Ostrom (1994).
2. One interesting account of this relationship is in Wittfogel 1957.
3. The entrepreneurial basis for government goes back further than this. Such explanations for the establishment of cooperative institutions were developed mainly since the argument by Mancur Olson (1965) that groups of individuals will not naturally overcome their predilection to free ride (but see Schumpeter 1943). So Salisbury (1969) and Wagner (1966) both responded to Olson's idea with the possibility of an entrepreneurial solution. Frohlich, Oppenheimer, and Young 1971 was the first sustained argument to establish the approach, and it was further developed in Frohlich and Oppenheimer 1978 and 1974. See also Skaperdas 2002 and Dixit 2001 for some of the latest thoughts on the matter, which complement those of Bates, Greif, and Singh.
4. As such, they break out of the narrow confines of Axelrod's binary assumptions.

References

Aivazian, V. A., and Jeffrey L. Callen. 1981. "The Coase Theorem and the Empty Core." *Journal of Law and Economics* 24: 175–81.

Aivazian, V. A., J. L. Callen, and I. Lipnowski. 1987. "The Coase Theorem and Coalitional Stability." *Economica* 54: 517–20.

Axelrod, Robert. 1984. *The Evolution of Cooperation*. New York: Basic Books.

Coase, R. 1960. "The Problem of Social Cost." *Journal of Law and Economics* 3: 1–44.

Dixit, Avinash. 2001. "Some Lessons from Transaction-Cost Politics for Less-Developed Countries." Lecture given in memory of Mancur Olson, October 26, University of Maryland Collective Choice Center.

Frohlich, Norman, and Joe A. Oppenheimer. 1974. "The Carrot and the Stick." *Public Choice* 19 (fall): 43–61.

———. 1978. *Modern Political Economy*. Englewood Cliffs, N.J.: Prentice-Hall.

Frohlich, Norman, Joe A. Oppenheimer, and Oran Young. 1971. *Political Leadership and Collective Goods*. Princeton, N.J.: Princeton University Press.

Hobbes, Thomas. 1950. *Leviathan*. New York: Dutton.

Ledyard, John O. 1995. "Public Goods: A Survey of Experimental Research." In *The Handbook of Experimental Economics*, ed. John H. Kagel and Alvin E. Roth, 111–94. Princeton, N.J.: Princeton University Press.

Mueller, Dennis C. 1989. *Public Choice II*. Cambridge: Cambridge University Press.

Nozick, Robert. 1974. *Anarchy, State, and Utopia*. New York: Basic Books.

Olson, Mancur. 1965. *The Logic of Collective Action*. Cambridge: Harvard Univerity Press.

Olson, Mancur. 1993 "Dictatorship, Democracy, and Development." *American Political Science Review* 87, no. 3 (September): 567–76.

Ostrom, Elinor. 1994. "Constituting Social Capital and Collective Action." In *Local Commons and Global Interdependence: Heterogeneity and Cooperation in Two Domains*, ed. R. O. Keohane and E. Ostrom. A special issue of *Journal of Theoretical Politics* 6.

Ostrom, E., J. Walker, and R. Gardner. 1992. "Covenants With and Without the Sword: Self Governance Is Possible." *American Political Science Review* 86: 404–17.

Salisbury, Robert. 1969. "An Exchange Theory of Interest Groups." *Midwest Journal of Political Science* 13 (February): 1–32.

Samuelson, Paul. 1954. "The Pure Theory of Public Expenditure." *Review of Economics and Statistics* 36 (November): 387–89.

Schapera, Isaac. 1956. *Government and Politics in Tribal Societies*. New York: Schoken Books.

Schumpeter, Joseph Alois. 1943. *Capitalism, Socialism, and Democracy*. London: G. Allen & Unwin.

Skaperdas, Stergios. 2002. "Restraining the Genuine Homo Economicus: Why the Economy Cannot Be Divorced from Its Governance." Lecture given in memory of Mancur Olson, February 8, University of Maryland Collective Choice Center.

Wagner, Richard. 1966. "Pressure Groups and Political Entrepreneurs: A Review Article." *Papers on Non-Market Decision Making*: 161–70.

Wittfogel, Karl August. 1957. *Oriental Despotism: A Comparative Study of Total Power*. New Haven, Conn.: Yale University Press.

2

The Rational Foundations of Social Institutions
An Evolutionary Analysis

Individuals and Institutions

THE GENERAL PROBLEM

How can we explain the universal emergence of institutions or their ubiquitous influence on human behavior? The problem is, of course, ancient. Indeed, we can think about major social science paradigms in the light of their assumptions about the relation between individuals and institutions. Methodological individualism in general and the rational choice paradigm in particular try to explain institutions based on the properties of individual actors. Hobbes, for instance, explains why rational citizens would create a powerful state, and Rawls derives his principles of justice by assuming individually rational decision making under uncertainty (the "veil of ignorance"). But can we construct similar explanations for other institutions, such as social norms?

If indeed all institutions, including all forms of social organization, can be derived from the conduct of rational individuals, then much of social theory may need to be rethought. Some fields of research operate on an assumption, either tacit or overt, that institutions cannot be derived from the properties of individual agents. A typical sociological analysis—for instance, Emile Durkheim's classic study of suicide—takes institutions (i.e., social structures) as given and studies their effects on the behavior of individuals. The two research programs—one trying to explain institutions by the properties of their individual members, the other trying to explain properties of actors by the institutions to which they belong—create a significant gap in social science research.

Recently, however, efforts have been made to narrow this divide in all of the social sciences.[1] In political science, one of the best-known recent efforts

is Putnam's study (1993) of political culture and politicoeconomic performance in Italy. In chapter 6, "Social Capital and Institutional Success," Putnam
explicitly melds the two types of analyses. On the one hand, he formulates
the problem in game theoretic terms; Italian communities face "dilemmas of
collective action."[2] On the other, he hypothesizes that various kinds of social
capital—especially networks and social norms—greatly ameliorate these
dilemmas in northern Italy, while their absence leaves southern Italy in a bad
equilibrium of little cooperation. For example, he asserts that communities
which follow the norm of reciprocity "can more efficiently restrain opportunism and resolve problems of collective action." Further, the norm addresses the core of collective action dilemmas by helping "to reconcile self-
interest and solidarity" (Putnam 1993, 172). Moreover, norms and social
networks are intertwined; "an effective norm of generalized reciprocity is
likely to be associated with *dense* networks of social exchange" (172, emphasis added). In such situations people can reasonably assume that cooperation
will be repaid. Thus together these two types of social capital sustain a good
equilibrium of ongoing cooperation.

These are important claims. In order to understand them, however, we
must grasp the exact nature of the dilemmas that social capital is purported
to ameliorate. Moreover, we must understand why it is no simple matter to
combine, as Putnam does, game theoretic and sociological analyses. To begin this process, let us examine the following simple example.

AN EXAMPLE

Consider three actors, A, B, and C, involved in repeated pairwise interactions and exchanges. Suppose, for instance, that a repeated cooperative interaction between two actors gives them both an income of 3, an exploitive relation results in an income of 6 for the exploiter and -3 for the exploited,
and an interaction involving mutual defection (noncooperation) gives both
players an income of 0. For simplicity, the reader may assume that these
numbers represent incomes in dollars.[3]

Let's think now about a variety of structurally different situations in
which A garners identical incomes. Figure 2.1 depicts a number of such situations. In Figure 2.1(a), for instance, A gets an income of 6 as a result of two
cooperative exchanges with B and C; in Figure 2.1(b), A gets the same income by exploiting B and defecting with C. If A were a homo economicus,
then as long as A's behaviors in two different situations generate the same income, his utility of these behaviors should be the same—for homo economicus, the utility of an income is independent of how the income is obtained.[4] Indeed, this is how we will informally define the notion of homo
economicus. Homo sociologicus will serve us as a complementary concept—defined as a non-homo economicus—denoting a player whose util-

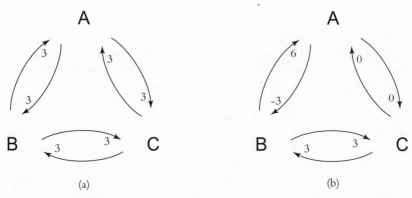

FIGURE 2.1 Two situations in which A's income is identical but his utility may vary. The arrows represent binary relations between the three individuals A, B, and C.

ity is a function of other factors in addition to income.[5] We will call any factor which affects A's utility an institution—an unusual but useful stipulation. Income will remain the only economic institution we will consider here. Following the distinction between homo economicus and homo sociologicus, all institutions other than income will be called social institutions. If we look at Figure 2.1, it should be easy to see how different social institutions might affect players' utilities.

Consider, for instance, an A who holds a norm against exploitative behavior. A's utility in situation (a) would then be larger, other factors equal, than his utility in situation (b). Or, consider an A who is an egalitarian (i.e., derives larger utility, other factors equal, from an income distribution with smaller variance), then his utility in (a) will be larger than in (b). Or consider a conformist A who derives a positive utility just from following the behavior of the majority. Assuming that in situation (a) players' incomes result from everyone following a norm or reciprocal cooperation, A's utility in (a) would then be larger than in (b). Or consider a B who holds a strong norm against exploitation, a norm that calls for defection against any exploiter in the group. B may then derive a significantly lower utility in (b) than in (a). Similarly, other social institutions, like envy, nonconformity, discrimination, social stratification, internalized norms, would alter utilities of a homo sociologicus.

But sufficiently large changes in utilities will induce changes in behaviors, and these changes in behaviors may in turn lead to different incomes obtained by players in a new equilibrium. Thus an egalitarian A who despises large differences in incomes may chose to reduce her income, and perhaps the income of others, in order to decrease inequality in the group. Similarly, if B's norm against exploitation were sufficiently strong, he would stop cooperating with A in order to punish A for exploiting C in (b), but this would destroy cooperation with A and decrease B's income. This means that utility maximizing behavior of an egalitarian in the first case or a player intervening on someone else's behalf in the second case can reduce the income of this player and of others in his group. Thus the social institution of egalitarianism and that of third-party sanctions would conflict, at least in some situations, with the principle of income maximization.[6] But the same argument can be made about any social institution. Since all social institutions act as constraints on income-maximizing behavior, they will all result, at least in some situations, in behaviors which are not income maximizing.

Hence, if we seek to explain the emergence of social institutions from a Hobbesian world without social institutions, we face the following problem: How does a world inhabited by income-maximizing homo economicus turn into a world inhabited by homo sociologicus players who value things beyond income, for whom utility maximization does not always result in income maximization. Or, we might equivalently ask, how does a market become a group? How does one form of rational behavior (one type of utility function) evolve into another? What are the origins of social preferences?

These queries induce us to rephrase the opening question: how do we explain the emergence of institutions that do not maximize the incomes of their members? Relatedly, at the micro level, how can we explain the shift from an income-maximizing homo economicus to homo sociologicus who values factors beyond income?

THE NATURE OF THE SOLUTION

To address these problems we first need to specify a theory of rational interactions. Only then can we see if social institutions can indeed be reconciled with the notion of utility-maximizing actors. Suppose, then, that we have specified a theory, in the form of a game, in which players, their actions, and payoffs are all well defined. Given this setup, we want to understand whether we can expect a specific social institution to exist.[7] If we can show that an institution is a necessary condition for an equilibrium, the critical part of the analysis turns on the assumptions under which the equilibrium exists. How constraining are these postulates and what do they imply about the players? As with any deductive analysis, the nature of the assumptions determines both the content and the meaning of the solution. Thus understanding the setup is, in a sense, equivalent to understanding the solution.

The necessary assumptions underlying our analysis are driven by two fundamental considerations. First, since our goal is to explain the emergence of social institutions, we must begin the analysis assuming a world without them. We will have to show that social institutions are bound to emerge even in a perfectly symmetric world of identical actors involved in identical interactions who value nothing but the income obtained in these interactions. At the same time, however, we would not want our solution to depend on any wrong assumptions. Thus, our second critical consideration concerns the generality of the assumptions. Since we hope to prove that some forms of institutions are robust and ubiquitous, it is critical that we derive them under appropriately general assumptions. The solution should not depend, for instance, on any strong assumptions about the degree of rationality of players, precise specification of payoffs, static properties of the game, the exact form of the dynamic governing adaptation, a uniform compliance of all players with the assumptions of the game, or any other knife-edge condition.[8]

The basic finding that underlies our explanation of different social institutions is a theorem that shows that stabilizing economic exchange requires social institutions. More specifically, whenever people interact with each other in certain cooperative exchanges with a long time horizon, social institutions are necessary to equilibrate their behavior. The essence of our general conclusion is that groups are markets which have evolved stabilizing mechanisms. Different social institutions, like social norms, envy, conformity, internalization of norms, and discrimination, can be shown to be necessary to stabilize behaviors under various conditions.

A theory which implies these results is deductive.[9] It has roots in game theory (more specifically, evolutionary game theory[10]), though it goes significantly beyond the standard analysis. By providing a link between the micro universe of individual incentives and the macro world of social institutions, our results shed a new light on the emergence and stability of social institutions.

Defining the Problem

THE NATURE OF INTERACTIONS BETWEEN PLAYERS

If interactions among players allow each person to secure the maximal payoff independently of the actions taken by anyone else, then players' choices are strategically trivial; since what is best for each individual can be obtained regardless of what others do, there is no conflict and no reason for an institution (i.e., a constraint on behaviors) to emerge. Hence, to understand the evolution of institutions, we ought to begin our analysis with interactions in which conflict might arise. To fix ideas, it makes sense to confine the analysis to a specific class of games. We will restrict our attention to the so-called games of cooperation (Bendor and Swistak 1997.)

To see the nature of the general problem as modeled by a game of cooperation, it is best to begin our discussion with a specific example. Consider, then, the simplest game-theoretic model (a one-shot two-by-two game) of the problem of cooperation as exhibited in the following market exchange problem between A and B. Suppose A has a can of cola and B has fifty cents. B would like to buy the cola for fifty cents, and A would profit by selling it to B for this price. Hence, both would benefit from the exchange. In the absence of law, however, the exchange may not occur. Note that the best outcome for A is to keep his cola and steal B's money, while the best outcome for A is to keep his money and steal B's cola; the second-best outcome for both is to exchange, the third-best outcome is not to exchange, and the worst outcome is to fall victim to theft. The problem of "steal or exchange" has the structure of the prisoners' dilemma game. The same logic underlies many other types of interactions, including social ones. Consider, for instance, an exchange of favors. Egoistically, it is always best to obtain favors without returning them (doing a favor is costly), and the worst is to give and not get; yet both parties are worse off when favors are withheld than they would have been had favors been exchanged. The essence of the problem can be seen more readily when we specify the details.

Consider, then, two players, A and B, choosing between two possible actions. A can either cooperate with B (exchange, do a favor, etc.) or defect; B's options are the same. Let's assume that if A defects while B cooperates, then A gets her best outcome, with a utility of $T = 5$. The second-best outcome ($R = 3$) results from mutual cooperation. If both defect, A gets the third-best outcome ($P = 1$), and the worst outcome for A is when A cooperates with B while B defects ($S = 0$). Assume, moreover, that the order of payoffs is the same for B, whose utilities are correspondingly $T^\star$, $R^\star$, $P^\star$, and $S^\star$. With $T > R > P > S$ and $T^\star > R^\star > P^\star > S^\star$, this is an instance of the prisoners' dilemma game. Defection is a dominant strategy; it yields a higher payoff regardless of the other player's action. Thus mutual defection is the only equilibrium in the one-shot game, and in equilibrium players get a payoff of $(P, P^\star)$, which is worse for both than the payoff for mutual cooperation $(R, R^\star)$.

A GAME OF COOPERATION

Though the prisoners' dilemma paints the problem of cooperation in its sharpest colors, there are many other games that exhibit, in varying degrees, problems of cooperation or coordination. Results described below hold for a class of games that is much larger than the prisoners' dilemma; we call them "games of cooperation" (cf. Bendor and Swistak 1997.) Informally speaking, a game of cooperation is defined as any symmetric game with a finite set of actions with a unique socially efficient cooperative outcome (in pure strategies), from which players may be tempted to deviate.[11] The definition encompasses a large class of games that involve many different kinds of cooperation problems including the prisoners' dilemma, some coordination games, an important type of chicken, stag hunt (also known as the assurance game; see Snidal 1991), and others.

Because, however, the basic prisoners' dilemma game is the best known and best understood instance of a game of cooperation, we will continue our discussion using the example of the prisoners' dilemma.

THE REPEATED GAME

If the prisoners' dilemma is played just once (and players know this and are rational), then the game's outcome is a Pareto inferior set of payoffs; both players could have done better had they cooperated. Suppose, however, that individuals interact repeatedly and they anticipate many future interactions with no definite termination date. Formally, we can model this situation by assuming that both players play a fixed one-shot game infinitely many times.[12] A (pure) strategy of player A in a game with B is defined as a complete plan of a game, that is, a function which specifies A's move in any period k depending on B's moves toward A in periods 1 through $k - 1$.

"Strategy," then, is a game-theoretic notion of a "behavioral norm." This concept of a strategy, of course, is much stronger than our colloquial understanding of a norm; a strategy is a full contingency plan for the game. No matter how the opponent moves, a strategy must tell us precisely what to do in all periods of the game. This strong notion of a complete plan is necessary for analytical reasons. We must be able to specify payoffs in a game. If the string of moves between two "norms" playing each other were not completely specified, we would be unable to assign payoffs to these norms. Later we will generalize the strict notion of a norm, as we will examine the stability of any behavioral rule, not just a fully contingent strategy.

The notion of a strategy implies a simple way to evaluate behaviors. When two players, each equipped with a complete (and deterministic) plan of the game (a pure strategy), interact with each other, what ensues is a uniquely specified string of one-shot interactions. Since players care about future payoffs, one reasonable index of how much a strategy is worth to them is the average per-period payoff it generates.[13] For instance, if both A and B play a strategy of Always Defect (ALL-D)—defect unconditionally in all periods—each player gets a payoff of $P = 1$ in each interaction, and hence the average per-period payoff to ALL-D is 1. Or consider A playing an unconditional strategy ALT (alternate)—cooperate in odd periods and defect in even ones. When ALT plays against ALL-D, its string of payoffs will be 0, 1, 0, 1, 0, 1, . . . (since $S = 0$ and $P = 1$), and hence its average per-period payoff is 0.5. Of course, the per-period average is a good index of the value of a strategy only if players care sufficiently about future payoffs. For this reason we will refer to these games as games in which the future is sufficiently important, and we will focus our analysis on this type of situation.[14]

EQUILIBRIA OF THE REPEATED GAME BETWEEN TWO PLAYERS

To see what kinds of strategies can be supported in equilibrium in games where the future is sufficiently important, consider, for instance, a strategy of Tit for Tat: cooperate in the first period of the game and thereafter in any period k do what one's partner did in $k - 1$. Suppose that player A is using Tit for Tat and player B, knowing A's strategy, is trying to maximize against it. If the future payoffs are important, then—given the retaliatory nature of Tit for Tat—it is best for B to cooperate with Tit for Tat in all periods. Defecting in any period can only lower the payoff, given that $P < R$ and $R > (T + S)/2$. Hence, B has an incentive to play Tit for Tat against A, since using any other strategy would yield either a lower or, at best, the same payoff. If we now apply the same reasoning to A, we see that neither player, given the other's strategy, has an incentive to change his own; the two strategies are in equilibrium.[15] But this is not the only equilibrium in a repeated game. If, for instance, A believes that B is playing Always Defect, A would have no incentive to do anything but to play Always Defect as well. Since the same reasoning holds for B, a pair of Always Defect strategies is also an equilibrium. In fact, it can be proved that any amount of cooperation can be sustained in equilibrium. A pair of strategies in equilibrium can support anything between o percent cooperation (e.g., a pair of Always Defect strategies) to 100 percent cooperation (e.g., a pair of Tit for Tat strategies).[16] In other words, with only two players in the game, the standard equilibrium concept predicts that a great many norms may emerge in their interaction. But is this still the case in more general contexts in which there are many players involved in pairwise games?

HOMO ECONOMICUS

In markets, taken in their ideal form, players are solely concerned with income maximization. Thus a homo economicus will prefer a strategy which yields a higher income, and if two strategies yield identical incomes, then homo economicus's utility for them will be the same.[17] What is more, an idealized market is characterized by all players knowing that all other players are income maximizers. Thus, for instance, a homo economicus A's maximizing strategy against B will be the same regardless of whether A and B are the only two players in the market, they are members of a larger group, or they are members of two different groups. In other words, if A is a homo economicus, then she will condition her moves toward B only on the past history of play between the two players. These conditions informally define the notion of homo economicus and the concept of a (pure) market.

To better grasp certain properties of homo economicus, it will be useful to briefly consider some implications of this concept. Suppose, for instance, that B is known to use Tit for Tat and A is torn between the possibility of doing likewise or playing the maximally retaliatory strategy of Grim Trigger (cooperate in the first period and never defect first; if the opponent defects in any period in the game, defect forever, from the next period on). In a game with B, A's problem seems simple. Since Tit for Tat and Grim Trigger generate an identical pattern of interactions with B's Tit for Tat (constant cooperation) and hence identical incomes, A, as a homo economicus, should be indifferent to which of the two strategies he should play; A's utility from playing Tit for Tat will equal the utility produced by Grim Trigger. Similarly, if A is a homo economicus and if two strategies give A the same income when used against B, then A's utility from playing these two strategies against B should be the same in all groups in which A and B interact. The behavior of a homo economicus should, thus, be group-independent; as long as the incomes generated in an interaction are identical, the strategies generating these incomes should have the same utility.

The notion of a homo economicus is probably the most useful analytical tool in the social sciences. At the same time it is also one of the most descriptively inappropriate notions we have. Since in most situations people do not behave the way a homo economicus would, it is crucial for rational choice analysis to explain why utility-maximizing players do not act as income maximizers. To explain departures from homo economicus and explain the emergence of homo sociologicus, we must generalize our conceptual framework in a way that allows social institutions to creep into the market. (To assume them away axiomatically would, of course, make it impossible to explain their emergence.)

HOMO SOCIOLOGICUS

Departures from the behavior of homo economicus are an essential aspect of human interactions. We do apply third-party sanctions and punish people not only for what they did to us but also for what they did to others (social norms). Our utility is often affected by the distribution of incomes in a group and not just by the income we obtain. We often derive lesser utility from the same income if it was generated in a group with big inequalities (egalitarianism). We sometimes try to improve the well-being of the worst off in a group even though doing so reduces our income (Rawlsianism). We often derive greater utility from our actions if the average income in the group is larger (utilitarianism) even if our own income declines. In the extreme case, our utility may be completely independent of the value we get and be solely a function of the values accruing to others (e.g., extreme altruism). Less virtuously, we often enjoy larger utility when others are worse off, even if it comes at a loss of income to us (envy). We often derive greater utility from following the behavior of the majority (conformity), though in other cases we feel better by going against the group's behavior (nonconformity). Often, following a norm has an intrinsic value, regardless of the income it generates in an interaction; such a norm is internalized. If, for example, we value the norm of "forgiveness," we would derive higher utility from playing Tit for Tat than from playing Grim Trigger, even when these two strategies generate identical income.[18] These and other departures from the notion of homo economicus fall into the following two categories: (1) players condition actions toward each other on what happens in other interactions in the group, and (2) the utility a player derives from a norm is not only a function of the income the norm generates. To explain the emergence of these departures, we will need to factor them in to the analysis. The first category calls for a more general notion of a strategy; the second one calls for a more general type of a utility function.

To explain the emergence of homo sociologicus, we need to generalize our framework in a way which would allow social institutions to creep into the world of homo economicus. It is also important not to err in the opposite direction by injecting structural constraints into the theoretical framework. Our objective is to explain the emergence of institutions in a world which initially is devoid of any structural constraints. Conceptually, then, we need to begin our explanation with a theory in which both homo economicus and homo sociologicus are possible. Only if we allow for all forms of behavior to emerge can we meaningfully explain why some of them have arisen and others have not.

A GENERAL NOTION OF A STRATEGY

If player A is a homo economicus, then by definition she conditions her moves toward B only on the past history of play between the two players. Always Cooperate or Tit for Tat are examples of such strategies. If we want to understand, however, why A may want to condition her moves toward B on how B behaves toward some third party, C, the notion of strategy should be appropriately generalized to allow for such departures. The extension is very straightforward; we assume that A may choose to condition her moves toward B not only on what has happened between A and B but also on what has happened between B and other people in the group. In fact, to allow for all possible patterns of conditioning, we will assume that A's strategy toward B allows A to condition her action toward B in any period on what has happened in all pairwise games in the group.[19]

A GENERAL NOTION OF UTILITY

If we want to explain the emergence of internalized norms, for instance, we must allow for a possibility that players' utilities are functions not only of the income generated by their strategies but also of the strategies' noneconomic effects. If we label the residual category of all possible noneconomic effects as "social," we will assume that the general form of an individual's utility function for a norm η is:

utility(η) = utility (income(η)) + utility (social value(η)).

Note that the utility of a pure homo economicus is a function of income only. A radical egalitarian whose utility takes value 1 if and only if all players obtain identical incomes and 0 otherwise is an (extreme) example of a homo sociologicus.

Properties of the Solution

THE EVOLUTIONARY GAME

Imagine now a group of players involved in pairwise interactions.[20] Assume that players hold certain norms, but as they learn about norms of the other players, they may be willing to change the norms they hold. The setup is thus dynamic; in particular, we assume that there is a learning process that exerts evolutionary pressure on norms. Whenever different members of a group adopt different norms and different norms have different utilities for players, selection will trigger change. Individuals will keep switching to norms that increase their utility; norms with higher utilities will have higher reproductive fitness, that is, more successful behaviors will be replicated and less successful ones abandoned. Given the initial distribution of strategies in the group, one can ask whether the system will stabilize, which norms will become extinct, which will survive, and so on. The question of stability, for instance, requires finding a norm which, when used by all players in the population, can resist invasion of mutant norms (i.e., no new norm will have higher utility than the native one). We will call such a norm evolutionarily stable. In our theory, evolutionarily stable norms constitute the notion of equilibrium.

EVOLUTIONARY DYNAMICS

The essence of evolutionary change is simple; the more fit a strategy is in the current generation, the faster it increases. In other words, an evolutionary process is a dynamic that is increasing in utilities; players adapt by switching to strategies which give them higher utilities. There are, of course, infinitely many types (functional forms) of evolutionary processes which have this property. In biology, for instance, the mechanism which drives adaptation is genetic (cf. Dawkins 1989) and hence the so-called replicator dynamics, or proportional fitness rule, is the appropriate function to study. The social sciences, however, don't have a similarly well-defined replication mechanism that would imply a specific functional form. When and how in-

dividuals change their behavior depends on their utility functions, on the social and cognitive processes that drive change, such as learning through, for
example, imitation or socialization (Axelrod 1984; Gale, Binmore, and
Samuelson 1995; Boyd and Richerson 1985; Cabrales 1993), on players' "level
of rationality," on what they assume about the rationality of others, and many
other factors that consciously or not affect our behavior. Hence, assuming
that the process is described by a specific type of dynamics is a risky way to
proceed. Empirically it may be impossible to discern precisely how strategies
replicate, or what equations approximate the dynamics. Consequently, the
only meaningful equilibria may be ones that remain stable under all
processes which are increasing in players' utilities. Therefore, when looking
for equilibria, we will require that they remain stable under all process spec-
ifications.

BELIEFS ABOUT OTHERS

Different players may have very different utility functions. Hence, an
analysis that relies critically on an assumption that all players have identical
preferences is very fragile. But an analogous claim can be made about other
important parameters of the game, including players' beliefs about each
other. In game theory, any player's best course of action generally depends
on what she believes the other players are going to do, which, in turn, depends on what you think their utility functions are. But players do not know
each other's utility functions and indeed cannot know them for certain.
They may have only reasonable conjectures about some properties of others' utility functions. We have assumed that in an ideal market all players
know that everyone else is an income-maximizing homo economicus. In a
more general world, however, where actors need not be homo economicus,
this assumption must be replaced by a less restrictive one. Given the generalized form of the utility function, the only obvious generalization is one
which assumes that players' utilities are increasing in incomes, ceteris paribus
(i.e., all other factors in the utility function held constant). Since players are
utility maximizers if their utility is also a function of a norm's social value,
then in equilibrium the norm's social value must increase utility.[21] Otherwise the player would revert to pure homo economicus. This simply means
that if in equilibrium people hold a social value, then they derive positive
utility from it.

We should note that this is a very general assumption which allows players to hold a great variety of beliefs about others. One such belief, for instance, may be that other people are homo economicus, and hence if the
group undergoes any change which generates a new set of strategies, the
players will adapt to the change by switching to strategies which maximize

their income. But one can also imagine an opposite belief. One may conjecture that for others in the group a norm's social value is so great that even if there is a sizable change resulting in a new set of strategies, the players will still hold to the norm even though abandoning it could raise their income significantly. We also want to allow for the possibility that players believe that the group is heterogeneous in some ways; for instance, a person might think that some group members are pure home economicus, some are pure homo sociologicus, and others have yet some other kind of utility function. In short, we want very general assumptions; players' beliefs should allow for all possible distributions of utility functions in the group, and our solution should be invariant to these beliefs.[22]

NORMS VERSUS STRATEGIES

Using strategies as models of human behavior presents a serious problem. Positing that every strategy in a repeated game corresponds to a complete plan of the game is absurd. Except for very simple strategies like Always Cooperate or Tit for Tat, it is clearly unreasonable to suppose that players have comprehensive plans of a game of any complexity (e.g., see Simon and Schaeffer 1992). People's behaviors are guided by simple rules of thumb which constitute behavioral norms. For instance, in the iterated prisoners' dilemma, one may follow a proscriptive norm of "niceness" (Axelrod 1984)—"never defect first"—or a prescriptive one of "vengeance" which requires punishing a partner's defection at the first opportunity; one could follow a saintly norm of Always Cooperate or a superstitious one of never defecting in period 13.[23] Thus we will define a norm as any constraint on players' strategies.[24] It is norms, then, rather than strategies that should be the proper object of the analysis. When we pose questions about the emergence and stability of behaviors, we will search for norms that emerge in equilibria, not just strategies.

EQUILIBRIA

Consider a group in which everyone plays the same norm. If the norm is the best reply to itself (Nash equilibrium), then no one has an incentive to change it and the ecology will be in equilibrium. But such an equilibrium may be very unstable; it may not hold if for some reason several of the players change their behaviors. To have a meaningful solution, we need a more robust concept of an equilibrium, and a robust equilibrium requires that if we perturb the ecology by allowing a few "mutant" behaviors to invade the group, the common norm will not be destabilized. If players who follow the common norm would still have no incentive to switch to some other behavior, no matter what the "mutant" behaviors are, then the norm will be stable. Thus an evolutionarily stable norm is one that, once it is sufficiently common in a group, can resist a small invasion of any new behaviors.[25] All the stability results which we describe below use this notion of stability.

Rational Foundations of Social Institutions

With the above sketch of the basic assumptions in hand, we now have the framework needed to present our results. To avoid frustration, it is important to keep in mind that the theory sketched above is deductive and the results listed below are theorems that require formal proofs. Some of the proofs are complex; some are less so. All are sufficiently complex, however, so that common intuition is not enough to see why the following propositions follow from our assumptions. In fact, as we shall see, some results are quite counterintuitive.

THE IMPOSSIBILITY OF STABLE HOMO ECONOMICUS

The problem with homo economicus is simple; in games of cooperation, a stable homo economicus does not exist in equilibrium.[26] Take, for example, three individuals, A, B, and C, interacting with one another in a repeated prisoners' dilemma. Suppose that while initially all cooperate with all, at some point A starts defecting toward B whereas B loyally continues to cooperate with A. Assume, moreover, that while B is being exploited by A, cooperation between A and C and between B and C continues. C's problem is now clear: should he start punishing A for A's exploitation of B or not? The norm which says that foes of your friends ought to be your foes requires that C defect toward A. But if C starts punishing A for A's mistreatment of B, C may jeopardize the beneficial cooperative exchange he has with A. By complying with the norm, C would reduce his income—which is irrational for homo economicus. This calculus is precisely what destabilizes a group of income-maximizing homo economicus.

The essence of the instability of homo economicus can be seen in an example which tells the above story of players A, B, and C in the context of the evolutionary prisoners' dilemma game (Boyd and Lorberbaum 1987). Suppose that a universal norm of Tit for Tat has evolved in a group. Since everyone is using a nice strategy—one that never defects first (Axelrod 1984, 33)—each player cooperates with everyone else in all periods; hence Tit for Tat's retaliatoriness (its readiness to punish defection) is never tapped. Because a latent property may decay, some Tit for Tat strategies may mutate into less provocable ones, say Generous Tit for Tat (cooperate in periods 1 and 2 and thereafter in any period $k > 2$ do what one's partner did in $k - 1$). Suppose, then, that a few of the mutant Generous Tit for Tats invade the group. Because Generous Tit for Tat is, like Tit for Tat, nice, everyone continues to cooperate and the invaders remain behaviorally indistinguishable from the native Tit for Tats. Assuming, as we have before, that the payoff to mutual cooperation is 3, the average per-period payoff in any game involving Tit for Tat and Generous Tit for Tat is 3. Suppose now that a behaviorally distinct mutation, Suspicious Tit for Tat, appears in the group. The non-nice version of Tit for Tat, Suspicious Tit for Tat, defects in period 1 and thereafter reciprocates its partner's previous move. Tit for Tat responds to this deviation by punishing Suspicious Tit for Tat in period 2, thus triggering a vendetta, with Suspicious Tit for Tat defecting in odd periods and cooperating in even ones and Tit for Tat defecting in even periods and cooperating in odd. This results in a string of alternating temptation and sucker's payoffs. With the temptation payoff of 5 and sucker's payoff of 0, both Tit for Tat and Suspicious Tit for Tat end up with an average per-period payoff of 2.5. Yet clearly a vendetta is not the best reply to Suspicious Tit for Tat. The best response to Suspicious Tit for Tat calls for ignoring the first defection and cooperating thereafter—exactly how Generous Tit for Tat behaves. Thus in a game between Generous Tit for Tat and Suspicious Tit for Tat both strategies end up with an average per-period payoff of 3. Finally, two Suspicious Tit for Tats will defect with each other in every period, thus getting an average payoff of L.

Consider now a group in which Tit for Tat is almost universal, with a frequency of $1 - \varepsilon$, and an ε fraction of mutant strategies: ε_1 Generous Tit for Tat and ε_2 Suspicious Tit for Tats ($\varepsilon_1 + \varepsilon_2 = \varepsilon$). Note now that in a group consisting of homo economics the payoff for Tit for Tat equals $3(1 - \varepsilon)$ + $2.5\varepsilon_2 + 3\varepsilon_1$, the payoff for Generous Tit for Tat is $3(1 - \varepsilon) + 3\varepsilon_2 + 3\varepsilon_1$, and the payoff for Suspicious Tit for Tat equals $2.5(1 - \varepsilon) + \varepsilon_2 + 3\varepsilon_1$. Clearly, since Generous Tit for Tat cooperates with all strategies, it obtains the highest payoff. But this means that players who use Tit for Tat may want to switch to Generous Tit for Tat or some other income-maximizing strategy which would destabilize the group norm of Tit for Tat.[27] The logic of this construction is exactly what makes homo economics unstable in equilibrium.

But if the world of homo economics were ridden with instability, then stabilizing mechanisms would enjoy a selective advantage. What sort of mechanisms will stabilize groups of homo economics? Any stabilizing mechanism must be a departure from the model of homo economics; hence any such mechanism must be a type of social institution. Hence the next question is, what kind of institutions will do the job?

SOCIAL NORMS INVOLVING THIRD-PARTY SANCTIONS

One of the most perplexing puzzles of rational behavior is the existence of group norms that induce us to reward and punish other players not for what they did to us but for what they did to other players in the group. In the preceding story of A, B, and C (where B was exploited by A, hence A was B's foe, while A and C and B and C continued to be "friends" and thus cooperated with each other), for instance, a norm which says that foes of your friends ought to be your foes would require C to defect toward A. A different norm which requires that friends of your foes are your foes would have the Tit for Tat players defect toward Generous Tit for Tat, who cooperates with Tit for Tat's foe (i.e., a player with whom Tit for Tat does not cooperate continuously), Suspicious Tit for Tat. But this suggests one way to solve the problem of homo economicus's instability. If Tit for Tat players altered their strategy by adding a third-party sanction requiring them to defect toward friends of your foes, the resulting payoff structure would be markedly different; the payoff for the new Tit for Tat would be $3(1 - \varepsilon) + 2.5\varepsilon_2 + \varepsilon_1$, Generous Tit for Tat would get $(1 - \varepsilon) + 3\varepsilon_2 + 3\varepsilon_1$, and Suspicious Tit for Tat would get $2.5(1 - \varepsilon) + \varepsilon_2 + 3\varepsilon_1$. In this case, the new version of Tit for Tat gets the highest payoff in the group (assuming, of course, that ε is sufficiently small) and the norm remains stable.

As it turns out, such rules involving third-party sanctions *are precisely what are sufficient to restore stability* (Bendor and Swistak 2001, 2000). If a norm is sufficiently common in the group, this property would give it an effective conformity-enforcing mechanism against all possible deviant norms; any deviation from the majority behavior will give the mutant a lower utility. This conformity-enforcing attribute turns out to be necessary to stabilize a norm. In fact, for games of cooperation, a sufficient condition for equilibria requires third-party sanctions that use the following two ancient rules: "a foe of a friend is a foe" and "a friend of a foe is a foe." That we can derive these norms under extremely weak assumptions explains, we believe, the prevalence of social norms in social, political, and economic systems.

GOSSIP

Punishing a departure from a social norm requires that player A know not only what happens between herself and B (which is most natural to assume) but also what happens between B and C and between any pair of people in the group. Hence, gossip, a powerful weapon in small communities, plays a functionally critical role; it is necessary for stability. This could explain why this type of social exchange—exchange of information about third parties' behavior—is a favorite form of interaction among humans. Of course, gossip will work only when the exchanged information is truthful and people trust it and each other. But what happens when information is not credible and people do not trust each other?

ENVY

When third-party sanctions cannot be applied because people distrust one another, we would expect that some other stabilizing mechanism would emerge. The question is what mechanism will induce stability when credible information is absent. Suppose, for instance, that even though members of a group do not observe all third-party interactions and cannot trust what they hear about them, they do observe the total wealth of each person in the group. If wealth is observable, then another group mechanism which is sufficient to ensure stability turns out to be envy; defect toward anyone whose wealth (total income) exceeds yours (Swistak 2000). Absent trust, envy is a functional equivalent of the two social norms which stipulate that a foe of a friend is a foe and a friend of a foe is a foe. Envy, of course, is not only an emotion but also a social norm, that is, a behavior that conditions what A does to B on information above and beyond what has happened between the two. What happens, however, if the information constraints are even more severe and players distrust each other and have no reliable indicators of a person's wealth? Are social norms the only form of social institutions that can stabilize behaviors?

CONFORMITY

Since each stabilizing mechanism requires a departure from the model of pure homo economicus, the new stability result requires the emergence of a new social institution. To see how the necessary stabilizing mechanism works, consider the following utility effect: Imagine that a player who holds a certain norm derives a small positive utility (the norm's social value) from interacting with another player who holds the same norm. This, of course, is conformity. It can be proved that an arbitrarily small conformity effect suffices to stabilize a strategy like Tit for Tat (Swistak 2001). The stabilizing mechanism in this case is an arbitrarily small correction to the utility function of homo economicus, which arguably corresponds to the most fundamental kind of social institution—conformity.

While conformity avoids the strong informational conditions required by third-party sanctions and envy, it still requires that a player be able to ascertain that sufficiently many others adhere to the same norm. Is it possible to stabilize behavior without this condition? Or is conformity the only type of social institution that can stabilize norms that don't use third-party sanctions, such as Tit for Tat? Interestingly, it can be proved that there is only one other type of a social institution that can stabilize a norm: the mechanism of internalization (Swistak 2001).

INTERNALIZED NORMS

Consider a person who holds a specific norm and derives a small positive utility (social value) from all interactions in which he exercises the norm. Or, equivalently, assume that switching away from the norm reduces his utility a bit. This, of course, is what can happen when norms are internalized. It can be shown that an arbitrarily small utility effect of internalization suffices to stabilize a norm (Swistak 2001). Interestingly, it can be shown that the three social institutions—social norms, conformity, and internalized norms—are the only independent mechanisms that are both sufficient and necessary to stabilize behavior in a group (Swistak 2001). More specifically, third-party sanctions are both sufficient and necessary to stabilize norms absent conformity and internalization. Conformity is sufficient and necessary to stabilize norms absent third-party sanctions and internalization. And finally, internalization is sufficient and necessary, absent third-party sanctions and conformity. This means that all other types of social institutions which can stabilize behavior must involve one or more of the three basic institutions: third-party sanctions, conformity, or internalization. In this sense, *these three elements of social organization are the foundation of all stable behaviors.*

We chose to focus here exclusively on the general type of norms, or social institutions, that must emerge in markets and other systems of exchange as stabilizing mechanisms. We did not comment on any of a number of important properties of these equilibrium behaviors that are clearly worth analyzing. Are the equilibrium norms efficient (cooperative) or not? And if both efficient and inefficient norms can be obtained in equilibrium, do these equilibria differ from each other? If so, how? These are important questions, but they are not central to the main objective of this chapter. Our goal here was to shed light on the microfoundations of social institutions, to entertain the idea that social structure can be derived as a set of mechanisms that have evolved in stable systems composed of (adaptively) rational players. If these few basic social institutions have indeed evolved (under different conditions) as mechanisms stabilizing behavior, then we should be able to explain other forms of human organization in a similar fashion.

Notes

1. In sociology, see, for example, Coleman 1986 and 1990; in economics, see Eggertsson 1990.

2. Putnam represents them as two-person or *n*-person prisoners' dilemmas.

3. Formally, of course, the concept of a payoff has a specific meaning in game theory and refers to the utility of the amount of good obtained and not the amount of good itself.

4. More precisely, these utilities may be different but should remain sufficiently close so that behavior is unaffected.

5. More precisely, for a homo sociologicus there are situations in which a player's behavior garners identical income but different utilities, and the difference in utilities is large enough to induce different behaviors and thus different equilibria in a game.

6. Note that homo sociologicus players, although not income maximizers, are still utility maximizers and are hence rational in this standard sense.

7. When we solve the game for equilibria, a social institution may or may not be a necessary part of an equilibrium. If an institution is simply an off-equilibrium phenomenon, then it is bound to disappear once we remove conditions which keep actors from reaching the equilibrium. The question of whether an institution is an off-equilibrium phenomenon or a property of an equilibrium is not just a matter of theoretical importance. An answer may have serious policy implications. For example, if discrimination is indeed a self-correctable market deviation, then we might be better off letting market forces take care of the problem. Regulation may not only slow down the process of dissolution but even intensify the discrimination problem. Yet if the market thesis is wrong and discrimination can be sustained in a robust equilibrium, then regulation may be necessary to restore efficiency.

8. Suppose we want to explain the emergence of third-party sanctions (social norms.) It would be difficult to accept an explanation which relied critically on a specific assumption about players' cognitive constraints or one which was sensitive to small changes in players' payoffs. These norms are ubiquitous precisely because they are robust with respect to small (or possibly even large) parametric changes. Hence a reasonable explanation of their emergence cannot rely in a critical way on any knife-edge assumption.

9. The precise formulation of the various results and assumptions has been advanced in a series of papers: Bendor and Swistak (1997, 2000, 2001) and Swistak (2000, 2001). The theory described here is formal and all our results are established deductively. Though this chapter is quite informal, it is important to keep in mind that all concepts presented here have precise definitions in the theory. Milton Friedman's old advice is to keep theory construction maximally formal or mathematical (as a safeguard against logical problems) and its presentation maximally informal. One drawback of this advice is that an informal presentation of formal ideas may induce in the reader the very problems against which theory construction was meant to serve as a safeguard.

10. Evolutionary game theory began in biology with the seminal works of Maynard Smith and G. Price (1973) and Maynard Smith (1982). This approach diffused early and rapidly in the biological sciences (see, e.g., Hines 1987, Axelrod and Dion 1988, and Vincent and Brown 1988 for review articles) and a bit later, in game theory, in economics and political science (see, e.g., Friedman 1991, Selten 1991, Mailath 1992, and Samuelson 1993 for review articles; recent books include Fudenberg and Levine 1998, Samuelson 1998, Vega-Redondo 1996, Weibull 1995, and Young 1998.) The early work of Robert Axelrod, in particular his book *The Evolution of Cooperation* (1984), was very important in bringing the paradigm of evolutionary games to

the attention of social scientists. Our work, which follows in the footsteps of this earlier line of research, focuses on trying to explain the emergence of norms.

11. Denote by $v(a, b)$ Player 1's payoff in a stage game when she plays action a against Player 2's b. A game of cooperation is then formally defined as a symmetric two-person game with M actions, $a1, \ldots, aM$ ($M > 1$), which has the following two properties: (1) there is a cooperative action ac such that $v(ac, ac)$ is the unique efficient outcome in pure strategies, that is, $2v(ac, ac) \geq v(ak, am) + v(am, ak)$, for all m, k, equality holding if and only if $m = k = c$, and (2) there exists an action ad, distinct from ac, such that $v(ad, a_j) \geq v(a_j, ad)$ for all $j = 1, \ldots, M$.

12. While this may seem like a very strong assumption and one that is empirically implausible (e.g., Hechter 1992), it is in fact a reasonable way to model repeated interactions without a specific termination point. See, for example, Rubinstein 1991 for an explanation.

13. Note that it makes sense to talk about payoff to a specific strategy only if we identify the strategy it plays against. Note also that there are other ways to specify the worth of a strategy in an infinite game (cf. Fudenberg and Tirole 1991.)

14. The reason why it makes sense to focus the analysis on games for which the future is sufficiently important is simple: the problem of cooperation is otherwise trivial. An equilibrium in an iterated prisoners' dilemma wherein players heavily discount future payoffs is the same as the equilibrium in the one-shot prisoners' dilemma defection. If future payoffs matter little, maximizing in a repeated game is effectively equivalent to maximizing in a current period and the Always Defect strategy becomes the best response to all other strategies in the iterated prisoners' dilemma. Hence the emergence and the stability of cooperative behaviors, and of institutions that can sustain them in equilibrium, becomes meaningful only in games where the future is sufficiently important.

15. In the language of game theory, this means that the pair of Tit for Tat strategies in the iterated prisoners' dilemma with sufficiently important future is in Nash equilibrium.

16. By a percent of cooperation, we mean the frequency of mutually cooperative moves. This is an unorthodox formulation of the so-called folk theorem, a well-known result in game theory (cf. Fudenberg and Tirole 1991).

17. Since in standard game theory the concept of utility is treated as a primitive term (it is not definable in terms of other concepts), some readers may be troubled by the fact that we seem to be working in a nonstandard framework where utility is defined in terms of economic value and social value. This, however, is *not* the case. The concept of income can be defined in terms of utilities derived by actors in different games which are a part of a more complex game (an evolutionary game) to be described later. More specifically, we define A's income, in a game with B, as the utility (calculated as a per-period average) that A *would* have gotten in this game in the absence of any other actors or interactions. (Informally speaking, this is as if A and B were the only people in the world involved in this single repeated interaction.) Note now that if A and B interact with each other in an analogous repeated game—but this game is a part of a "larger game" where A interacts with C, D, and so on—then, given the possibility of certain social effects on utility, the utility A de-

rives from the game with B need not be equal to what it would have been had A and B been the only two actors.

18. Tit for Tat has an important property of being forgiving; an opponent's co-operation will always be reciprocated regardless of his earlier moves. Grim Trigger, on the other hand, is maximally unforgiving; a single defection in any period is punished by permanent defection thereafter. For instance, in a game against Tit for Tat, Grim Trigger and Tit for Tat generate identical incomes, yet a player who values the norm of forgiveness may derive greater utility from playing Tit for Tat even though the norm of forgiveness is never exercised in this particular interaction.

19. Note that this general notion of a strategy does not require a player to condition her moves on other interactions in the group; it merely allows for such a possibility.

20. We assume that interactions among players are unstructured. This lack of structure means that in every period every individual has the same probability of interacting with any other player in the group. We also assume that each interaction has a fixed form (for example, of a one-shot prisoners' dilemma game) and that each player is in the game for the long haul so that his value of an interaction with any other player in the game can be reasonably indexed by an average per-period payoff, as we have discussed before. Every two players in a group are thus involved in a repeated interaction with each other. If a group consists of n individuals, each of them plays $n - 1$ separate repeated games (each game with one of the $n - 1$ other members of the group). Each of the $n - 1$ pairwise repeated games generates a payoff (i.e., as measured by the average per-period payoff) for an individual playing a specific strategy. If an actor is a homo economices, then his total payoff in the game will equal the sum of payoffs garnered in all pairwise interactions. For a technical introduction to evolutionary analysis, see, for example, Weibull 1995.

21. More specifically, we assume that players believe that if a norm is present in the group in equilibrium, then it cannot decrease players' utilities. If, however, a norm is not present in the group in equilibrium, then its impact on players' utilities is not known.

22. See Bendor and Swistak 2000 for formal definitions.

23. Note that some norms, for example, the superstitious one, constrain players' behavior only slightly, while others, like the norm of unconditional cooperation, are so demanding that they uniquely determine behavior in all periods of the game. This last type of a norm is equivalent to a game-theoretic strategy.

24. Douglass North (1990, 3) defines institutions as "the rules of the game in a society or, more formally, . . . the humanly devised constraints that shape human interaction." Our definition of a norm follows this very general formulation. Formally, we define a norm (Bendor and Swistak 2000) as any set of strategies.

25. Intuitively, "resist an invasion" may be understood in two reasonable ways: stronger, if the invaders decline in frequency under the evolutionary dynamic, and weaker, if they do not increase. Since in repeated games the best the native strategy can do is prevent the mutant from spreading, the weaker form of stability is the only type of stability attainable (cf. Selten 1983; van Damme 1987). More specifically, we will call a norm stable if it does not decrease in frequency in any group (with a fi-

nite number of strategies) where its frequency is sufficiently high. Others have referred to such strategies as semistable (Selten 1983), neutrally stable (Sobel 1993), or neutral ESS (evolutionarily stable strategies) (Warneryd 1993). If a native strategy is weakly stable, then certain mutants may be just as fit as the native and hence may remain in the population indefinitely.

26. In fact, it does not exist in any nontrivial game (Bendor and Swistak 1998).

27. In general, the payoff-maximizing strategy depends on what players believe about the future behavior of other players and how quickly they change their norms. Since we require stability under all evolutionary processes and under all beliefs, the norm of Tit for Tat is unstable.

References

Axelrod, Robert. 1984. *The Evolution of Cooperation*. New York: Basic Books.

Axelrod, Robert, and Douglas Dion. 1988. "The Further Evolution of Cooperation." *Science* 242 (December 9): 1385–90.

Bendor, Jonathan, and Piotr Swistak. 1997. "The Evolutionary Stability of Cooperation." *American Political Science Review* 91: 290–307.

———. 1998. "Evolutionary Equilibria: Characterization Theorems and Their Implications." *Theory and Decision* 45: 99–159.

———. 2000. "The Impossibility of Pure Homo Economicus." Working Paper.

———. 2001. "The Evolution of Norms." *American Journal of Sociology* 106: 1493–1545.

Boyd, Robert, and Jeffrey Lorberbaum. 1987. "No Pure Strategy Is Evolutionarily Stable in the Repeated Prisoners' Dilemma Game." *Nature* 327 (May 7): 58–59.

Boyd, Robert, and Peter J. Richerson. 1985. *Culture and the Evolutionary Process*. Chicago: University of Chicago Press.

Cabrales, Antonio. 1993. "Stochastic Replicator Dynamics." *Economics Working Paper* 54. Barcelona: Universitat Pompeu Fabra.

Coleman, James S. 1986. "Social Theory, Social Research, and a Theory of Action." *American Journal of Sociology* 91: 1309–35.

———. 1990. *Foundations of Social Theory*. Cambridge: Harvard University Press.

Dawkins, Richard. 1989. *The Selfish Gene*. Oxford: Oxford University Press.

Eggertsson, Thrainn. 1990. *Economic Behavior and Institutions*. Cambridge: Cambridge University Press.

Friedman, Daniel. 1991. "Evolutionary Games in Economics." *Econometrica* 59: 637–66.

Fudenberg, Drew, and David K. Levine. 1998. *The Theory of Learning in Games*. Cambridge: MIT Press.

Fudenberg, Drew, and Jean Tirole. 1991. *Game Theory*. Cambridge: MIT Press.

Gale, John, Kenneth Binmore, and Larry Samuelson. 1995. "Learning to Be Imperfect: The Ultimatum Game." *Games and Economic Behavior* 8 (January): 56–90.

Hechter, Michael. 1992. "The Insufficiency of Game Theory for the Resolution of Real-Life Collective Action Problems." *Rationality and Society* 4: 33–40.

Hines, W. G. S. 1987. "Evolutionary Stable Strategies: A Review of Basic Theory." *Theoretical Population Biology* 31: 195−272.

Mailath, George J. 1992. "Introduction: Symposium on Evolutionary Game Theory." *Journal of Economic Theory* 57: 259−77.

Maynard Smith, John. 1982. *Evolution and the Theory of Games*. Cambridge: Cambridge University Press.

Maynard Smith, John, and G. Price. 1973. "The Logic of Animal Conflict." *Nature* 246: 15−18.

North, Douglass C. 1990. *Institutions, Institutional Change, and Economic Performance*. Cambridge: Cambridge University Press.

Putnam, Robert D. 1993. *Making Democracy Work*. Princeton, N.J.: Princeton University Press.

Rubinstein, Ariel. 1991. "Comments on the Interpretation of Game Theory." *Econometrica* 59: 909−24.

Samuelson, Larry. 1993. "Recent Advances in Evolutionary Economics: Comments." *Economics Letters* 42: 313−19.

———. 1998. *Evolutionary Games and Equlibrium Selection*. Cambridge: MIT Press.

Selten, Reinhard. 1983. "Evolutionary Stability in Extensive 2-Person Games." *Mathematical Social Sciences* 5: 269−363.

———. 1991. "Evolution, Learning, and Economic Behavior." *Games and Economic Behavior* 3: 3−24.

Simon, Herbert, and Jonathan Schaeffer. 1992. "The Game of Chess." In *Handbook of Game Theory*, vol. 1, ed. R. J. Aumann and S. Hart. New York: Elsevier Science Publishers B.V.

Snidal, Duncan. 1991. "Relative Gains and the Pattern of International Cooperation." *American Political Science Review* 85 (3): 701−26.

Sobel, Joel. 1993. "Evolutionary Stability and Efficiency." *Economic Letters* 42 (2−3): 301−12.

Swistak, Piotr. 2000. "The Evolution of Envy." Manuscript.

———. 2001. "The Economic Origins of Social Order." Manuscript.

van Damme, Eric. 1987. *Stability and Perfection of Nash Equilibria*. Berlin: Springer-Verlag.

Vega-Redondo, Fernando. 1996. *Evolution, Games, and Economic Behavior*. Oxford: Oxford University Press.

Vincent, Thomas L., and Joel S. Brown. 1988. "The Evolution of ESS Theory." *Annual Review of Ecology and Systematics* 19: 423−43.

Warneryd, Karl. 1993. "Cheap Talk, Coordination, and Evolutionary Stability." *Games and Economic Behavior* 5 (October): 532−46.

Weibull, Jorgen. 1995. *Evolutionary Game Theory*. Cambridge: MIT Press.

Young, Peyton. 1998. *Individual Strategy and Social Structure*. Princeton, N.J.: Princeton University Press.

Young, Peyton, and Dean Foster. 1991. "Cooperation in the Short and in the Long Run." *Games and Economic Behavior* 3: 145−56.

ROBERT H. BATES, AVNER GREIF, AND SMITA SINGH 3

The Political Economy of Kinship Societies

THIS CHAPTER seeks to deepen our understanding of the process of development by exploring the political economy of kinship societies. Looking first at the economics, it emphasizes the manner in which families link labor and land in the process of production and the impact of diminishing returns upon material life. Turning to the politics, it focuses on the manner in which families provide defenses for persons and for property and the impact of this arrangement upon personal security. Dissenting from those who view kinship societies as static (see discussion below), it treats them as dynamic. Families, it argues, provide means for transacting across time, enabling people to save, to invest, and thus to enhance their future well-being.

Despite their capacity to form capital, kinship societies remain poor. To explore the economics of kinship societies is thus to explore the economics of underdevelopment. A major lesson to be drawn from this exploration is the significance of political institutions and their impact upon the level of prosperity that such societies can secure. Given the properties of their institutions, we find that kinship societies remain trapped in equilibria in which their members must trade off peace for prosperity—values that stand near the core of the meaning of development.

For the purposes of this chapter, two literatures prove most relevant. The first originates in economics and views development as the process of "structural transformation" (Kuznets 1966; Chenery and Taylor 1968). As economic development proceeds, economists argue, labor shifts from agriculture to industry and the percentage of the gross domestic product originating from agriculture falls while that originating from manufacturing rises. The second originates in sociology and views development as the process of "the great transformation" (Polanyi 1944). Whether in the form of Tönnes's (1963) juxtaposition of gemeinschaft and gesellschaft, Emile Durkheim's

(1949) notions of mechanical and organic solidarity, or Talcott Parsons and Edward Shills's (1951) comparison of societies in which status is ascribed with those in which it is achieved, the process of development is viewed as a transition from a social order governed by kin and community to one based on legality, bureaucracy, and institutions.

Kinship societies prevailed in Europe prior to the great transformation, whether in the form of the Celtic communities of Britain and western Europe, the Germanic tribes of northern and central Europe, or the Hungarian and Slavic Tribes of eastern Europe (Bloch 1961a, 1961b; Bartlett 1993). And as stressed by students of developing societies in the modern world, they dominate much of the social terrain in the developing world today, be it in Africa, Southeast Asia, or the mountainous communities of southern Asia, the Caucuses, or Latin America. To better grasp the origins and nature of the development process, then, this chapter probes the political economy of kinship societies.

The Economics of Agrarian Societies

Agriculture forms the economic foundation of kinship societies. Table 3.1 captures the relationship between land, labor, and output that characterizes agrarian economies. For any given quantity of labor, land of grade A is the most productive and grade E the least. And as more labor is applied to each plot, the additional amount of output declines.

The first person to work grade A land produces 100 bushels; when an additional person also works the soil, total output increases to 180 bushels. Doubling the input of labor produces a less than proportionate increase in output. Table 3.2 presents the same data in a different manner; the figures in that table record the difference in total output produced by the addition of units of labor. The first person who works grade A land adds 100 bushels to the total output; the second adds but 80. As shown in Table 3.2, when added to a given unit of land, each additional unit of labor produces a smaller increment in output. It is as if the addition of a new worker impedes the operations of those already present, with the magnitude of the interference increasing with the total number of workers. Alternatively, the first worker may be the most productive—say, a middle-aged adult—with younger, older, or less healthy workers entering the labor force at later stages.

Just as movement down the columns of Tables 3.1 and 3.2 leads to diminishing output per additional unit of labor, so too does the movement across the rows. One person working the land with the richest soils—grade A land—can produce 100 units of output. As the soils decline in quality—moving from grade A to grade E land—output declines from 100 bushels per unit of land to a mere 20 in the lowest-quality soils. The same relation

TABLE 3.1

Total Output per Unit of Land and Labor (in bushels)

Units of Labor	Land				
	Grade A	Grade B	Grade C	Grade D	Grade E
1	100	90	70	50	20
2	180	160	130	70	30
3	240	210	150	80	38
4	280	230	160	87	43
5	300	248	168	92	46
6	310	255	173	95	48

SOURCE: Drawn from J. P. Quirk, *Intermediate Microeconomics* (Chicago: Science Research Associates, 1976).

holds no matter the number of workers; were six people to be placed on a hectare of grade E land, they would produce less total output on its inferior soils—48 bushels—than they could on lands of higher quality—say, land of grade B, where the six could produce a total of 255 bushels per year. Returns thus decline along both the internal margin (i.e., as more labor is added to a single plot of land) and the external margin (as a given labor force works additional units of land). The relationship between land, labor, and output thus exhibits decreasing returns (Ricardo 1819).

Over much of history, societies have remained agrarian. Production in such societies has therefore been subject to diminishing returns. This remains true in agrarian societies today. And because populations increase while the increment of output generated by additional workers declines, average incomes fall over *la longue durée* (the long term).[1] Such societies are therefore not only agrarian but also poor.

DYNAMICS

Sociologists who study contemporary societies (e.g., Lerner 1958) and those who focus on history (e.g., Max Weber; see Gerth and Mills 1958) view kinship societies as governed by tradition and, by implication, as therefore resistant to change. And in economics, neoclassicists (e.g., Schultz 1976) join Marxists (e.g., Marx and Engels 1979) in exploring the manner in which traditional technologies constrain the capacity of such societies to develop. While modern anthropologists emphasize the dynamic nature of kinship societies, their predecessors often cast them in the "timeless present," as

TABLE 3.2

Increment in Output per Additional Unit of Labor

Units of Labor	Land				
	Grade A	Grade B	Grade C	Grade D	Grade E
1	100	90	70	50	20
2	80	70	60	20	10
3	60	50	20	10	8
4	40	20	10	7	5
5	20	18	8	5	3
6	10	7	5	3	2

if they were immune to historical change (e.g., Ortner 1999). Students of kinship societies have thus tended to treat kinship societies as static.

We instead view these societies as dynamic. Central to these dynamics is the behavior of families. One manner in which families impart dynamics to societies is through the process of reproduction. All else remaining constant, an increase in population alters the ratio between land and labor, setting in motion numerous adjustments in relative prices and incomes. When studying preindustrial Europe, historians mark the passage of *la longue durée* in terms of the "great demographic cycle" associated with the early increase in Europe's population, its collapse in the fourteenth century, and its subsequent slow recovery, punctuated by the recurrence of the plague and the outbreak of wars (Postan 1937; Goldstone 1991; Wrigley and Schofield 1989; but see Brenner 1976). Over *la longue durée*, average incomes tended to decline as population rose (Wrigley and Schofield 1989); with static technologies, societies failed to escape from the tyranny of diminishing returns, leading to lower average incomes.

In the midst of such aggregate dynamics, the family provides a means for defending and enhancing individual welfare. As suggested in Fortes 1958, the element of time structures the relationship between kin (see Figure 3.1); families exist not only at moments of time but also across units of time. On the one hand, the passage of time marks the life span of individuals who proceed from youth (Y), to middle age (M), and thence to old age (O) before exiting the family group; thus the horizontal axis. On the other hand, the passage of time defines the structure of generations; thus the vertical axis. Taken together, the two effects yield a structure in which generations overlap and middle-aged persons cohabit with members of the older and

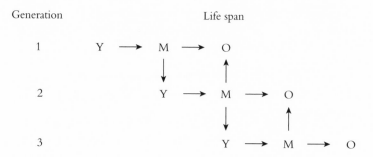

FIGURE 3.1 Overlapping generations and the family over time
Y = young
M = middle-aged
O = old
The arrows indicate the flow of resources.

younger generations. They also thereby yield a structure through which people can invest. The middle-aged can sacrifice their own consumption possibilities at one point in time by channeling resources to the young in anticipation of enhancing their consumption possibilities at a later period in time when they (now old) are supported by the young (now middle-aged); the verical arrows in Figure 3.1 indicate the flow of resources between generations. The result is that people in agrarian societies employ families not only to organize production and consumption but also—pace both the neoclassical and Marxist economists—to form capital.

While the central tendency of average incomes is to decline with time in kinship societies, all else being equal, through the family, individuals can strategize against the impact of diminishing returns and enhance their future prospects by investing in their young. Most commonly, the formation of capital in this manner takes the form of migration and resettlement (Bates 1976; Stark and Bloom 1985).

Migration as a Rational Investment

Consider the "history" of a representative family settled on the most desirable lands of the region whose economic properties are captured in Table 3.1, assuming that it was the first family to settle in the grade A land. Mixing its labor with land, the family produces one hundred bushels of output. As the family matures, it grows. Its subsequent generations then encounter diminishing returns; with the passage of time and the increase in population, prosperity in the subregion (grade A) yields to poverty as average incomes decline.

Under such circumstances, the middle-aged and younger generations find a common interest: provisioning ventures by the young. The elders dispatch them to the extensive margin, there to open up, settle, and bring into production new lands. By helping to defray the costs of resettlement, families generate a stream of young households from the economically declining and densely populated core to the sparsely populated periphery, where land is more abundant and the prospects of prosperity higher than at home. Families in locations where incomes have become depressed owing to diminishing returns escape to the extensive margin, locating on soils that while possibly inferior may yet be lightly inhabited and so capable of yielding a higher level of average income.

For the elders, such ventures yield two benefits. By reducing population density in the core, the elders defend the prevailing wage; they thus buy time in their struggle against the impact of diminishing returns. And insofar as the cadets they dispatch to the periphery secure the rewards that accrue to successful pioneers, the elders stand to benefit from the remission of a portion of their newfound prosperity. As demographic pressures mount in settled territories, the result is a spawning of migratory ventures; flows of settlers pulse forth from the core, journeying to the periphery, and claim property there. Manipulating links between kin, the elders thus render the family a means of investing.

Far from being static, agrarian societies are thus dynamic. Writing of eleventh- and twelfth-century Europe, Marc Bloch (1961a; 1961b, 69) notes not only the growth of population but also the movement of people which led to the "incessant gnawing of the plough at forest and wasteland," the creation of "completely new villages clutching at . . . virgin soil(s)," the "extensions of the assarters,"[2] and the waves of colonization "of the Iberian plateau and the great plains beyond the Elbe." And writing of modern Africa, Marshall D. Sahlins (1961) emphasizes the expansionary nature of kinship societies, such as the Nuer and the Tiv. Such societies, he argues, are best thought of as "predatory," as they use kinship as a means of invading neighboring territories, colonizing them, and establishing rights of property. Impelled by diminishing returns in the core, then, generations combine and expand the range of settlement by venturing into new territories.

While emphasizing resettlement as a response to diminishing returns, it is important to note the existence of other strategies. In particular, rather than altering their location, families may instead invest, seeking thereby to improve the yield from existing farms (Boserup 1965; North and Thomas 1973; Ladurie 1976). By leveling fields, manuring and mulching and altering the depth and structure of the soils, families improve the yields from their lands. By planting fodder crops and stall-feeding their livestock, they increase the extent of the arable. By damming watercourses and constructing reservoirs, they lengthen the growing season and secure the multiple planting of crops. And by experimenting with new varieties and new rotations, they increase the output they secure per unit of land and labor. Sacrificing leisure, farmers invest labor in the improvement of their farms. The increase in yields often persists beyond the lifetimes of the family head whose sacrifice made them possible. Because they create a valuable asset for future generations, these efforts also constitute investments.

The Politics of Agrarian Societies, Part I: Within Kin Groups

Families in agrarian societies thus respond to the threat posed by diminishing returns by investing. The sacrifices made by the elders when staking the ventures of the young are made in the belief that the young will subsequently repay. For this behavior to be rational, the conduct of the young must be consistent with the belief of the elders; were their behavior to be otherwise, beliefs would have to be revised—or be revealed as irrational.

When portrayed sequentially, the problematic nature of the junior members' conduct becomes plain. As shown in Figure 3.2, the seniors can choose to invest (I) or not ($\sim I$). If the seniors choose not to invest ($\sim I$), the game terminates. If they choose to invest (I), the young then choose. They can choose either P (for "perform," i.e., to repay the loan), or D (for "defect," i.e., to migrate, to settle abroad, and to abscond with the funds). The payoffs for the seniors and young appear at the end points of the game; those of the elders come first; and the numbers rank the outcomes at each end point from 1 (for the highest) to 3 (for the least preferred). The elders prefer to invest in the young and to receive their support in old age; they would prefer not to invest in the young at all rather than investing in the young only to have the young subsequently defect with the funds. By contrast, the young would do best by defecting. And from their point of view, they would prefer to receive payments from the older generation, even if they need to repay them, to not receiving such contributions.

Applying backward induction, the incentives become clear, as do their significance for society. The elders can see that the youths would do best using their contributions to settle abroad and then sever their family ties. In anticipation of this behavior, the elders' best response is not to invest. Unable to achieve the first best outcome (which results from the choices of I, P), the elders then steer the family toward the third-best (that resulting from their choice of $\sim I$).

The general problem facing the family can be characterized as one of time consistency.[3] Even were the youths to pledge to repay, their pledges would not be believed. For when it later comes time for them to choose between P and D, their interests would be best served by the latter (i.e., defecting). Maximizing in each period, the youths would do best by first making, and then breaking, their promises. Their pledges to repay are therefore

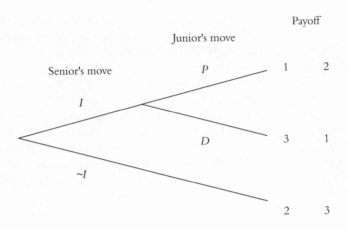

FIGURE 3.2 Game between generations

I = invest
$\sim I$ = don't invest
P = perform
D = defect

not credible, and in the absence of corrective measures, the elders' best response is to refrain from investing—a response that makes this two-genera-
tion "society" worse off.

Agrarian societies, like others, appear to have responded to this problem
by lodging the private arrangement of the family within a structure of public institutions.[4] Specifically, they place the senior generation in positions of
power (Meillassoux 1981). Elders often dominate the councils that adjudicate
property rights, be they over cattle, land, or people. They dominate the
councils that rule on matters of family law, resolving disputes over marriages,
divorces, or the inheritance of property. They select among competing
claimants for public office, allocate titles, and control access to desired positions, be they membership in an age grade or in a secret society. Those who
wish to marry, to gain social recognition of their child, or to be laid to rest
among ancestors and kin must first pass through a "veto point" controlled by
the older generation. In gerontocracies, elders govern.

In terms of the game captured in Figure 3.2, when the family is lodged
within a polity in which the elders hold power, the strategic situation includes an additional move—one in which the elders can reward, or penalize,
the youths, depending upon whether they have behaved opportunistically or
honored the terms of the contract between generations. So long as the reactions of the elders are sufficient to render the payoffs to choosing P greater
than those from choosing D, the pledges of the youths to repay can be
trusted. For knowing that the elders can sanction them—whether by de-

priving them of honors and offices, marriage opportunities, or favorable rulings in disputes with neighbors—the youths possess an incentive to curry their favor by honoring their promises and repaying their debts.

In kinship societies, families not only regulate both consumption and production but also superintend the polity. As stated in Radcliffe-Brown 1965, "For the understanding of any aspect of the social life of [such societies]—economic [or political] . . .—it is essential to have a thorough knowledge of their system of kinship" (1). And the structure of the polity is such that the older generation governs. In societies in which the elders move last, beliefs that the youths will perform find subsequent validation. The nature of political institutions is therefore such that investment becomes a rational act.

The Politics of Kinship Societies, Part II: Between Families

In agrarian societies, relationships within families thus pose threats to economic well-being; absent the presence of institutions to counter the incentives for youths to defect from intergenerational contracts, such societies would be worse off. But relationships between families also threaten to undermine the economic welfare of agrarian societies. Each family seeks to enhance its material well-being. One way of doing so is by engaging in production. Another is by engaging in predation and seizing the goods produced by others. Rather than expending costly effort on labor, families can instead devote their energies to raiding. Each family must therefore protect itself and allocate its endowment of labor not only between leisure and productive effort but also between peaceful activities and military training as it prepares to raid or to defend against raids by others.

The temptation to raid arises in the core (i.e., in the most productive region), where some people have improved their land, accumulated livestock, or amassed possessions. To ward off attempts to appropriate the fruit of their labors, families in the core arm themselves, seeking thereby to deter predation by threatening punitive retaliation. Similar tensions arise in the periphery, as new entrants encounter established settlers in the less densely populated margin and seek to seize their lands.

By modeling the behavior of families thus endowed, thus motivated, and thus situated in relation to others, we can achieve additional insights into the properties of kinship societies. In particular, we learn how their institutions—polities in which each family provides its own military—shape the choices of private individuals in ways that place limits on the attainable level of well-being.

A MODEL OF KINSHIP POLITIES

As emphasized by students of agrarian societies, from the point of view of their members, kin groups appear infinitely lived; members of younger generations replace the ranks thinned by the deaths of the elders. Such societies exhibit an additional characteristic: relationships take the form of face-to-face interactions. Given the small scale of such societies, this is as true of political relationships between families as it is of economic relationships within them. Given these characteristics, when exploring political interactions between families, we direct our attention to the equilibria that can arise in games in which persons choose in the expectation that interactions will be repeated an infinite number of times. And we also direct our attention to equilibria that arise in games in which the families can play trigger strategies, conditioning their choices upon those previously made by others.

When playing a trigger strategy in an extended game, a player adopts the strategy of punishing another for having taken opportunistic actions in earlier plays of the game. The familiar strategy tit for tat, for example, is a trigger strategy and one in which a defection triggers a one-period punishment (see Axelrod 1984). But the punishment can run in principle for several periods; were the player to play a "grim trigger" strategy, punishment would continue to the end of the game. In the context of our model of kinship politics, as will be seen, punishment takes the form of entering a stage of the game in which everyone defects, resulting in low payoffs for all players.

SOME TABLE SETTING

For simplicity, we assume there exist two families, $i = 1,2$, equally endowed with a unit of labor, T_i, which it can allocate to work, w_i; to military preparation, m_i; or to leisure, $l_i = T_i - w_i - m_i$. Labor is productive; expenditures of effort, w_i, result in output, $F(w_i)$.[5] Military activity is unproductive. If player i attacks and player $-i$ defends, then $M(m_i, m_{-i})$ is the share of player $-i$'s wealth that player i is able to expropriate if she allocates m_i units of effort to perfecting her military capabilities, while the other player, player $-i$, allocates m_{-i} units. Each player derives utility from income and from leisure denoted by $U(I_i(\bullet), l_i)$, where I_i is that player's income and l_i represents the resources allocated to leisure.[6]

In the context of a game that extends through time, a strategy specifies one player's response to the anticipated actions of the other at each node of the game. In equilibrium, each player's strategy will maximize her payoffs; her best response to the anticipated (maximizing) choice of the other and her anticipations will be confirmed by the choices actually made.

Our notion of equilibrium is subgame perfection. In a subgame perfect equilibrium, each player's strategy contains her best response at each node of the extended game. In each subgame, the strategy thus calls for responses that are credible; they are credible because if the actors enter the subgame choosing the action specified by that strategy, it then constitutes a payoff-maximizing choice. Opponents will thus avoid choices that lead them to subgames in which their rivals will punish them; the threats to punish are credible. Strategies that are subgame perfect therefore specify both actions that lie on the equilibrium path of play and so will be chosen as well as the punishments that will be inflicted should the game veer off the path of play.

Analyzing the game between two families, we explore a variety of subgame perfect equilibria. One supports the first-best, in which the equilibrium outcome results in payoffs that maximize the welfare of both families. Arguing that the attainment of the first-best is in fact unlikely, we then explore two alternative (and second-best) equilibria: the No Military (NM) and Positive Military (PM) equilibria. In the first, there is peace; neither family invests resources in preparing for conflict. In the second, each family devotes resources to military preparedness. Exploring the properties of these equilibria, we learn that the political institutions of kinship societies impose limitations upon the level of welfare that their members can attain. While the members of kinship societies may value both peace and prosperity, the nature of their institutions forces them to consume lower levels of the one in order to enjoy higher levels of the other.

We model the extended game between the two families as a stage game in which each period is divided into two parts. At the start of the first, players simultaneously allocate their resources among working (w_i), acquiring military capabilities (m_i), and leisure (l_i), where $w_i, m_i, l_i \geq 0$, and $T_i = w_i + m_i + l_i$. In the second, after observing the allocation of the other player, each player decides whether to raid the wealth of the other.

Define $r_i = \{0, 1\}$ to equal 1 if player i raids and equal 0 if she does not attack. The net income of player i, I_i, then equals her income from work and raiding (if any), less her losses from having herself been raided:

$$I_i(\bullet) = F(w_i) + r_i F(w_{-i})M(m_i, m_{-i}) - r_{-i}F(w_i)M(m_{-i}, m_i)$$

Any resources not devoted to w_i or m_i result in increased amounts of leisure, l_i, that a player consumes. At any stage of the game, the abandonment of an equilibrium choice of strategies marks the entry into a subgame, the equilibrium of which is called the All-Defect (D) equilibrium.

In the All-Defect (D) equilibrium, to secure the fruits of their labor, $F(w_iD)$, both players devote resources to military activity.[7] At best such efforts result in mere redistribution; more commonly, they result in losses as goods are destroyed in struggles over their appropriation. Because such activity is unproductive, such expenditures of effort lower the families' welfare. In repeated play, it is the prospect of these reduced payoffs that supports the choice of alternative strategies in equilibrium. The reversion to the All-Defect (D) equilibrium choice of strategies represents a punishment phase of the game.

THREE INFORMATIVE EQUILIBRIA

We begin with what many would consider a standard result.[8] Because the game is infinitely repeated, the families can interact in ways which yield the first-best (FB) as a subgame perfect Nash equilibrium.

Because military preparedness is costly but nonproductive, the strategies that characterize the First-Best (FB) equilibrium must include choices in which m_i^{FB} and $r_i = 0$, so long as the other player has neither raided nor deviated from the first-best allocation of effort. Given that defection provokes a reversion to the All-Defect (D) equilibrium, the payoffs that accrue in the First-Best (FB) equilibrium must yield a flow of future benefits that exceeds in value the one-period benefits achieved by defecting (i.e., engaging in predation) and the resultant future losses that accrue under the All Defect (D) equilibrium (i.e., during the punishment phase). That is, the condition for the First-Best to be achieved in equilibrium is as follows

$$\frac{\pi_i^{FB}}{(1 - \delta_i)} \geq \pi_i^{D,FB} + \frac{\delta_i \pi_i^{D}}{(1 - \delta_i)} \tag{1}$$

where π_i^{FB} stands for the payoffs that result under the First-Best (FB) equilibrium; $\pi_i^{D,FB}$ for the payoff for defecting from the first-best strategy while the other player maintains the first-best allocation of labor, leisure, and military preparedness; and π_i^{D} for the payoff under the All-Defect (D) equilibrium. δ_i is the discount factor, or the weight placed on future payoffs.

Equation 1 can be rewritten as follows:

$$\frac{\pi_i^{FB} - \delta_i \pi_i^{D}}{(1 - \delta_i)} \geq \pi_i^{D,FB} \tag{2}$$

The right-hand side of equation (2) is finite, but the left-hand side approaches infinity as $\delta_i \to 1$. As noted above, δ_i is the discount factor. The more the player discounts the future, the more weight she places on immediate benefits and the less she fears future punishment. Equation 2 suggests that as player i becomes more patient, the inequality becomes easier to fulfill. The fear of future penalties yields an increased appreciation for the benefits of the first-best in comparison with the payoffs that would result from defection. In accordance with the Folk Theorem, the first-best is thus attainable as an equilibrium and results when the shadow of the future—the magnitude of which is determined in part by δ_i—is of sufficient weight that neither family feels that it can gain from raiding.

In international relations, as in kinship societies, no government possesses a monopoly over the means of coercion; force is controlled by the constituent units of international society. And some, such as Robert Keohane (1984), see in the Folk Theorem a reason to doubt the necessity of international government for the attainment of global welfare. Others, such as Michael Taylor (1987), explicitly address the properties of kinship societies and herald the Folk Theorem as suggesting that governments may not be necessary for the attainment of the collective welfare and that societies that lack states nevertheless can achieve high levels of well-being.

In probing the properties of kinship societies, however, it is important to note the limitations of this result. For the first-best to prevail in equilibrium, the discount factor must be sufficiently high that even were one player to lack any means of defense (i.e., were $m_i = 0$), the other would place so great a weight on future losses that she would resist temptation. Crops standing undefended in the field, cattle roaming freely and without protection, houses laden with possessions and left unguarded—under the conditions that define this equilibrium, none can provoke a transgression, so high is the discount factor; and no one need therefore prepare militarily in anticipation of possible predation. The conditions that support the first-best choice of strategies as an equilibrium thus appear highly improbable. It appears unlikely that they would be fulfilled. In our exploration of the properties of life in societies governed by kinship, we would do well, then, to explore other equilibria.

Given the restrictive nature of the assumptions underlying the Folk Theorem, and thus the implausibility of attaining the first-best as an equilibrium in repeated play, we turn to equilibria in which the discount factor is insufficiently high to dissuade those subject to temptation. The properties of two such equilibria appear enlightening.

The first is the No Military (NM) equilibrium, in which a player devotes no resources to m_i as long as the other player has never raided or produced more than w_{-i}^{NM}, w_i^{NM} units of resources to productive work, and $T - w_i^{NM}$ units to leisure, and reverts to the D equilibrium strategy otherwise. The choice of NM strategies yields a (symmetric) subgame perfect equilibrium, if

$$\frac{\pi_i^{NM}}{(1 - \delta_i)} \geq \pi_i^{D,NM} + \frac{\delta_i \pi_i^{D}}{(1 - \delta_i)} \tag{3}$$

or

$$\frac{\pi_i^{NM} - \delta_i \pi_i^{D}}{(1 - \delta_i)} \geq \pi_i^{D,NM} \tag{4}$$

where π_i^{NM} constitutes the payoffs under the No Military (NM) equilibrium, π_i^D constitutes the payoffs under the All-Defect (D) equilibrium; and $\pi_i^{D,NM}$ stands for the payoffs to be secured from a one-period defection from the NM equilibrium. The right-hand side of equation 4 registers the gains from defection. For a given rate of discount, equation 4 suggests, the choice of NM strategies yields an equilibrium if the payoffs to predation are sufficiently small. They must be smaller than the future stream of benefits that result from the combination of the payoffs from the No Military (NM) equilibrium and the losses experienced under the All-Defect (D) equilibrium.

The most informative way to view this result is to realize that payoffs for defection increase insofar as others labor, generating output that is tempting to steal. In the No Military (NM) equilibrium, let w_{-i}^{NM} stand for the highest level of work that can be sustained without inciting investments in military preparedness. If the other player were to devote more than w_{-i}^{NM} to work, player i would find it rational to devote some units of resources to m_i since the marginal productivity of military expenditure would increase. If player $-i$ devoted more than w_{-i}^{NM} to work, then the right-hand side of equation 4 would increase in magnitude and, ceteris paribus, the incentives to behave in ways that render it unnecessary to invest in military preparedness in equilibrium would decline.

In kinship societies, political institutions rest upon the private provision of security. The lesson of the No Military (NM) equilibrium is that for people in such societies to refrain from military preparations, the immediate rewards for predation must be small. Put another way, they must possess few goods worth stealing.

Now suppose there was some incremental increase in military preparedness that might allow a player to shift resources from leisure to productive work.[9] Might such an equilibrium yield higher levels of welfare? In other words, if, as suggested above, poverty is the price of peace, could investment in the capacity to fight lead to greater prosperity? To evaluate this possibility, we turn to a last equilibrium: the Positive Military (PM) equilibrium.

A Positive Military (PM) equilibrium resembles the No Military equilibrium except that each agent devotes positive amounts of effort to the acquisition of military capabilities. A family contributes m_i^{PM} units of effort to military preparedness (where $0 < m_i^{PM} < m_i^D$) and w_i^{PM} units to work (where $w_i PM > w_i D$), and refrains from raiding as long as the other player has never raided and has herself allocated w_{-i}^{PM} to work and m_{-i}^{PM} to military preparedness.[10]

The condition for the Positive Military (PM) equilibrium is as follows:

$$\frac{\pi_i^{PM}}{(1 - \delta_i)} \geq \pi_i^{D,PM} + \frac{\delta_i \pi_i^D}{(1 - \delta_i)} \tag{5}$$

where $\pi_i^{D,PM}$ is the highest payoff attainable from one period deviation when the other player continues to play her *PM* strategy.

Analysis of this equilibrium further deepens our understanding of the political institutions of kinship societies. Despite the wasteful investment in military resources, the payoffs under the Positive Military (*PM*) equilibrium can Pareto dominate those under the most efficient No Military (*NM*) equilibrium. In other words, in seeking increased well-being, people in stateless societies may do better investing resources in preparing to fight.

In the *NM* equilibrium, the amount of effort devoted to work is constrained by the need to reduce the productivity of the other player's raids; families devote residual resources to leisure rather than to labor. But because they devote more resources to deterring raiding, those who adopt a *PM* equilibrium strategy can devote more resources to productive activity as well. The *PM* equilibrium can therefore dominate the *NM* equilibrium when a redistribution of effort in the *NM* equilibrium from leisure to work and military preparedness yields an increase in economic output that compensates for the loss of leisure, while still being low enough to ensure that raiding (which entails a reversion to the All-Defect (*D*) equilibrium) remains unprofitable.

Under the political institutions that mark kinship societies, then, each family provides its own defenses. Using the framework of an infinitely repeated game, we have learned that the political institutions of such a society place an upper limit on the level of welfare that people can attain. People prize both peace and prosperity. But when defense is privately provided, to be prosperous, families may have to invest in military preparedness. And as seen in the analysis of the No Military (*NM*) equilibrium, the price of peace is prosperity. And as shown by the Positive Military (*PM*) equilibrium, the price of prosperity is preparation for fighting. The political institutions of kinship societies thus pose a cruel trade-off. In so doing, they impose a constraint upon the level of welfare that such societies can attain.

THE GREAT TRANSFORMATION

By focusing on kinship societies, this chapter has clarified the meaning of underdevelopment. Contrary to the assertions of many, such societies are dynamic, not static; their members do in fact form capital. But they remain poor. Productive relations remain subject to diminishing returns, such that average incomes fall as the population rises. And while their institutions safeguard the formation of capital, when incomes rise, then so too do political tensions, as persons find it necessary to invest in defense of their persons and property. Given that military preparedness is necessary but unproductive, these societies appear caught in a low-income trap. The trap is formed in part by the structure of their institutions.

The members of such societies strive to escape from poverty. In some, they invest in means of extracting wealth, be it in the form of gemstones, timber, or precious minerals. As witnessed in contemporary Africa, however, the result then is increased violence, as families and communities coalesce into warring armies to prey upon, or to defend, valuable resources (see, e.g., Cilliers and Dietrich 2000).

In other instances, people find new ways of combining land, labor, and capital, with the result that output increases more than proportionately with increases in inputs. By combining diverse productive activities in a single location, they generate external economies, such that the effort expended in one activity lowers the costs of another. Or by combining productive activities within a single organization, they generate internal economies, with the result that the product of the team exceeds the sum of what the individuals could produce working separately. The first innovation takes the form of the town (Krugman 1991); the second, the firm (Alchien and Demsetz 1972; Holmstrom 1982; see also Cooper 1999). As town replaces country and firms replace farms as the basic units of production, the economy begins to elude the forces of decreasing returns; per capita incomes rise, and the society enters the great transformation (Wrigley and Schofield 1989).

Just as events in contemporary Africa suggest the political dangers that accompany the increase in incomes, so too do events in history suggest those that accompany the transition to an economy based on commerce and manufacturing. In northern Europe, the new economy first appeared in the lowlands, where the Rhine, the Schedlt, and the Meuse enter the North Sea. The towns in that region numbered among the most prosperous in medieval and early modern Europe; specializing in commerce and finance, they also pioneered the first major industry—the manufacturing of textiles, be it from flax or from wool. Of great relevance to the argument of this chapter, however, is that these towns were·not only wealthy but also sanguinary. Throughout medieval and early modern history, they served as the cockpit for rebellion, invasion, and violence.

The private provision of coercion thus fails to secure peace with prosperity. The achievement of order, it would appear, requires the state. But central to the study of development is recognition of the significance of the "Weingast Paradox" (Weingast 1995, 1): "a government strong enough to protect property rights . . . is also strong enough to confiscate the wealth of its citizens." The creation of the state thus reintroduces the problems of time consistency and commitment, as addressed above. Progress in the study of the political economy of development has been marked by the analysis of the impact of political institutions upon the credibility of policy makers in the advanced industrial societies (Persson and Tabellini 2000; Drazen 2000). This research represents an attempt to address the political economy of developed

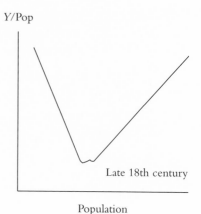

FIGURE 3.3 Average income and population
Y/Pop = per capita income
SOURCE: Loosely adapted from
Wrigley and Schofield (1989).

societies; this chapter can be regarded as an attempt to contribute to the political economy of those that remain underdeveloped.

Conclusion

One way to synthesize the broader lessons of this chapter for the study of development is to present two figures, Figures 3.3 and 3.4(a.) The first highlights a core feature of the economics of development; the other, a key feature of the politics.

Figure 3.3 is drawn from a study of the demographic history of England (Wrigley and Schofield 1989). The x-axis registers the rate of growth of population; the y-axis captures changes in the level of per capita output. Edward A. Wrigley and Roger S. Schofield enter a point on the graph whose coordinates indicate the two quantities for a given year. As suggested by the initial portions of the graph (those nearest the origin), the relationship between population and (average) income tends to be downward sloping; as population increases, the level of per capita output declines, and when, as in the period of the Black Death, population declines, then per capita incomes rise. Throughout much of recorded history, the data thus suggest, the people of England were caught in an economy subject to decreasing returns. Each additional unit of population added a smaller increment to total output than had the previous unit, such that average incomes fell.

As can be seen toward the lower right-hand side of the graph, around 1780, something changed. The two aggregates began to increase together. Beginning in the late eighteenth and early nineteenth centuries, for the first time in recorded history, England's economy began to grow.

Figure 3.3 thus portrays the economic story of "the great transformation."

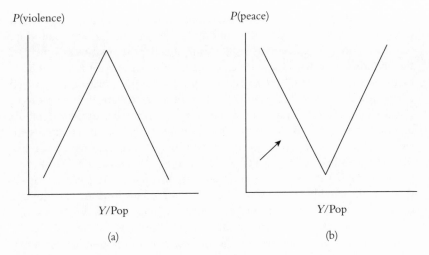

FIGURE 3.4 Political order and economic prosperity
   P = probability; Y/Pop = per capita income
   NOTE: The arrow in (b) indicates the direction of increasing utility, or that people desire higher levels of peace *and* prosperity.

Figure 3.4(a) illustrates the political. The x-axis portrays levels of income per capita, running from low levels at the origin to higher levels to the right. The y-axis records the probability of violence, which runs from a value of zero at the origin to one at the top. Reading along the x-axis, the graph suggests that at lower levels of per capita income, as incomes increase along the x-axis, so too does the level of violence. But the relationship then alters; among societies that enjoy higher incomes, increased prosperity associates with higher levels of peace, not violence. Thus the contribution of the state.

Taken together, the Figures 3.3 and 3.4(a) highlight core features of the development process. Economically, societies escape from the tyranny of diminishing returns; they gain the capacity to become wealthy, even as their populations increase. Politically, as societies develop, they elude the trade-off between peace and prosperity and gain the capacity to preserve political order in the midst of abundance.

Figure 3.4(a) can be recast such that the y-axis registers the probability of peace rather than that of violence (see Figure 3.4(b)).[11] Doing so helps to communicate a central theme of this chapter. As suggested by the arrow, welfare increases with increases in the levels of peace and prosperity; people seek more of both. But the degree to which they can do so is constrained by the downward sloping line that is generated by the political institutions of kinship societies—a line that represents the need to trade off peace for prosperity.

Upon reflection, we can extract a last broad lesson from this chapter, that of the significance of time to the notion of development. Growth, transition, transformation, development—each term suggests the passage of time. For the economics of development, recognizing the centrality of time implies a focus on capital. Capital is the factor of production that spans time; created at one moment, it makes possible higher levels of welfare in later periods. For the politics of development, recognizing the centrality of time implies a focus on institutions. Because capital spans time, its formation is fraught with risk; not only acts of nature but also actions by other human beings can bedevil the fortunes of investors (Williamson 1985). By creating political institutions, people can reduce the rewards to opportunism and gain the capacity to make credible promises. The existence of institutions can thereby render the choice to form capital a rational act. Taken together, the two observations point to the interaction between the formation of capital and the institutions of politics as forming the analytic core of the political economy of development.

By implication, then, in political science, the study of development should therefore stand on its own; that is, it should be separated from the field of comparative politics, where it conventionally resides. Within that field, research traditionally proceeds cross-sectionally; scholars analyze political development by contrasting the political economy of nation states in poor regions with those in the advanced industrial world. To capture the significance of time, however, it is clear that they should proceed longitudinally rather than cross-sectionally. Indeed the close match between phenomenon and approach may help to account for the impact achieved by historical work in this field (Tilly 1975; Skocpol 1979; Levi 1988)—something that is ironic, give the tensions between historically based researchers and those who employ the formal forms of analysis used in this chapter.

Notes

This essay was written with the support of the Carnegie and National Science Foundations (Grant SES 9905568), and while Bates was a visiting scholar at the Economic and Social Research Foundation, Dar es Salaam. It draws heavily on materials included in Bates 2001 and from an earlier formulation of the arguments subsequently published as Bates, Greif, and Singh 2002.

1. Some variables, such as consumption decisions, can be altered in the short run; others, such as capital stock, can be changed only in the longer run. *La longue durée* refers to even longer time periods, as are relevant for changes in the magnitude of the population or in the structure of institutions.

2. Or those claiming farms and land rights in waste or forested lands.

3. People's preferences can change over time. What they may prefer in one period may not be what they want later. And should they maximize in each period, then

they would be reluctant in the second to keep promises made in the first. In the face of such problems, those engaged in strategic interaction seek ways of rendering their promises credible; they face the problem of commitment. For a lucid discussion, see Persson and Tabellini 2000.

4. An example of other societies that have responded similarly is offered by the literature on central banks; see the review in Drazen 2000.

5. F($\bullet$)is assumed to be a twice continuously differentiable concave function that maps from player i's effort to her income.

6. We maintain the usual assumptions with respect to the function U($\bullet$), including concavity in each of its elements.

7. Where D stands for the level chosen under the All-Defect equilibrium.

8. This is, of course, the famous Folk Theorem (Fudenberg and Maskin 1986).

9. But the increase was less than the amount that characterizes the All-Defect equilibrium, $0 < m_i^{PM} < m_i^D$.

10. Furthermore, the strategy calls for raiding and then reverting to playing the All-Defect strategy forever if the other player has ever allocated units m_{-i} not equal to m_{-i}^{PM} to military preparedness or more than $w_{-i}PM$ units to productive labor.

11. That is, 1 - probability of violence.

References

Alchien, A., and H. Demsetz. 1972. "Production, Information Costs, and Economic Organization." *American Economic Review* 62: 777–95.

Axelrod, R. 1984. *The Evolution of Cooperation.* New York: Basic Books.

Bartlett, R. 1993. *The Making of Europe: Conquest, Colonization, and Cultural Change, 950–1350.* Princeton, N.J.: Princeton University Press.

Bates, R. H. 1976. *Rural Responses to Industrialization.* New Haven and London: Yale University Press.

———. 2001. *Prosperity and Violence.* New York: Norton.

Bates, R. H., A. Greif, and S. Singh. 2002. "Organizing Violence." *Journal of Conflict Resolution* 46(5): 599–629.

Bloch, M. 1961a. *Feudal Society: Social Classes and Political Organization.* Chicago: University of Chicago Press.

———. 1961b. *Feudal Society: The Growth of Ties of Dependence.* Chicago: University of Chicago Press.

Boserup, E. 1965. *The Conditions of Agricultural Growth.* London: Allen and Unwin.

Brenner, R. 1976. "Agrarian Class Structure and Economic Development in Pre-Industrial Europe." *Past and Present* 70 (February): 30–75.

Chenery, H. B., and L. J. Taylor. 1968. "Development Patterns: Among Countries and Over Time." *Review of Economics and Statistics* (November): 391–416.

Cilliers, J., and C. Dietrich, eds. 2000. *Angola's War Economy.* Pretoria, South Africa: Institute for Security Studies.

Cooper, R. W. 1999. *Coordination Games.* Cambridge: Cambridge University Press.

Drazen, A. 2000. *Political Economy in Macroeconomics.* Princeton, N.J.: Princeton University Press.

Durkheim, E. 1949. *The Division of Labor in Society*. Glencoe, Ill.: The Free Press.

Fortes, M. 1958. "Introduction." In *The Developmental Cycle in Domestic Groups*, by J. Goody. Cambridge: Cambridge University Press.

Fudenberg, D., and E. Maskin. 1986. "The Folk Theorem in Repeated Games with Discounting or with Incomplete Information." *Econometrica* 54(3): 533–54.

Gerth, H. H., and C. W. Mills, eds. 1958. *From Max Weber*. New York: Oxford University Press.

Goldstone, J. A. 1991. *Revolution and Rebellion in the Early Modern World*. Berkeley and Los Angeles: University of California Press.

Holmstrom, B. 1982. "Moral Hazard in Teams." *Bell Journal of Economics* 13: 324–40.

Keohane, R. 1984. *After Hegemony*. Princeton, N.J.: Princeton University Press.

Krugman, P. 1991. *Geography and Trade*. Cambridge: MIT Press.

Kuznets, S. 1966. *Modern Economic Growth*. New Haven and London: Yale University Press.

Ladurie, E. L. R. 1976. *The Peasants of Languedoc*. Urbana: University of Illinois Press.

Lerner, D. 1958. *The Passing of Traditional Society*. New York: Free Press of Glencoe.

Levi, M. 1988. *Of Rule and Revenue*. Berkeley and Los Angeles: University of California Press.

Marx, K., and F. Engels. 1979. *Pre-Capitalst Socio-economic Formations*. London: Lawrence and Wishart.

Meillassoux, C. 1981. *Maidens, Meal, and Money*. Cambridge: Cambridge University Press.

North, D. C., and R. P. Thomas. 1973. *The Rise of the Western World*. Cambridge: Cambridge University Press.

Ortner, S. B. 1999. "Resistance and the Problem of Ethnographic Refusal." In *The Historic Turn in the Human Sciences*, ed. Terrence J. McDonald. Ann Arbor: University of Michigan Press.

Parsons, T., and E. Shills. 1951. *Toward a General Theory of Action*. Cambridge: Harvard University Press.

Persson, T., and G. Tabellini. 2000. *Political Economics: Explaining Economic Policy*. Cambridge: MIT Press.

Polanyi, K. 1944. *The Great Transformation*. Boston: Beacon Press.

Postan, M. 1937. "The Chronology of Labour Services." *Transactions of the Royal Historical Society* 70: 169–93.

Quirk, J. P. 1976. *Intermediate Microeconomics*. Chicago: Science Research Associates.

Radcliffe-Brown, A. A. 1965. "Introduction." In *African Systems of Kinship and Marriage*, ed. A. R. Radcliffe-Brown and Daryll Forde. London: Oxford University Press for the International African Institute.

Ricardo, D. 1819. *On the Principles of Political Economy and Taxation*. Georgetown, D.C.: J. Milligan.

Sahlins, M. D. 1961. "The Segmentary Lineage: An Organization of Predatory Expansion." *American Anthropologist* 63: 322–45.

Schultz, T. W. 1976. *Transforming Traditional Agriculture*. New York: Arno Press.

Skocpol, T. 1979. *States and Social Revolutions*. Cambridge: Cambridge University Press.

Stark, O., and D. Bloom. 1985. "The New Economics of Labor Migration." *American Economic Review, Papers and Proceedings of the Ninety-Seventh Annual Meeting of the American Economic Association* 75(2): 173–85.

Taylor, M. 1987. *The Possibility of Cooperation*. New York: Cambridge University Press.

Tilly, C. 1975. "Reflections on the History of State Making." In *The Formation of National States in Western Europe*, ed. C. Tilly. Princeton, N.J.: Princeton University Press.

Tönnes, F. 1963. *Community and Society*. New York: Harper Torchbooks.

Weingast, B. 1995. "The Economic Role of Political Institutions." *The Journal of Law, Economics, and Organization* 7(1): 1–31.

Williamson, O. E. 1985. *The Economic Institutions of Capitalism*. New York: The Free Press.

Wrigley, E. A., and R. S. Schofield. 1989. *The Population History of England, 1541–1871: A Reconstruction*. Cambridge: Cambridge University Press.

PART II

Institutional Design

POLITICAL SCIENCE has been from its beginnings (the works of Aristotle are one conventional starting point), and largely still is, both empirical and practical. As an empirical science it aims to describe and explain how the political world works. As a practical science it hopes to guide actions that influence that world. One important theme in the history of political science is the tension between these two tasks. Some believe that only descriptive and explanatory tasks are legitimate for a science (as they would be in a physical science). Others believe that physical sciences are not an appropriate model for the study of politics and that it is the distinctive task of political science to provide guidance to the practitioner: the prince, the statesman, the constitutional drafter, the lawmaker, the policy maker, and the citizen.

The common view of rational choice puts it in the first of these two camps, rejecting the legitimacy of practical tasks for political science. No doubt a great deal of rational choice research is purely empirical, but the tradition has made many significant contributions to understanding the practical tasks of politics, including constitutional and institutional design, as the chapters in this section illustrate.

The ancient (and continuing) *practical* problem of political science revolves around two fundamental tasks: how to improve existing political arrangements, and how to protect them from deterioration or destruction. These imply a second-order task: creating political arrangements which are relatively easy to improve and to protect.

To deal with these problems, we need to answer two questions. First, what constitutes improvement? This requires some form of normative argument, on the basis of which we can distinguish better from worse arrangements. Second, what are the most important threats to existing arrangements, sources of possible deterioration or destruction? How much attention we give to each of these questions, when we attempt to influence politics, will give us a rough location on the political spectrum. The more we look for potential improvements, the more we are identifiable as progressive. The more concerned we are with protection, the more conservative we appear. But political science must be concerned with both protection and improvement. And so we can develop our understanding of both tasks separately, without necessarily specifying the optimal balance between them.

The rational choice tradition has made significant contributions to both the identification of improvements and the identification of threats. On the normative side, guiding improvement, at least one commonly accepted end of politics is to pursue what is good for individuals, or providing them with what they want, or doing simply what they decide to do. For many people, of course, this is the only legitimate end of politics. But the rational choice elaboration and analysis of these ends is relevant and useful for anyone for whom these ends at least belong *among* the legitimate ones. They need not have a monopoly of legitimacy.

On the protective side, among the most widely recognized threats to the survival, integrity, or goal achievement in political arrangements, we have, first, the problem of faction, as it is known in Madison's famous formulation. It is the threat that narrowly interested action will undermine the common good. The second widely recognized source of difficulty in institutional design is the limited competence of decision makers. In a democracy this is above all the problem of citizens.

Thanks to work in the rational choice tradition, we have today a deeper understanding in three areas relevant to institutional design: (1) how institutional arrangements can be made into impartial instruments of all affected individuals (serving what is good for individuals, or what they want, or what they decide), in a manner we may find desirable; (2) how they can resist becoming instruments of individuals or factions; and (3) how they can make decision makers more competent, either by allocating decision authority to those who know what they are doing or by creating better incentives for decision makers to learn. Let us consider each in turn, under the headings of "the sovereignty of the people," "the problem of faction," and "the problem of citizen competence."

The Sovereignty of the People

When monarchs were sovereign, the king's death was greeted by the cry "The King is dead! Long live the King!" emphasizing the institutional continuity of the monarchy as contrasted with the mortality of individual kings. But when Louis XVI was executed, the institution of the sovereignty of the monarch died with him (at least for the moment), and the eyewitnesses cried, "Long live the nation!" If they were English speakers, they might have cried, "Long live the people!" We entered the democratic age as the sovereignty of the monarch was replaced by the sovereignty of the people, even if it was not at all clear initially what that meant. It is still not entirely clear what it means. But we certainly have a better idea. And the rational choice tradition has made a major contribution to the clarification of what the sovereignty of the people can and cannot mean.

According to one interpretation, "the people" is a corporate body with its own distinctive purposes, in the way a formal organization will have purposes distinct from the purposes of its individual members. A profit-maximizing firm is one example. This is roughly Rousseau's understanding of popular sovereignty, distinguishing the will of all (what people individually want in fact) from the general will, the purposes and ends of the people as a corporate body, which may not correspond to what the people want. The general will is something we may need to discover; it does not necessarily correspond with what real empirical people want.

Rousseau's conception of popular sovereignty has not been widely accepted recently among political scientists. But it has also not been entirely rejected, either by rational choice theorists or by others. The research within the rational choice tradition most directly relevant to a Rousseau-style conception of general will derives from Condorcet's jury theorem and related work, identifying the effect of voter competence and voting procedure on the probability of obtaining the right answer to some question, such as the determination of the guilt or innocence of the accused in a trial (as in jury decisions) or the identification of the general will (Grofman, Owen, and Feld 1983; Miller 1986; Ladha 1992; Ladha and Miller 1995; Austen-Smith and Banks 1996).

According to another interpretation, a liberal alternative to the "populist" Rousseau, we need to disaggregate the sovereignty of the people. Sovereignty is not transferred as a bundle from the monarch to the people as a group. It is instead divided up among individual people. Politics, law, and the state must then serve individual people, whatever they want or decide. A contract is a good example here, and it is widely used as a model or a metaphor. In contract law, the legal system provides an instrument, which anyone can use for whatever purposes they want (within some legally specified limits). The courts will enforce a broad range of agreements without imposing their judgment about the wisdom of these agreements (again, within limits). Contract law is thus a good approximation of a neutral instrument for whatever individuals choose to decide. The people are sovereign individually; whatever they decide (in a contractual agreement) is law.

The Austrian social theory, which Russell Hardin praises in Chapter 4, can be seen as a kind of elaboration and justification of the contract idea transferred to the society as a whole. The legal concept of the contract, or some more abstract model of contract, are not of course necessary to express the idea, and Hardin's Austrians do not use it. Many others do, however, and rational choice contributions to political philosophy and to practical political science are full of different versions of contract theory, including Buchanan and Tullock (1962), Rawls (1971), Kolm (1985), Gauthier (1986), and Mueller (1996).

There is a third possibility, roughly intermediate between these two. According to this idea, something like the will of the people as a corporate body does exist, but it is constructed out of what individual people want, or what individual people decide. We aggregate individual wants, or individual desires, or individual preferences and obtain a social desire or preference. This idea has been most fully developed in the utilitarian family of approaches. One typical version identifies as improvements all and only those changes which increase the average utility, or welfare, or happiness of all the individuals affected. The rational choice tradition has contributed perhaps the most to this line of thought. It has contributed rational choice–based justifications of utilitarianism (Harsanyi 1982), but also many critiques and refinements. Perhaps the most famous result is Arrow's Impossibility Theorem.

The Problem of Faction

If we accept the sovereignty of the people in any of its forms outlined above, we will favor making politics into an instrument of what the people want (or what is good for them, or what they decide). But we will do so on condition that some form of equality or impartiality is maintained; each person's happiness, or each person's preference, or each person's vote counts the same. When we now turn from ideals which politics can serve to threats which it needs to avoid, we will still be concerned with individual desires, but this time as these are pursued in the spirit of faction, without regard for equality or impartiality.

Thanks to work in the rational choice tradition, we understand today much more deeply the pervasiveness and the nature of the problem of faction (and related problems), the conflicts between the rational pursuit of narrow interest and the achievement of a collective good. The simplest illustration is the prisoners' dilemma, a situation in which it is absolutely clear what is rational for each player to do individually, and it is also absolutely clear that the result of all doing this is worse than an alternative outcome produced if they all reject the rational pursuit of their interest. The prisoners' dilemma can be seen as a simple, clear, and vivid illustration of a generalized version of the problem of faction. Individuals, or factions making decisions as uni-

fied agents, act in pursuit of their own interest and produce a result clearly
contrary to the collective good. For the rational choice tradition, the simple
idea of a prisoners' dilemma was the beginning of a long research program,
which we discussed in the Introduction, including the problem of the provision of public goods and the logic of collective action.

Chapter 5 shows the pervasiveness and depth of the problem. Selective
incentives will not provide a solution, because the provision of selective incentives is itself a public good subject to the same logic. Political entrepreneurs will not solve the problem, because they will have an incentive to allocate to themselves as much as their entrepreneurial position allows,
without regard for the effect on the collective interest. A solution can be obtained only if the pursuit of self-interest is restrained.

The Problem of Citizen Competence

Institutions work well when decision makers have the right incentives and
the right skills. The problem of faction identifies, roughly speaking, the issue
of getting the incentives right. But what about the skills? Here we can go in
two directions. We can make sure, first, that decision-making authority is allocated to those with the relevant knowledge and skill. For some, this justi-
fies rule by experts. But others, notably the Austrian theorists Hardin writes
about in Chapter 4, argue that much of the relevant knowledge is specific
and particular, it is a highly decentralized knowledge of local conditions and
individual preferences. Decision-making authority should not be given,
then, to the experts and technocrats; it should be decentralized as in a market or in a free society more generally.

In this way we adapt institutions to the existing distribution of competence. But we can also go the other way and use institutions to modify the
distribution of competence. So, for example, in a democracy some key institutions are designed to make the citizens more competent. But they often do
not work well, in part because their design does not take into account the
incentives the parties face. Various forms of deliberation, information transfer, persuasion, and argument are among the most significant methods of improving citizen competence and decision maker competence more generally. But such deliberation does not occur in anything like the "ideal speech
situation" Habermas writes about, where the force of argument is the only
force. The originator of the argument can be presumed to be in part self-
serving, and so can the recipient. Their incentives distort what is communicated and what is accepted of the communication. This is true in general,
but it is more true in some situations than in others. So those concerned
with citizen competence, or with the recently popular subject of deliberative
democracy, must ask, what conditions, and what systems of incentives, allow

deliberations to be effective in improving decision maker competence? This is a big question, and Chapter 6 is a kind of progress report from the research frontier exploring it.

References

Austen-Smith, David, and Jeffrey Banks. 1996. "Information Aggregation, Rationality, and the Condorcet Jury Theorem." *American Political Science Review* 90: 34–45.

Buchanan, James, and Gordon Tullock. 1962. *The Calculus of Consent: Logical Foundations of Constitutional Democracy*. Ann Arbor: University of Michigan Press.

Gauthier, David. 1986. *Morals by Agreement*. Oxford, England: Clarendon Press.

Grofman, Bernard, Guillermo Owen, and Scott Feld. 1983. "Thirteen Theorems in Search of the Truth." *Theory and Decision*, 15: 261–78.

Harsanyi, John. 1982. "Morality and the Theory of Rational Behavior." In *Utilitarianism and Beyond*, ed. Amartya Sen and Bernard Williams. Cambridge: Cambridge University Press.

Kolm, Serge-Christophe. 1985. *Le Contrat Social Liberal*. Paris: Presses Universitaires de France.

Ladha, Krishna. 1992. "The Condorcet Jury Theorem, Free Speech and Correlated Votes." *American Journal of Political Science* 36: 597–634.

Ladha, Krishna, and Gary Miller. 1995. "Political Discourse, Factions, and the General Will: Correlated Voting and Condorcet's Jury Theorem." In *Social Choice and Political Economy*, ed. Norman Schofield. Boston: Kluwer.

Miller, Nicholas. 1986. "Information, Electorates, and Democracy: Some Extensions and Interpretations of the Condorcet Jury Theorem." In *Information Pooling and Group Decision-Making*, ed. Bernard Grofman and Guillermo Owen. Greenwich, Conn.: JAI Press.

Mueller, Dennis. 1996. *Constitutional Democracy*. New York: Oxford University Press.

Rawls, John. 1971. *A Theory of Justice*. Cambridge: Harvard University Press.

Rational Choice Political Philosophy

MUCH OF MODERN political theory has focused on the problem of collectively providing for individual welfare. This was de facto the whole point of Thomas Hobbes's political theory, and it is arguably the central point of David Hume's.[1] Even the theory of justice of John Rawls ([1971] 1999) is supposedly rationally mandated for anyone with a modicum of risk aversion, and it is mutually advantageous (66, 110). Rawls refers to the mutually disinterested nature of citizens (111–12). The central move of such theory is typically to create an institutional structure that will guarantee the welfare of individuals who act sensibly, which is commonly to say, who act according to the simple rational choice rules of game theory. We create institutions that will secure collective results through individualistic actions by citizens. Such political theory therefore does not require a specific moral commitment from citizens.

Why should we go this way? Why not build political theory on normative commitments that are not individualistic? After all, we know that people often do behave morally against their own interest, for example, when acting on behalf of their families or larger groups, or when following moral rules of some kind, or when being altruistic. In general, however, these motivations are sporadic and particular; they do not govern all behavior, and we could not expect to achieve high levels of, for example, altruistic action if we designed our institutions to work well only if altruistic motivations were common or pervasive. One might aspire to creating a society of people for whom such motivations are very strong, as in the desire to create a new, publicly oriented Soviet man, a few of whom probably were created, or in the desire to create devout Muslims in Iran and Afghanistan, where many of whom surely have been created. But, in a mild variant of Hume's ([1742] 1985) dictum that we should design political institutions that would work well even if they were staffed with knaves, we can say that we should design social institutions that would work well even for citizens who are not generally and pervasively altruistic.

We commonly can expect noninterested motivations to accomplish relatively specific and idiosyncratic—and usually local—purposes, but not to accomplish systematic public purposes. Moreover, we can generally expect individuals to see public interests or welfare as analogous to own-interests or welfare. That is, public welfare is merely the aggregation of individual welfares, especially when a particular action serves the welfare of virtually all. Much of what we must want of our political institutions is that they provide the collective equivalent of own-welfare. In an ordinal assessment, this is simply mutual advantage, which is the collective implication of own-welfare generalized to the collectivity. When altruistic and other ideal motivations enter, they can produce results that mutual advantage considerations could not produce, and some of us may be grateful for such motivations in helping to eliminate racial inequality before the law and in attempting to reduce economic inequality through welfare programs. But we should also be grateful that general social order and much of the vast array of welfarist policies do not require such motivations. Indeed, we might even be grateful, with Albert Hirschman (1977), that interests have generally displaced passions in public debate and policy in many societies, as they did in England a few centuries ago.

There presumably are and often have been societies that were governed relatively systematically by religious views, so that on many matters individuals might act for collective purposes or altruistically out of religious conviction. It is the initial legacy of liberalism that it cannot be grounded in the hope of any such resolution, because it was historically a response to religious division and deep disagreement. The first and still a central tenet of liberalism in politics is the toleration of varied religious beliefs, as enunciated especially forcefully in the U.S. constitutional provision of the separation of church and state. Moreover, much of the religious conviction at the time of Hobbes and John Locke, who were among the progenitors of liberal thinking, was specifically other worldly and antagonistic to welfare in this world (Locke [1689] 1950). The seventeenth-century English Diggers, for example, preferred that people live the relatively poor life of subsistence farming because, they believed, one could attain to proper Christian humility only in such a life (Winstanley [1652] 1973).

Virtually all of political philosophy in the rational choice mode has been directed at achieving relatively high levels of welfare, and Hobbes was very forceful in refusing to allow the focus of his concern to depart from welfare onto religious qualifications. Indeed, Hobbes's ([1651] 1968, 376; see also 188) starting point was to found an all-powerful government to secure the safety of individual citizens and to secure their possibilities of furthering their own welfare. We seek "not a bare Preservation, but also all other contentments of life." Few Western political theorists since Hobbes have looked back from this stance, which is essentially foundational for modern Western political theorists. Indeed, the nearest competitors with welfare as a moral political concern have been fairness and egalitarianism, which are themselves generally about the distribution of welfare and the resources for providing welfare, and consent, which is an ex ante concern and is often about welfare, fairness, or egalitarianism.

The rise of welfarist political theory was accompanied by the rise of individualistic economic theory, as developed by Bernard Mandeville ([1714] 1924), Hume ([1739–40] 1978), Adam Smith ([1776] 1976), John Stuart Mill ([1848] 1965), and many others. Many of these theorists simultaneously presented rational choice political philosophies and individualistic market economic theories. Perhaps no one integrated the two better than Hume and Mill, for whom the two are clearly of a coherent piece. Most of them were utilitarians in political philosophy and more or less laissez faire market economists in economics. The development of economic theory and of political philosophy largely separated over the course of the nineteenth century in Anglo-Saxon thought, and economic theory left political theory and utilitarian moral theory far behind in their technical developments in the twentieth century. The last major theorists who gave relatively equal consideration to moral and political theory on the one hand and to economic theory on the other were the philosopher Henry Sidgwick and the economist F. Y. Edgeworth.

Given the view of Hume and Mill that political and economic theory are of a piece, the separation of the two was a disaster for political theory after Sidgwick. Indeed, Peter Laslett (1956) asserted that political theory was a dead letter only shortly before Rawls helped revive it. But Rawls came to the task just as moral theory was about to be radically shifted to a grounding in Kantian theory to replace the previously dominant grounding in utilitarian theory. In a related development, Anglo-Saxon and positivist legal theory moved away from its grounding in utilitarianism to a grounding (perhaps only briefly) in conceptions of rights (Hart [1979] 1983). The rights revolution in legal theory seems to be past after a relatively short heyday, and legal theory is now relatively diverse and incoherent with several unifying principles in contest, including efficiency in law and economics, autonomy (Raz 1986), and pragmatism (Posner 1999).

The reign of Kantianism in moral theory and its invasion of political theory in the later work of Rawls and of many others are far from past. But they are increasingly abstracted from actual life to an astonishing degree, to a degree that only the silliest divergences in utilitarian theory ever reached.

For example, G. E. Moore's (1903) dictum that a beautiful stone out in the universe that will never be experienced by any sentient being nevertheless contributes value to the universe was a travesty of the central utilitarian concern with welfare. The abstract appeal of such silliness took utilitarianism out of the world of the senses and into the world of the nonsenses, where it languished in philosophical circles during the early twentieth century just when economic theories of welfare became creative and incisively able to resolve central problems that had plagued such theory for a century.

Already Kant himself took Kantianism into the silly sphere with his (perhaps senile) claim that one should never lie no matter what. Benjamin Constant challenged this dictum with reference to real-world contexts in which telling the truth might entail the death of an innocent. For example, if an assassin comes to my door and asks whether his intended victim is inside, Kant supposed that I must answer truthfully even if that means the likely death of the innocent person. Kant ([1797] 1909) wrote, "we must not understand [the issue as one of] the danger of *doing harm* (accidentally), but of *doing wrong*; . . . and, although by a certain lie I in fact do no wrong to any person [such as the intending murderer], yet I infringe the principle of justice in regard to all indispensably necessary statements *generally* (I do wrong formally, though not materially); *and this is much worse than to commit an injustice to any individual*" (365, final emphasis added). Moore's value theory was merely silly and irrelevant to life. Kant's dictum was vicious and outrageous in elevating the moral theory for rational beings into such hallowed status that it should actually allow, through the exercise of moral duty *on behalf of the theory*, the destruction of rational beings. No major thinker of our time with Kantian leanings ascends into such abstract perversity. But much of contemporary political philosophy escapes into claims that cannot have much footing in the real world of actual people.

Austrian Social Theory

Let us turn now to a body of theory that is perhaps the most empirically grounded of any major body of economic or political theory: Austrian economic and social theory. Not all its contributors have managed to stay grounded in empirical assessments of the nature of knowledge and its use and to avoid ascents into the metaphysical, but when they spiral into nonsense or excess artfulness, they clearly violate the tenets of their own theory. In the Austrian view of economic relations, the knowledge of how to produce and market vast numbers of commodities cannot be centralized in any person or agency. Knowledge is inherently distributed and local, and most of it is inaccessible to any one person or agency. This is an unchallengeable descriptive claim from which various theoretical implications seem to follow.

The chief policy implication of the Austrian vision of the nature and distribution of knowledge in a society is that the central design and very extensive management of a modern economy are therefore unlikely to be as effective in creating great prosperity and innovation as is a relatively loosely run market economy. This claim could turn out to be false under certain circumstances such as, for example, conditions of extreme exigency when central management might, for all its inefficiencies and errors, get us through better than an unmanaged system could. For example, during wartime, when the value of immediate production overrides various economically future-oriented values, central managerial control of production might be far more successful for the short term than operating by standard market principles would be. It might be wasteful and inefficient in many ways and might even slow some kinds of innovation, but it would be highly efficient in the one way that matters most at the time, as, for example, in producing vast numbers of jeeps or other military vehicles rather than in innovatively redesigning them.

Unfortunately, the successful experience of wartime mobilization in World War I may have contributed to the later centralization of the Soviet economy and, largely just because central control could be readily extended, of many other irrelevant values, such as artistic taste and science. James Scott (1999, 97–102) supposes that the efforts of Walter Rathenau to manage the production of materiel and other goods for the war effort of imperial Germany during World War I inspired Lenin ([1917] 1954, 195; quoted by Scott 1999, 100, emphasis added) to believe that the war "had accelerated the development of capitalism to such a tremendous degree, converting monopoly capitalism into *state*-monopoly capitalism." He then drew on Rathenau's model to design the Soviet economy. It was a drastic error to suppose, as Rathenau and Lenin did, that the management of a dynamic, innovative economy could be similar enough to the management of a highly and narrowly focused wartime economy to justify its central management by the state. Lenin should have taken a bit of the Austrian tonic and thereby spared three generations of Soviet citizens from the malaise of the planned economy.

I do not wish to expound Austrian economic theory here. Rather, I wish to argue for an essentially Austrian theory of social relations more generally. These cannot be managed or even overseen by any central agent or agency. Indeed, the argument for an Austrian social theory must be even more compelling than that for an Austrian economic theory. The earliest understanding of liberalism is that individuals should be allowed to go their own way on very many social issues. That vision was the equivalent of the social version of Austrian economics.

Much of the argument for Austrian economics is predictive and explanatory, although it is motivated by a central normative concern, which is productivity. That concern is imputed to or assumed for virtually everyone, so that the normative concern is itself factually determined and not theoretically imposed. Arguably, normative concerns are more important in an Austrian social theory because it must often say simply that we should let people go their own way merely for their own sake and not for the sake of greater productivity in the larger society or anything else that would have such universal collective appeal. While virtually all might acknowledge the value of greater productivity, many might not grant the value of letting others lead their lives in certain ways. In many societies, however, it seems that the common view of politics is that it is to serve the welfare of citizens, so that its normative vision is the same as the normative vision of Austrian economics. The causal argument of Austrian economics is that, typically, individual welfare and aggregate productivity will be enhanced by decentralization of decisions that matches the actual decentralization of knowledge. The causal argument of an Austrian social theory is the same.

I think that one can actually go further to say that there are collective implications of individual liberty and that these may actually entail benefits to others from my own private liberty. In brief, the argument is this.[2] If, for example, my rights of free speech are abridged, typically by some local authority, I can take that authority to court to seek to have my rights protected and honored. When I do that, I automatically help to secure the rights of others in my society. Hence, although I ostensibly seek an individual benefit, I effectively help to provide a collective good. One might speak of this, in Mancur Olson's (1965) terminology, as an instance of a group that is privileged in the provision of its collective good. One person values the good highly enough to provide it essentially for all. Collective action on behalf of a whole society is typically hard to motivate. Action that has benefits to an enormous collection of people but that is justified already for a single individual is a rare category. Yet, through a bit of legal magic, the defense of individual rights has this extraordinary collective quality. One often hears of the logic of rights. This bit of magic in securing collective interests through individual actions is the grand logic of rights.

One might raise two objections to this argument. First, some might not actually value the right to free speech and might prefer to be able to block many kinds of speech rather than to protect it. Of course, that can be true; and it probably is true of most of the individual rights that are protected in any constitution that some people would rather they not be protected. It is still the case, however, that in defending my right to free speech I am simultaneously defending your right, whether you want to exercise that right or not.

Second, one might argue that, case by case, there will commonly be losers in any decision to protect someone's right. The reason to take one's case to court would be that someone else has blocked one's exercise of a right, and presumably that someone loses if the courts protect the right. Moreover a claim of right for one party often entails a claim that some other party has a duty. Again, the issue here is not that each individual defense of a right is itself not without losers but rather that protecting the right generally is desirable for certain citizens or even virtually all citizens. The design of rights is ex ante, and it generally would not make sense to argue for a right exclusively in an individual context or case by case ex post. My defense of my right in a court case is, of course, ex post, but it is in defense of a right that was created ex ante. My successful defense helps secure that right for others ex ante.

Incidentally, although Thomas Jefferson and others characterized certain rights as natural, the defense of the original Bill of Rights of the U.S. Constitution seems clearly to have been animated by the view that protection of these rights would serve the mutual advantage. Many of those rights were directed at abusive practices of the British Crown. There was possibly little chance that the new U.S. government would ever have commandeered private homes to house soldiers, but the English practice of doing so still rankled; and the U.S. Congress strongly supported the adoption of an explicit constitutional prohibition of any such actions by the U.S. government. Today, it is probably far more common to defend rights in terms that were not those of the generation of James Madison by claiming that they contribute to Kantian or Millian autonomy. Madison's welfarist defense did not depend on such later views.

In this respect, political theory is similar to legal theory. The best way to protect me legally against, say, theft is to have prohibitions on everyone, including me. I cannot expect any support for solipsistic law that prohibits all others but that allows license to me alone. As Hobbes ([1651] 1968, 315) noted, law was arguably brought into existence to limit the "natural liberty" of particular men. It does that by limiting all, but some of us, perhaps even the overwhelming majority of us, might not require the constraints of law to keep us from major offenses against others.

If individuals give heavy weight to welfare values, this Austrian vision is essentially utilitarian (ordinal utilitarian, as in Hardin 1988, chap. 3). But even if individuals do not focus on welfare values, one could still think that a kind of Austrian laissez faire is correct for social relations. Some society might not give heavy weight to welfare values and therefore need not be particularly utilitarian, but that would be because its citizens, as individuals, did not give heavy weight to welfare values. In the Austrian vision each citizen in such a society should be left free of constraint—subject to some variant of Mill's ([1859] 1999, chap. 1, pp. 51–2) harm principle—with the result that welfare would not be collectively very important even though it might be important to some individuals. The welfare of those to whom welfare was important might suffer substantially from the low level of overall productivity because, for example, my welfare is arguably more the result of the overall welfare of my own society than it is of my personal efforts. And in any case my welfare is heavily influenced by the range of opportunities provided by my society.

In our actual world, with the virtually inescapable interaction between states and peoples, it might be very difficult for any society to become autarkic in its social values and to give little weight to welfare values. It is difficult because, in any society that is left very far behind in economic development, large sections of the populace are likely to want greater prosperity and to consume the kinds of things available elsewhere. Hence, we may experience what the critics of globalization bemoan, which is the seeming westernization of every society. A distressing aspect of such forces is that, although many people might wish to live in a nonwesternized society, they can generally do so only at the price of suppressing the desires of their many compatriots who share many of the supposedly Western values. It is not practically possible to create genuinely autarkic societies that can survive without at least some of their citizenry succumbing to the blandishments of greater material prosperity.

It is perhaps in this Austrian vision of social order that we can see most clearly why economic and political theories were joined in the work of Hume and others in the rational choice school. They were joined not because they had the same value theory, even though they generally assumed utilitarian values. The central, fundamental feature was, rather, that they were grounded in individual values, whatever those might be. Political philosophy need have no value theory at base. It can merely posit the structure of institutions that enable people to seek their own individual values.

It would be wrong, in the shibboleth of our time, to say that the institutions could be neutral, that is, that they would have no effect on what values people sought. A massively coercive religious state could have great impact on individual values, as seems to be shown by the cases of Iran under the Ayatollahs and of Afghanistan under the Taliban. But liberal economic and political institutions likely would substantially undercut such values. One individual immersed in a licentious society can find it difficult to sustain personal adherence to a rigidly religious or moralistic value system. Some value systems therefore seem likely to require specific institutional supports. Hence, it is prima facie false to suppose that any institution can be neutral with respect to all values or value systems.

What seems to be evident, however, is that individuals who are left to their own values commonly have strong welfarist preferences. Market economic and liberal political institutions allow them to pursue those values. In both cases, the central theoretical move is to create institutions that let individuals seek their own values, which in experienced fact generally means to seek their own welfare to a substantial extent. The institutions of market economics and of liberal politics are mutual advantage, and in both economics and politics the underlying individual value theory is own-welfare. These two—own-welfare and mutual advantage—work very well together, the first at the individual level and the second at the aggregate level.

Critics of consumerism and welfarism (can one genuinely object to welfare?) often suppose that people are manipulated into having the strong welfarist urges that we witness. Barry Schwartz (1986), for example, frames his criticism of contemporary welfarism as "the battle for human nature." The battle that he sees is carried out by academics with variant visions of human nature. That would be merely an academic debate, perhaps even in the derogatory sense of that phrase. Sometimes, Schwartz's claim seems, however, to be that economic theory has itself reformed the values of masses of people. This seems implausible without a lot of argument to demonstrate the intervening causal connections between academic visions and popular visions. What seems far more likely is that individuals put in the way of various material and nonmaterial pleasures find them to be very appealing and they seek them, work for them, and give over much of their lives for them.

The drive for many of these pleasures is programmed into us biologically, and all the blandishments of advertising and commercial exposure can at most only heighten them or make them more urgent. Even under the most rigorous institutions to block such drives, they will out. Some of our pleasures, such as opera and very high-style food, seem so artful and removed from most human existence that one might even think them contrived. But many people seem genuinely and deeply motivated by such pleasures, and one could as well say that their beauty is among the great achievements of civilization as say that their appeal is somehow false or unnatural. It is not economic or social theory that has produced preferences for such consumptions, but experience itself. Indeed, such consumptions do not much appeal to some of the academic theorists whom Schwartz and others think to be misguided.

Ironically, at least one of those critics, Allan Bloom (1987), was among the most sybaritic of academics and among the most dependent on the larger framework of the commercial society that he seemingly deplored. It is possible that he fully understood his relationship to that commercial society and that he thought it reasonable to value that society for what it did for him even while holding it to be a corrupting influence for others. In such a view, he would be, like Edmund Burke, a conservative elitist whose criticisms were more of other people than of the society itself, because no society could be built on an elite class by itself.

The Economic and Political Realms

To open, I asked why political philosophy should be welfarist. In the preceding section I gave reasons for why Austrian economic and social theories hang together. Now I wish to narrow the second category to specifically political theory, and to leave out broader social theory. In broader social theory it would be surprising if there were not manifold values at stake in addition to welfare values and, in particular, to own-welfare values. Politics is a much narrower realm, however, and we might sensibly ask whether it narrows the normative focus. In the abstract, the answer must be no, because all values that we seek to fulfill can be laid before the political system for support. In pragmatic fact, however, political systems commonly rule many values out of play politically. In liberal democracies, for example, certain kinds of special privileges are ruled out. In the U.S. Constitution, specifically religious values are ruled out. In actual fact, such values cannot be completely kept out of political adjudication, and we see politics over religiously based policies on a large variety of issues, such as pacifist commitments, education, and abortion.

What I wish to argue, however, is that politics does in fact focus far more sharply on welfare issues than on other values and that it therefore has even more in common structurally with economic concern than with broader social concerns. An Austrian theory of politics does not differ very much from an Austrian theory of economics except that it likely requires even more substantial institutions and institutional devices.

In brief, the reason that politics resembles economics is that, when we engage in politics, as when we engage in economic activities, we are generally motivated by interests. For some people, interests and own-welfare might dominate virtually all their concerns, from politics to private relations. But even for those whose social lives are filled with collective and altruistic concerns or with moral or religious concerns, recourse to politics commonly has an especially strong welfarist focus. We speak of interest groups for the very good reason that most of them seek to enhance the interests of those who might be their members or clients or of those whose interests they work for. To call them interest groups is no dogma, merely natural usage. There are many politicized issues that are not interested (Schattschneider 1960). For example, both sides in the abortion debates seem to be motivated primarily by concern for others—although they focus on different others. The politics of racial equality in the era of civil rights was also partly over noneconomic concerns. Some ostensibly noneconomic issues are, however, genuinely economic in at least the degree to which they are politicized successfully by interested parties. For example, the gun lobby is funded very heavily by gun manufacturers and dealers, who have a large stake in the sale of vast numbers of guns.

Even when we find interest groups that claim to seek policies that are not strictly self-interested, we commonly find that those policies serve their members' interests significantly better than they serve the interests of apparently conflicting groups. For example (there are many easy examples), the Sierra Club's members tend to be predominantly people who live near and benefit substantially from the use of some of the natural preserves that they struggle to protect. Indeed, critics complain that the Greens of many wealthy communities, such as Palo Alto and Marin County in California, push environmental policies whose coincidental effect is to enhance their own property values substantially.

A recent past mayor of Palo Alto once exemplified the coincidence of values to a striking degree. A regular gossip column in the *Palo Alto Weekly* (5 July 2000, p. 6) reported that "Mayor Liz Kniss and her husband, Agilent Technologies Senior Vice President Richard Kniss, have purchased a $2 million plot of land . . . in Palo Alto's foothills. . . . 'It's an investment for when we're old and gray,'" Kniss said. On the immediately facing page, in a news article reporting on the environmental impact statement for Stanford University's planned use of some of its own land in the foothills, the same Mayor Kniss said, "Keep development this side of [the foothills]."

One might read Kniss's views as unduly cynical, except that one can imagine she was not being consciously cynical at all. She may genuinely have seen her own invasion of a pristine part of the foothills as a strictly private matter while she saw anything Stanford did as a public matter. In particular, she may have seen Stanford's vast land holdings as partly in trust for the larger society rather than merely for Stanford's own purposes. But that one can have such a view today is already a sign of the politicization of relevant issues to attempt to capture resources from some people and institutions and to make them available to others. That is the core of much of politics, which is conflict over my welfare versus yours.

Why are such welfare issues, many of them involving great conflict of interests between groups, so central to politics? Much of what is at stake in politics is expenditures and taxation. Much of it, however, is legal principles and policies that control activities of various kinds without specific regard to economic implications. The latter, however, very often do have enormous impact on interests, and the reason for politics over them is to attempt to secure various groups' welfares or to protect their welfares against the claims of others. Sometimes, government policies merely shift resources from some to others. Often, however, such shifts are costly because they involve expending funds for the transactions. And often they are costly because they change what can be done in the larger society. Politics over resources often therefore entails net losses.

Despite the net losses, however, most economic policies have beneficiaries who are likely to support the actions of the government and even to support government itself. Many social policies without economic import have virtually no beneficiaries but many losers. For example, if I am required to dress or worship in a particular way, you do not gain a clear benefit other than the satisfaction of knowing that you and your party have successfully imposed on me and my party. (The history of dress codes and codes on hairstyles in American schools would make for reading that would be at once very funny and very dispiriting.) Keeping such issues out of politics often benefits political candidates for public office. The striking fact is that such issues can commonly be kept out of politics, far more readily than economic issues can be. In the United States in particular, this is true in part just because politics is itself expensive and money is apt to be spent more readily when the returns from the expenditure will make it pay off.

None of this rises to the level of demonstrable theory, although it should be researchable and testable. On the other side, of course, we have lived through many political movements that were almost entirely about normative issues, such as racial equality. Antiequality forces put enormous energy into fighting against African-Americans and their supporters. In this and other instances, politics can be invested heavily with essentially normative concerns that are not primarily issues of material welfare. (Even the contest for racial equality may have been exacerbated by the fact that poor whites in some areas were apt to lose status and possibly even employment if African-Americans gained more nearly equal opportunities.)

As a matter of descriptive fact, however, politics is very heavily welfarist in advanced industrial societies of our time. It often gives us opportunity to secure collective goods—including order—that we could not secure through voluntary cooperation, and that is its foremost value to many of us. It similarly gives us collective ways to secure individual protections that commonly stand in the way of success for any politics over normative conflict. In this, liberal government inadvertently secures politics for welfarism against many normative claims of other kinds. In the main, therefore, both market economics and liberal politics are safe homes for primarily welfarist concerns. Other concerns are privatized, and if they cannot stand on their own as private concerns, they tend to fail. That is to say that liberal politics is welfarist in its working, and other values commonly get short shrift in politics, as they do in the economy.

Concluding Remarks

The central principle of rational choice political philosophy is not that it is built on a particular value theory but that it is based, rather, on the very limited (but not genuinely neutral) principle of individual choice. Six conclu-

sions follow. First, with actual individuals, the theory commonly backs welfarist values, but this is entirely because the theory yields to whatever values
individuals pursue. Again, what joins rational choice political philosophy and
economic theory in the tradition of Mandeville, Hume, Smith, and Mill is
that they are both fitted to the individual's concern with own-welfare. It is
not theoretically required that individuals have a dominant concern with
own-welfare, but it is factually true that for many individuals own-welfare is
a central concern and for some it is the chief concern. Other values can be
brought into the political sphere, but so long as these are also the values of
individuals, they can fit within the quasi-Austrian vision of rational choice
political philosophy.

Second, the Austrian vision of distributed knowledge is consistent with
Mill's ([1859] 1999, chap. 4, p. 124) grounding for his principle of liberty, that
individuals have the best knowledge of what their interests are. This claim
can be qualified, of course, in ways that the individual would allow. For example, I would defer to judgment by medical professionals on some things
that might be in my interest but that I could not understand adequately
without professional advice. The Austrian, Millian vision coupled with the
seeming fact that people place very high value on welfare, often especially
own-welfare, yields a welfarist political theory that is essentially a mutual advantage theory. Third, mutual advantage is not imposed or assumed, however, as it is an ordinal utilitarian theory (Hardin 1988) or in contractarian-
ism. Rather, it results from the aggregation of individual values.

Fourth, that such a theory de facto depends on what people actually
value makes its foundations pragmatic rather than strictly normative, unless
we add some normative principle that what people want is good or, alternatively, that arranging for people to get what they want is good. Most of the
writers in the long tradition of rational choice political theory would be
content with some variant of Mill's ([1859] 1999, chap. 1, p. 53) claim as a
fundamental assumption: "I regard utility as the ultimate appeal on all ethical questions; but it must be utility in the largest sense, grounded on the
permanent interests of man as a progressive being." But we can reach rational
choice political philosophy without assuming or imposing this utilitarian
value theory.

Fifth, rational choice political institutions are organized to achieve their
outcomes through the ordinary choices and actions of individuals who act
from their own pragmatic incentives. They do not require extensive individual commitment to values other than own-welfare. This works because the
mutual advantage of all is de facto the collective implication of self-interest.
And finally, because mutual advantage is a collective principle, not an individual principle, and is therefore normatively different from own-welfare, the
theory is inherently both normative and pragmatic in its implications.

Rational choice political philosophy is democratic in the sense that it commends aggregation of the own-welfares of citizens into a mutually advantageous outcome. Against the last two claims above, we might note that institutions often fail to represent mutual advantage because they are, for example, captured by well-organized groups or corporations that can use the institutions to their own advantage. Seeking own-welfare is not equivalent to seeking mutual advantage outcomes. Institutional design can mitigate these problems by channeling the urge to enhance own-welfare in less destructive ways. Rational choice political philosophers must put such design issues at the core of their applied theory.

Notes

1. On Hobbes's theory, see Hardin 1991, 156–80; on Hume's theory, see Hardin 1988, chap. 2.
2. This discussion draws on Hardin 2001.

References

Bloom, Allan. 1987. *The Closing of the American Mind*. New York: Simon and Schuster.

Hardin, Russell. 1988. *Morality Within the Limits of Reason*. Chicago: University of Chicago Press.

———. 1991. "Hobbesian Political Order." *Political Theory* 19 (May): 156–80.

———. 2001. "Democratic Aggregation." In *Level-of-Analysis Effects on Political Research*, ed. Yung-ming Hsu and Chi Huang, 7–33. Taipei, Taiwan: Weber Publication.

Hart, H. L. A. [1979] 1983. "Between Utility and Rights." In *Essays in Jurisprudence and Philosophy*, 198–222. Oxford: Oxford University Press.

Hirschman, Albert O. 1977. *The Passions and the Interests: Political Arguments for Capitalism Before Its Triumph*. Princeton, N.J.: Princeton University Press.

Hobbes, Thomas. [1651] 1968. *Leviathan*. Ed. C. B. Macpherson. London: Penguin. (Originally published, London: Andrew Cooke.)

Hume, David. [1739–40] 1978. *A Treatise of Human Nature*, 2nd ed. Ed. L. A. Selby-Bigge and P. H. Nidditch. Oxford: Oxford University Press.

———. [1742] 1985. "Of the Independency of Parliament." In *David Hume: Essays Moral, Political, and Literary*, ed. Eugene F. Miller, 42–46. Indianapolis, Ind.: Liberty Classics.

Kant, Immanuel. [1797] 1909. "On a Supposed Right to Tell Lies from Benevolent Motives." In *Kant's Critique of Practical Reason and Other Works on the Theory of Ethics*, 6th ed., ed. Thomas Kingsmill Abbott, 361–65. London: Longman's.

Laslett, Peter. 1956. "Introduction." In *Philosophy, Politics, and Society*, 1st series, ed. Peter Laslett, vii.

Lenin, V. I. [1917] 1954. *The Agrarian Programme of Social-Democracy in the First Russian Revolution, 1905–1907*, 2nd rev. ed. Moscow: Progress Publishers.

Locke, John. [1689] 1950. *A Letter Concerning Toleration*. Indianapolis, Ind.: Bobbs-Merrill.

Mandeville, Bernard. [1714] 1924. *The Fable of the Bees: Private Vices, Publick Benefits*. Ed. F. B. Kaye. Oxford: Oxford University Press (reprinted by Liberty Press, 1988).

Mill, John Stuart. [1848] 1965. *Principles of Political Economy*. In *Collected Works of John Stuart Mill*, 7th ed., vols. 2 and 3, ed. J. M. Robson. Toronto: University of Toronto Press.

———. [1859] 1999. *On Liberty*. Toronto: Broadview.

Moore, G. E. 1903. *Principia Ethica*. Cambridge: Cambridge University Press.

Olson, Mancur, Jr. 1965. *The Logic of Collective Action*. Cambridge: Harvard University Press.

Posner, Richard A. 1999. *The Problematics of Moral and Legal Theory*. Cambridge: Harvard University Press.

Rawls, John. [1971] 1999. *A Theory of Justice*, rev. ed. Cambridge: Harvard University Press.

Raz, Joseph. 1986. *The Morality of Freedom*. Oxford: Oxford University Press.

Schattschneider, E. E. 1960. *The Semi-Sovereign People*. New York: Holt, Rinehart and Winston.

Schwartz, Barry. 1986. *The Battle for Human Nature: Science, Morality, and Modern Life*. New York: W. W. Norton.

Scott, James C. 1999. *Seeing Like a State: How Certain Schemes to Improve the Human Condition Have Failed*. New Haven, Conn.: Yale University Press.

Smith, Adam. [1776] 1976. *An Inquiry into the Nature and Causes of the Wealth of Nations*. Oxford: Oxford University Press (reprinted Indianapolis, Ind.: Liberty Classics, 1981).

Winstanley, Gerrard. [1652] 1973. *The Law of Freedom in a Platform or, True Magistracy Restored*. Ed. Robert W. Kenny. New York: Schocken Books.

Constraining Rational Choice

If a man knocks on the door, and says that he will stab himself on the porch unless given $10, he is more likely to get the $10 if his eyes are bloodshot.

Thomas Schelling

Introduction

"Rational choice" is, by many measures, a successful paradigm for understanding social phenomena (for a favorable review of the rational choice paradigm, see Friedman 1996; for criticisms, see Green and Shapiro 1994 and Hogarth and Reder 1987). This success is due, in large part, to the paradigm's ability to draw deep insights from a relatively simple analytical framework. In turn, this framework builds upon the axiom that units of social analysis (e.g., individuals, families, firms, governments, etc.) behave "optimally," where optimality is defined with respect to stable preferences. From this parsimonious foundation emerges a rich set of insights into how social agents respond to changing constraints.

For example, models built upon the assumption that voters (Downs 1957), legislators (Mayhew 1974), and bureaucrats (Niskanen 1971) engage in maximizing behavior have markedly improved our understanding of related political processes. As a description of how these political agents behave, however, rational choice is clearly a poor modeling assumption—even microeconomic theorists do not (with any frequency) explicitly solve the optimization problems that, according to rational choice theory, govern social actors. Why, then, has rational choice become such a powerful analytical tool?

Seminal contributors (e.g., Alchian 1950, Becker 1976) argue, in effect, that "rational choice" is a model of selection mechanisms, not behavior per se. In short, they suggest that competitive forces conspire to select those units of analysis that behave "as if" they are rational. Treating rationality as axiomatic can thus facilitate valid insights to social systems, even if elements of that system are not explicitly rational.

In this chapter, we take issue with this interpretation of the "as if" principle. Others have criticized it because it lacks insight where competition is insufficient to select against irrationality. This line of criticism is frequently unsatisfactory, however—without reference to a fundamental force like competition, social scientists must offer ad hoc descriptions rather than refutable explanations. Hence, for this line of criticism to produce value, it must also offer an analytical framework whereby social scientists can identify, *ex ante*, whether competitive forces are sufficient for rational choice theory to be valid. To our knowledge, no such framework exists.

Hence, we offer here what may be a more constructive criticism; namely, not only can irrational behavior survive in competitive settings, but competition can select for irrationality. In addition, we identify a class of social phenomena where this apparent paradox is likely to invalidate more naïve applications of the rational choice paradigm. Hence, we identify not only a shortcoming in the rational choice paradigm but also how social scientists, without departing from first principles, can augment the paradigm to make better sense of complicated social phenomena.

We begin in the following section by reviewing seminal contributions to the industrial organization literature (Holmstrom 1982; Eswaran and Kotwal 1984). These contributions imply that, rather than facilitating optimality, unconstrained rationality necessarily produces inefficient or unstable outcomes in team production processes. This implication highlights the potential for competitive forces to select agents that embody something other than simple conceptions of rationality. In particular, it suggests that competitive settings adopt agents who can credibly commit against acting rationally!

We then identify an important class of social phenomena where this apparently paradoxical implication is prevalent. In particular, we argue that any social phenomenon that is logically reducible to a team production problem must exhibit this paradox. Since one such phenomenon is that of public goods, an important conclusion for the present research is that unconstrained rationality produces inferior outcomes in the state as well as the firm. Consequently, the "as if" principle does not hold in these settings—competition will select for constrained, rather than unconstrained, rationality.

While rational choice theorists might interpret constraints on rationality as inherently irrational, our arguments have the opposite implication. Moreover, relative to other criticisms of the rational choice paradigm, this one is constructive since it does not impose limits on rationality in an ad hoc manner. Rather, we argue that constraints survive for the same reason that rationality purportedly survives—that is, competition selects social agents that either implicitly or explicitly credibly constrain behavior that could be rational in settings other than team production. By showing how competitive forces can select for a particular form of "irrationality," we identify how rational choice theorists in particular and social scientists more generally can augment their analytical tools to gain deeper insights into important social phenomena.

Constraining Rationality, Team Production, and Public Goods

Institutions that constrain self-interest have earned the attention of scholars in both politics and economics. For example, Douglass North and Barry Weingast (1989) argue that to understand British political economy after 1688 one must understand how institutions emerged to constrain self-interested rulers. Others address institutional constraints on central banks (Friedman 1962; Kydland and Prescott 1977; Barro 1983; Rogoff 1985; Cukierman and Meltzer 1986), the presidency (Ingberman and Yao 1991), and firms (Williamson 1985).

In the present section, we address an important and largely open question; that is, why do institutions that constrain self-interest emerge in these particular settings? We argue that the incentive to "constrain rationality" follows from the inability of collectives to fully escape moral hazard when producing a joint product. Feasible production schemes cannot perfectly align individual self-interest with group efficiency. Moreover, attempts to refine such mechanisms can only move moral hazard from one actor to another, but never eliminate it. Since no mechanism completely extinguishes moral hazard, the "best" ones can only place opportunistic incentives with agents who are relatively incapable of acting on them. In other words, feasible mechanisms optimize production by credibly constraining self-interest as opposed to simply encouraging its pursuit.

Implications of this proposition are truly paradoxical. In firms, shareholders have an incentive to expropriate the product of their agents. In collective action organizations, entrepreneurs inevitably face temptations to exploit the organizations they create (Frohlich, Oppenheimer, and Young 1971). In autocratic states, leaders' self-interests (i.e., their stakes in the size of residuals) are necessarily at odds with the states' efficiency (a generalization supported by North's economic history). More generally, the classic political distribution question ("who gets what, when, and how") is an inevitable stumbling block on the road to social order: at some point self-interest is at odds with social efficiency. It follows that if social forces select for efficiency at the group level, the motivation to credibly constrain self-interest is omnipresent.

THE PROBLEMS OF TEAM PRODUCTION AND PUBLIC GOODS

We develop this argument by first showing that no incentive system can eliminate moral hazard when information asymmetries and externalities exist. This implication follows immediately from Bengt Holmstrom's (1982) frequently cited but little used impossibility result.

For Holmstrom, a team production process is one in which individuals $i \in N$ contribute effort levels $a_i \in A_i \in R+$ that when aggregated produce a joint product $Q(a)$ (where $a \in \underset{i \in N}{\times} A_i$). Holmstrom assumes that the production technology Q exhibits externalities in the sense that each individual's effort-choice affects the output available for sharing among all team members (i.e., $Q_i \neq 0 \; \forall i$). In addition, the production process exhibits information asymmetries, since Holmstrom assumes that monitors can observe only Q, not the individual effort levels a_i.

Given this fairly general setting, Holmstrom searches for a sharing rule, $s(Q)$, that distributes the team's joint product in a manner that simultaneously satisfies three properties:

1. Budget balancing. The sharing rule, $s(Q)$, allocates the team's joint product, Q, entirely amongst the team's members.

2. Nash equilibrium. Given the manner in which members' joint product is to be shared (i.e., $s(Q)$), there exists at least one set of self-enforcing strategy profiles. Under such a profile, no individual wants to defect from his or her individual effort contribution, a_i, given that others are contributing effort according to the profile's prescription.

3. Pareto optimality. The sharing rule, $s(Q)$, induces an outcome from which no player can be made better off without making another worse off.

Holmstrom shows that any budget-balancing sharing rule cannot simultaneously satisfy the conditions of Nash equilibrium and Pareto optimality. In other words, any group (e.g., a polity) that wishes to allocate its joint product (e.g., a public good) entirely among its members cannot do so in a manner that induces a stable and efficient outcome.

To see this, consider a budget-balancing sharing rule that is well behaved in the sense that it induces at least one Nash equilibrium. In equilibrium, each member contributes effort until the marginal cost of doing so equals the associated marginal benefit, given the contributions of all other members. But since the team's technology exhibits externalities in production, this benefit is not private to the team member—rather, it is public to the team. Hence, if a sharing rule does not transfer the entire benefit (private and public) to the individual whose actions induced it, then the set of Nash equilibrium effort-contributions will not maximize social welfare (i.e., efficient equilibria will not exist).

The question thus becomes, Can a budget-balancing sharing rule align private incentives with public objectives in this manner? It cannot—it is impossible for a sharing rule to allocate shares of the team's "public good" in a manner that just compensates each member for the marginal cost of his or her unobserved effort. But a sharing rule that doesn't just compensate each team member cannot "balance the budget"—there must exist a residual that is not allocated to the team's members. In short, production externalities coupled with hidden action make it impossible for sharing rules to distribute a team's joint product entirely among its members in a manner that simultaneously satisfies the conditions of Nash equilibrium and Pareto optimality.

Holmstrom characterizes this result as follows: "As long as we insist on budget-balancing . . . we cannot achieve efficiency. Agents can cover improper actions behind the uncertainty concerning who was at fault. Since all agents cannot be penalized sufficiently for a deviation in the outcome, some agent always has an incentive to capitalize on this control deficiency" (1982, 327). Note that Holmstrom's setup does not restrict this implication to firms. Rather, the setup is sufficiently general to apply to any collective organization, the state as well as the firm, where the product of joint effort (e.g., a public good) is shared and individual effort (e.g., productive activity serving as a tax base) is costly to observe.

This generality is further evidenced by its deep relationship to preference-revelation mechanisms. Theodore Groves (1973) and Edward Clarke (1971) independently show that when preferences over public goods are unobservable budget-balancing mechanisms cannot induce individuals to truthfully reveal their preferences in a manner that induces an efficient equilibrium. Fundamental to these results are the conditions of externality (i.e., externalities in production for Holmstrom and consumption for Groves and Clarke) and costly information (i.e., hidden actions for Holmstrom and preferences for Groves and Clarke). Since the relationship between preference relations and choice rules is "almost" isomorphic (e.g., see Mas-Colell, Whinston, and Green 1995, 11–14), the conditions giving rise to Holmstrom's theorem and that of Groves and Clarke are nearly identical. This symmetry furthers our argument that Holmstrom provides important insights to political economies in general, not only to firms.

THE ROLE OF "BUDGET BREAKING"

Scholars such as Clarke, Groves, Holmstrom, and others show that under conditions that characterize team production systems (e.g., social organizations), a budget-balancing allocation mechanism cannot simultaneously satisfy the conditions of Nash equilibrium (i.e., incentive compatibility) and Pareto optimality. To exhibit desirable welfare properties, therefore, sharing rules must "break the budget" (i.e., allocate some of the team's joint product

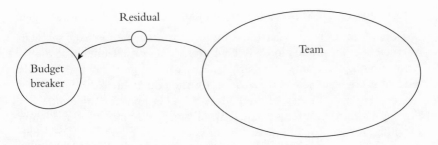

FIGURE 5.1 The residual must be allocated to an "external agent"

outside of the team). An important question for social engineers thus becomes who should "own" the budget-breaking residual.

Note that Holmstrom's theorem implies that the residual owner cannot be an actor whose actions directly affect the social output. By default, the residual must be allocated to an "external agent," as illustrated in Figure 5.1.[1] Budget breaking is essential for neutralizing the effort-retarding incentives associated with externalities in production.

As long as a passive repository for the residual exists, an efficiency-inducing incentive scheme is feasible. Holmstrom provides one such example. Suppose that a residual owner (e.g., a shareholder) cannot observe individuals' effort-choices within the firm but can observe output. Also suppose that the owner knows the efficient level of output since he or she may be presumed to know individual effort cost functions. Then the owner can offer a "group punishment scheme" where the team's joint product is distributed among its members, unless the team produces less than the Pareto efficient quantity. In that case, no member receives any remuneration—all of it accrues to the external agent.

This type of "forcing contract" is one of many possible schemes that induce a stable and efficient outcome among the team's members. Under these mechanisms, each employee's effort choice is pivotal in determining his or her own share. Consequently, no employee has an incentive to shirk. The external agent does not need to identify the shirker, as long as everyone receives the same punishment when the Pareto suboptimal outcome is observed.

And of course the common characteristic of all such efficient incentive schemes is that the payments to the members of the team do not equal the revenue generated by their efforts. In this scheme, the residual is presumably positive.[2] Since every team member, pursuing his or her self-interest, exerts effort at a level that supports an efficient outcome, there exists a residual for the passive owner.

THE MORAL HAZARD OF BUDGET BREAKING

Does Holmstrom's budget-breaking incentive scheme solve the problem of efficient team production? By definition, it aligns self-interest and efficiency among the team's members. It necessarily creates a residual, but that residual is the justifiable compensation for the budget breaker's contractual services. Holmstrom viewed the budget-breaking joint forcing contract as aligning incentives in teams plagued by information asymmetries, and doing so without exhausting resources on monitoring team members' efforts. This "solution" is, nevertheless, problematic.[3] It removes the moral hazard from the team members and places it with the budget breaker.

To see this, let us ask about the self-interest of the budget breaker—for example, the firm's owner, the residual-claiming public good entrepreneur, or the totalitarian state's ruler. Does the budget breaker's interest in the residual motivate efficient action? The answer must be no. The budget breaker's self-interest is necessarily subversive of organizational efficiency.

To see this, imagine the opposite—that is, there is an efficient budget-breaking incentive scheme for the N team members, and the budget breaker finds that maximizing its residual requires it to support the Pareto optimal outcome among those N team members. We have already reached a contradiction, as the N team members plus the budget breaker constitute a closed budget-balanced system. All of the revenue generated by the team members is distributed among the team members and the budget breaker. By Holmstrom's theorem, every such budget-balanced sharing rule cannot induce an efficient equilibrium—the incentive to play morally hazardous actions cannot be extinguished from the system. Since by construction it is not the N team members, then the moral hazard must be present for the budget breaker (Eswaran and Kotwal 1984).

The budget breaker's rational pursuit of the residual-claim must be inconsistent with Pareto optimality; that is, the budget breaker always prefers a different incentive scheme that increases the residual's size at the expense of overall efficiency in the organization. This must be true whether we are talking about a business firm, a political organization, or the state.

The moral hazard facing the budget breaker is apparent even in Holmstrom's proposed group punishment scheme, designed to create incentives for efficiency among team members. The residual-claiming budget breaker will have reason to contact just one employee, and that employee to shirk. As a result of this one employee shirking, no one would get paid. The residual, defined as the difference between total revenue generated by employees and payouts to them, is significantly larger when the bribe subverts efficiency. The point of this example, given a result attributed to Mukesh Eswaran and Ashok Kotwal (1984), is that the residual owner's self-interest must be at odds with organizational efficiency.

For every efficient incentive scheme, another exists that creates a larger residual for the owner—but is inefficient. Maximizing the owner's residual is inconsistent with efficiency for the team as a whole. It is this logical implication of the Holmstrom theorem that lies behind the rational suspicions of the employees of profit-maximizing firms.

RATIONAL SUSPICIONS

Casual empiricism suggests that "team members" are frequently suspicious of superiors who might expropriate their teams' product. The impossibility results that we synthesize here, of which Holmstrom's is an element, rationalizes such suspicions. It does so by showing that any agent, acting as a budget breaker (e.g., a sovereign set of shareholders), has the incentive to capture rents created by the members' collective efforts. Left unchecked, this incentive can preclude team members and budget breakers from attaining their shared goals.

As an initial example of this, let us consider once again Holmstrom's efficient group punishment scheme. Notice that the group punishment scheme is punitive—that is, it creates the possibility of efficiency by creating a punishment that is sufficiently bad to deter any shirking. Nevertheless, team members might voluntarily contract to such an incentive scheme with the rationale that it is necessary to generate efficient levels of (shared) revenue.

However, as Eswaran and Kotwal (1984) point out, there is every reason for employees to mistrust any efficient incentive scheme offered to them, precisely because of the residual owner's incentives to subvert. Employees offered Holmstrom's efficient group punishment scheme may well think, "I would be willing to take this job under a group punishment scheme if I knew that the contract would be honestly administered. But why should the owner not seek to subvert the scheme by bribing a coworker to shirk? I must expect that a bribe—and no payment to the employees—will be the ultimate outcome; therefore, it would be stupid of me to accept the contract." The group punishment scheme is not credible precisely because of the owner's moral hazard to subvert it. Concerns about the owner's self-interested actions are not peripheral to the performance of the firm. The owner's self-interest inevitably conflicts with overall efficiency.

Holmstrom's group punishment scheme is a metaphor for all such rational awareness of the moral hazard inherent in the leader's position. Any leader who is strong enough to manipulate selective incentives for the efficient supply of public goods is also strong enough to manipulate incentives for the maximization of leader rents—and Holmstrom tells us that those two leader goals cannot be made consistent.

Gary Miller and Thomas Hammond (1994) offer a similar argument with respect to demand-revealing mechanisms. Demand-revealing mechanisms, in

eliciting hidden information, can work efficiently only by creating a residual. A defense of demand-revealing mechanisms is that this residual can be
made to be a diminishingly small fraction of the benefits generated by the
scheme (Tideman 1977). However, the point is that the budget breaker does
not have an incentive to make that residual as small as possible; on the contrary, the budget breaker has every incentive to make the residual as large as
possible.

With hidden preferences, as with hidden action, budget breaking is not a
real solution but an indicator of a profound problem—that is, tension over
the distribution of collectively generated benefits can undermine the generation of those benefits. This observation has to be one of the strongest generalizations about social organization: leaders with a capacity to appropriate
the residual have a self-interest at odds with that of the organization as a
whole. An implication of budget breaking is Maurice Duverger's "Iron Law
of Oligarchy": as organizations become more hierarchical (more controlled
by their leaders), those in positions of command increasingly divert organizational resources toward perquisites of office and less toward supply of those
public goods that were the organization's original purpose.

This conflict between residual profit maximization and group efficiency
can be seen in firms, political interest groups, and the state. For example, for
firms to perform efficiently, their employees and suppliers may have to make
costly investments that are more productive within the firm than they are in
the market. But employees and suppliers often forgo those investments when
the residual owner can expropriate their rents (i.e., the difference between
their investment's productivity within the firm and on the market). The efficient level of these firm-specific investments, therefore, tends to obtain
only when stakeholders observe credible constraints on owners' incentives or
abilities to pursue opportunistic strategies (Kline, Crawford, and Alchian
1978).

Similarly, effective operation of the piece rate and other incentive systems
depends on the workers' belief that productivity improvements generated by
their efforts and ideas will not result in piece-rate cuts and eventual firing in
the face of large stockpiles (Miller 1992). Deferred earnings and steep earnings profiles may motivate high (unmonitored and unrewarded) effort early
in a worker's career in the expectation of promotions, job security, and retirement benefits (Lazear 1981); but this works only if employees are confident that shareholders will not benefit from leveraged buyouts, corporate
takeovers, downsizing, or raids on pension funds before the end of their ca-
reers.[4] As we highlight in section 2, separating ownership from control can
shift, but not extinguish, the incentive for morally hazardous action—just as
free riding among team members is inconsistent with efficient production,
so is a narrow pursuit of profits among owners.

Another example of owner opportunism is accepting hostile takeover bids. Andrei Shleifer and Lawrence Summers (1988) argue that accepting a hostile takeover is a "breach of trust" in which shareholders renege on implicit contracts and opportunistically expropriate wealth that would have gone to other stakeholders.

Norman Frohlich, Joe Oppenheimer, and Oran Young (1971) make a similar case regarding political organization in general. Following Mancur Olson, they agree that contributions for public goods in such organizations are generally induced by selective incentive. However, provision of the selective incentives is itself a public good for the organization. This infinite regress is resolved in the form of an organizational entrepreneur, who supplies selective incentives and public goods from the contributions induced by those selective incentives; the entrepreneur's self-interested motivation for taking on this role is precisely the residual profits available. The authors argue that this entrepreneur is necessary for the efficient provision of public goods. Paradoxically, however, they point out that the entrepreneur's stake in the residual profits may take precedence over, and undermine, the provision of the public goods. We take Holmstrom's and Eswaran and Kotwal's results to be stronger—the entrepreneur's goal of residual maximization must be inconsistent with Pareto optimality in public goods economies. Diversion of collective resources to the leadership diminishes the effectiveness of selective-incentive-based voluntary organizations, and cynicism about group leadership consistently undermines the ability of such groups to attract support.

Finally, in his sweeping economic history, North (1981) claims that ruler self-interest has always been at odds with economic efficiency. From the redistributive societies of ancient Egyptian dynasties through the slavery system of the Greek and Roman worlds, to the medieval manor, a tension persisted between ownership structures that maximized the ruler's (and his group's) rents and sustained efficient outcomes (25).

This does not mean that there is no such thing as an efficient incentive scheme for the state; it means that the ruler, as owner of the residual, will have no incentive to seek out such a scheme. Or more strongly, the owner of the residual will always have an incentive to replace an efficient scheme with an inefficient scheme that increases the residual.

In the autocratic state, the ruler (like the shareholders of a firm) may be thought of as the residual claimant. The leading kleptocracies of the twentieth century used the power of the state to extract huge proportions of their respective societies' wealth. Ex-president Suharto extracted up to $40 billion from Indonesia during his thirty-two-year reign. Mobutu Sese Seko ruled for the same number of years, piled up a comparable amount of wealth, and in the process transformed his ancestral village into a city of thirty thousand, with the main job of its citizens being to provide personal services at the three palaces and the luxury hotel and conference center that he had built there. Former Ukrainian prime minister Pavlo Lazarenko purchased a mansion from Eddie Murphy in Marin County with $6.75 million in cash; he claimed that he was not a thief but someone who was "fighting to bring about gradual reform leading to an improved economic climate" in the Ukraine. The population of Pakistan objected very little to the recent military coup in their country, evidently because the corruption of the previous administration was well known and the incoming military regime promised to do something about it. But of course military regimes are not immune to corruption, as illustrated by the millions stashed in American banks by members of the military elite that ruled Nigeria for fifteen years.

It is relatively easy to see that residual maximization by the ruler is inconsistent with efficiency as a whole. The anticipation that accumulated wealth will become a target for extraction creates a disincentive for entrepreneurial activity. Contracts are not trusted because political appeal to the ruler's clique trumps contract rights. Property rights are made uncertain by the ruler's vagaries. The economic costs to autocratic states of the kleptocrat's actions far exceed the wealth stolen by the ruler—much greater is the cost of deferred economic growth discouraged by the incentives imposed by the ruler's self-interested reign.

PERSISTENT INEFFICIENCIES

More generally, the classic political distribution problem ("who gets what, when, and how") is insoluble. Self-interest is always at war with efficiency at some point in every hierarchical organization. How then do social organizations (including the state) exist when they can never "solve" this paradox, in the sense of perfectly aligning self-interest with efficiency?

The easy answer, of course, is that social organizations often go under, or totter along burdened by whatever levels of inefficiency their leaders choose to burden them with, in the interest of better exploitation. North's examination of economic history was motivated by this empirical generalization: that states seem in general to persist in inefficient equilibria for very long periods of time indeed.

The same may be true of substate organizations. Organizations die all the time. Internal organizational conflict always appears associated with organizational death. How many interest groups have simply gone out of existence because of exposures of corruption by organizational leaders? How many organizations have persisted in weakened states because of conflicts over distributions of residual profits?

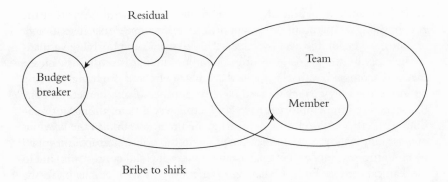

Residual

Team

Budget
breaker

Member

Bribe to shirk

FIGURE 5.2 A bribe from the budget breaker increases the residual but decreases team efficiency.

Producing Credible Commitments

As widespread as organizational failure and inefficiency are, some organizations and states demonstrate a capacity for persistent economic success and long-run growth. How can the successes of these social organizations be reconciled with the inevitable potential for inefficient rent extraction?

CREDIBLE COMMITMENT INSTITUTIONS IN THE FIRM

If the self-interest of everyone in an organization cannot be perfectly aligned with organizational efficiency, then the self-interest of some organizational actors must be credibly constrained. As an example, let us return for a last time to Holmstrom's budget-breaking group punishment incentive plan.

Remember that, while the Holmstrom plan has an equilibrium (among the team members) in which each member contributes an efficiency-inducing effort level, the resulting set of strategies is not a Nash equilibrium because, as in Figure 5.2, each team member will anticipate not getting paid as a result of a side payment between the owner and some other team member, subverting the efficiency of the joint-forcing contract. As a result, Eswaran and Kotwal point out, the predicted outcome of Holmstrom's "efficient" incentive scheme is inefficiency.

But the owner does not benefit from inefficiency. *Ex ante*, the owner prefers to commit to not pursuing greater profits by bribing one of the team members. The owner recognizes its budget-breaking capacity and thus anticipates the employee mistrust that this capacity, left unconstrained, can induce. The owner would therefore be better off "tying its hands" *ex ante*—that is, controlling its own capacity to opportunistically pursue greater profits.

Thus, we claim, the real message of Holmstrom's impossibility result is credible commitment. As Holmstrom demonstrated, it is possible to create incentive-compatible sharing rules that induce efficient outcomes. But he has not shown how to create credible efficient incentive schemes. *Ex post*, the owner and the employees have conflicting interests regarding distribution of an efficient level of benefits generated by the team. But *ex ante*, the owner and the employees have a shared interest in constraining the owner.

Holmstrom advances the separation of ownership and control as a simple mechanical process; budget balancing is inconsistent with efficiency, so we have to create an external owner who will accept the residual profits and losses that inevitably arise from an efficient scheme. However, separating ownership from control is more than a simple mechanical process. To be effective, separation must solve a fundamental constitutional problem of credible commitment; it must check the owner's opportunity to pursue his or her own self-interest via firm politics. Separation is in fact a metaphor for the constitutional problem addressed in *The Federalist*: how to keep self-interested social actors from exploiting others.

Practically speaking, this means that separating ownership from management of the firm is not sufficient. Not only must the owner be distinct from the firm—the owner must also be made impotent.

For most of the twentieth century, American firms employed one such commitment device—namely, shareholder fragmentation. As long as shareholders are numbered in the tens and hundreds of thousands, with no individual shareholder owning even as much as 1 percent of the firm's total value, collective action costs serve as a visible and tangible impediment to the kind of reneging described by Shleifer and Summers.

In fact, we can use Holmstrom's theorem itself to formalize this concept. Think of individual shareholders as a "team" whose action can result in increased monitoring of the firm, increased diversion of revenues away from employee wages and managerial perquisites, and increased extraction of firm revenues in the form of profits. We may think of the firm as a resource that generates profits that are distributed among the shareholders. Of course, the profits extracted from the firm are distributed exactly among the shareholders. Consequently, the shareholders can be thought of as a "team" that "produces" profits, the distribution of which respects the constraint of "budget balancing"—profits (by definition) go to no one other than shareholders. But because this sharing rule balances the budget, we know that shareholders cannot efficiently extract profits in equilibrium; there is no profit-sharing rule that will produce efficient behavior from shareholders.

The net result, then, is that shareholders can only inefficiently pursue their common interest to extract residual profits from the firm. This inefficiency is itself a form of credible commitment—restraining the very force that is inconsistent with efficiency for the firm as a whole.

As ownership becomes increasingly concentrated in retirement funds or other suppliers of capital, the credibility with which shareholder fragmentation can constrain owner interests diminishes. But if our analysis here is correct, then a concentrated owner could see the advantage of inventing other forms of credible commitment to substitute for shareholder fragmentation.

For example, the relationship between a firm's owners and its managers is frequently characterized as one in which owners are principals and managers are agents. This framework implies that forces exist in firms that induce managers to play self-interested actions, even if doing so detracts from achieving the owners' objectives. To the extent that this force pervades firms, management shirking increases as the ability of firm owners to constrain their agents decreases. If management-insulating institutions such as golden parachutes increase manager utility while working against owner objectives, and if the capacity for firm owners to constrain their agents (e.g., via monitoring) is a positive function of ownership concentration, then the incidence of golden parachutes should decrease as ownership becomes more concentrated.

Dino Falaschetti (2002a) examines the incidence of golden parachute agreements in this context. If golden parachutes evidence destructive managerial insulation, then they should presumably disappear when owners are sufficiently concentrated and powerful to eliminate them. In other words, these severance packages should exist only when shareholders are so fragmented that managers can force them upon the firm.

Falaschetti finds just the opposite, however. Firms tend to maintain golden parachutes precisely when owners are theoretically most capable of efficiently producing monitoring services, that is, when ownership is concentrated and thus forces associated with the team production problem are relatively weak. If concentrated sets of owners are relatively efficient monitors, why is the incidence of golden parachute agreements positively associated with shareholder concentration?

Our arguments in the present chapter rationalize this pattern. If concentrated groups are more efficient at pursuing common objectives, then concentrated owners incur relatively little cost to opportunistically expropriate their teams' products. Because owner opportunism threatens firm efficiency, firms face selection pressures to implement institutions that insulate stakeholders from associated consequences. The empirical distribution of golden parachute provisions is thus consistent with institutional constraints acting as efficiency-enhancing credible commitment devices.

CREDIBLE COMMITMENT INSTITUTIONS IN THE STATE

Just as diffusing ownership can credibly constrain shareholders' moral hazard in the firm, diffusing decision-making authority can credibly constrain political agents' moral hazard in the state. North and Weingast (1989) anticipate this argument in their analysis of 1688's Glorious Revolution. They argue, consistent with Holmstrom, that only by credibly constraining the British king was it possible to make the efficiency gains of the Industrial Revolution. In the Glorious Revolution, Parliament took control of finances and the courts. It required auditing of government expenditures and guaranteed that the highest priority for tax revenues would be to repay government loans. Loan administration was placed with professional bankers at the newly created Bank of England. Each of these organizational features helped divorce the king from management of the state's affairs, credibly committing the state to property rights and contract enforcement. As lenders' confidence improved, interest rates dropped and relatively cheap financing was made available for entrepreneurs to pursue their projects. The king was constrained from actions that would endanger property rights and contract enforcement. The result was enhanced productivity. During this period, Parliament credibly constrained the Stuart kings. But what prevented Parliament from reproducing the kings' abuses and thus the consequent costs to contract enforcement, property rights, and economic development?

If Parliament had been as unified as the king, then it could have easily undone the Glorious Revolution's reforms. Parliament could have sold monopolies, written laws that negated previous legal protections for property owners, and created entry barriers to protect favored economic actors. Parliament's advantage over the king lies in its diffusion of authority and thus the consequent increase in cost to coordinate morally hazardous actions.

The exception that proves the point is the power of sugar planters in eighteenth-century Parliament. With wealth sufficient to buy a large number of "rotten boroughs," Parliament's members were positioned to pursue a rent-seeking strategy, prohibiting other sources of sugar from the English economy and obtaining subsidies and privileges of various sorts. If Parliament had agreed on other aspects of policy as well, then it clearly would have had no compunction about pursuing rent seeking at the cost of economic efficiency in other policy dimensions. Rather than Parliament members' superior moral nature protecting England from the Stuarts' abuses, the increased cost of organizing Parliament to act like a Stuart king appears to have facilitated protection.

Of course, it was precisely the political corruption of eighteenth-century Parliament that motivated further reforms in nineteenth-century Great Britain. These reforms can be seen as further manifestations of credible constraints on morally hazardous rent seeking—and again, through further diffusion of political authority. By the early nineteenth century, the economic role of the middle class was clear. Among other things, middle-class taxation was critical to the government's strength. Disaffected by a corrupt court and bureaucracy, the middle class was increasingly reluctant to cooperate with the British taxation system. Gladstone and other reformers felt they had to constrain political leaders—that is, themselves!—to keep expenditures from continuing to rise inefficiently. As John Daunton (1998) writes, "The links of the chains which bound Leviathan were forged by politicians and bureaucrats who were well aware of the temptations to themselves and the electorate of allowing government expenditure to rise" (161). The elite willingly bore a new income tax and abandoned the Corn Laws from which they had benefited. These and other retrenchment laws were a move in the right direction—but of course they might be undone as easily as they were passed. The long-term commitment came when political reforms eliminated rotten boroughs, reformed the judiciary, reduced the church aristocracy's political power, and extended the vote broadly within the middle class. The political reforms provided visible assurance that the economic reforms would not be reversed.

The incentive for rent extraction cannot be eliminated, so the best protection is to make rent extraction relatively costly. This implies that any formal institutional framework may be subverted with a sufficiently concentrated coalition of economic and political power. For example, let there be a set of democratic institutions imposed on a social system with highly concentrated wealth. But wealth owners could "buy" a sufficient level of cooperation from agents across the institutions and recognize the capacity to profit from controlling those institutions—to the detriment of others' property rights, the rule of law, and long-term economic development.[5] Indeed, a number of Latin American countries with wealth concentrated in a small number of families have been able to accomplish just this when a constitution virtually identical to the U.S. Constitution was imposed on their political system. This is one of the implications of the logical argument in this chapter. Credible commitment is not obtained by an institutional "magical formula," but is painfully and tentatively constructed out of perceived obstacles to unified action by those with a claim to residuals generated by the polity.

Concentration of political power can subvert a formal diffusion of power as well, causing a collapse of credible commitment. For example, the purpose of a political party is, in large part, to overcome constitutional diffusions of power. In the nineteenth century, New York's Tammany Hall exemplified a unified political force that transcended a constitutional separation of powers. When both houses of the state legislature, the governor, and judges are obliged to the same party boss or machine, then formally diffusing authority counts for little as a source of credible commitment, and economic actors will assume that constitutional protections of their legal rights are only as good as their rapprochement with the party boss.[6] This makes clear that any political force with sufficient unity and coherence to pursue a rent-seeking strategy can work through a variety of formal institutions to undermine economic efficiency.[7] In the United States, the Progressive reform movement can be seen as a counterattack by economic forces that hoped to protect their economic investments by reestablishing the reality, rather than simply the form, of diffusion of power. Civil service laws, nonpartisan elections, city manager charters, and other reforms were all intended to reduce the coordinating power of the party boss and thereby reestablish de facto diffusion of political authority in American politics as a source of credible commitment (Miller 1989). Had the Progressive reformers failed, the United States might well have come to resemble states like Mexico, where the PRI (Partido Revolucionario Institucional, i.e., Institutional Revolutionary Party) sufficiently concentrated power to enrich the few members of the political economic elite at the expense of overall development.

Conclusion

Social scientists since at least Bernard de Mandeville (writing in the early eighteenth century) argued that private egoism can advance the public good (Copleston [1957] 1985, 5: 178). Neoclassical economic theory formalizes this argument via the first theorem of welfare economics—equilibria that emerge from the unconstrained pursuit of self-interest have desirable welfare properties.

Nevertheless, when monitoring is costly and externalities in production exist, unconstrained egoism does not induce efficient equilibria. In the competitive environment that surrounds modern firms and states, unconstrained egoism contributes to relative failure. The typical predatory state, such as Zaire, is a model for unconstrained pursuit of self-interest—and for social failure on a catastrophic scale.

The most successful firms and states will be those that address the inevitability of moral hazard by unleashing self-interest where it is most beneficial, but constraining self-interest where it is bound with moral hazard. We believe that the modern firm's evolution has seen such a development of self-interested constraints in the form of diffuse ownership, corporate law, and separation of ownership from professionalized autonomous managers. The net effect is to allow those contracting with the firm to have confidence that the firm's obligations will not (usually) be abrogated in the interest of greater corporate profits. This constraint has been beneficial even (or especially!) for those who experience the constraints most powerfully—the shareholders themselves, who benefit from the fact that the firms they own can make more profits when their contractual partners recognize the constraints operating on their firms.

Similarly, while the least successful societies have been those in which political elites are least constrained in their pursuit of self-interest, the most successful societies have been, as North insists, those with the most institutional and constitutional limitations on the political interest of political actors. These include a constitutional separation for a professionalized autonomous court, a separate and distinct central banking system, a system of competitive (and therefore mutually distrustful) political parties, and protections for basic liberties of speech, association, and press. Each of these constitutional features serves to limit the ability of those with political power from expropriating wealth from investors and entrepreneurs—and thus encourage an intensity of economic activity that enhances social strength. In the state, as well as the firm, competition selects for credible constraint of rational action.

Notes

Thanks to Jack Knight, Norman Frohlich, Joe Oppenheimer, and Ken Shepsle for early comments helpful in writing this paper.

1. An agent is "external" to a system if it is not a party to contracts between members of that system. For example, members of a political system may be various constituencies and an external agent a legislature and executive.

2. This type of side payment from team members to the external agent is sometimes referred to as a "Clarke tax" (Varian 1992, 428).

3. Holmstrom recognizes this difficulty (e.g., see Holmstrom 1999) but does not address it before turning to other issues regarding principal-agent relationships.

4. For recent popular accounts of such incidents, see "Companies Find Host of Subtle Ways to Pare Retirement Payouts," *Wall Street Journal*, July 27, 2000, p. A1, and "Phase Retirement Option for Workers Is Mainly a Boon for Their Employers," *Wall Street Journal*, July 27, 2000, p. A6.

5. Thanks to Joe Oppenheimer for pointing this out.

6. Beck et al. 2000 and Henisz 2000 exploit this insight to formally measure protections across countries and time.

7. Keefer and Stasavage 1999, Henisz 2000, Stasavage 2000, and Falaschetti (2001, 2002b) offer formal evidence of this phenomenon.

References

Alchian, Armin. 1950. "Uncertainty, Evolution, and Economic Theory." *Journal of Political Economy* 58(3): 211–21.

Barro, Robert J. 1983. "Rules, Discretion and Reputation in a Model of Monetary Policy." *Journal of Monetary Economics* 12(1): 101–22.

Beck, Thorsten, George Clarke, Alberto Groff, Philip Keefer, and Patrick Walsh. 2000. "New Tools in Comparative Political Economy: The Database of Political Institutions." Policy Research Working Paper #2283, The World Bank.

Becker, Gary. 1976. *The Economic Approach to Human Behavior*. Chicago: University of Chicago Press.

Black, Duncan. [1958] 1987. *The Theory of Committees and Elections*. Cambridge: Harvard University Press (Boston: Kluwer Academic Publishers).

Buchanan, James M., and Gordon Tullock. 1962. *The Calculus of Consent*. Ann Arbor: University of Michigan Press.

Calvo, Guillermo. 1978. "On the Time Consistency of Optimal Policy in a Monetary Economy." *Econometrica* 46(6): 1411–28.

Clarke, Edward H. 1971. "Multipart Pricing of Public Goods." *Public Choice* 11: 17–33.

Copleston, Frederick. [1957] 1985. *A History of Philosophy*, vol. 5. New York: Doubleday.

Crain, Mark W., and Robert D. Tollison. 1993. "Time Inconsistency and Fiscal Policy: Empirical Analysis of U.S. States, 1969–89." *Journal of Public Economics* 51(2): 153–59.

Cukierman, Alex, and Allan H. Meltzer. 1986. "A Positive Theory of Discretionary Policy, the Cost of Democratic Government and the Benefits of a Constitution." *Economic Inquiry* 24(3): 367–88.

Daunton, John. 1998. "Trusting Leviathan: British Fiscal Administration." In *Trust and Governance*, ed. Valerie Braithwaite and Margaret Levi. New York: Russell Sage

Downs, Anthony. 1957. *An Economic Theory of Democracy*. New York: Harper & Row.

Eswaran, Mukesh, and Ashok Kotwal. 1984. "The Moral Hazard of Budget Breaking." *Rand Journal of Economics* 15: 578–81.

Falaschetti, Dino. 2001. "Credible Commitments and Investment: Do Checks on the Ability or Incentive to Play Opportunistic Actions Matter?" Presented to the Public Choice Society, San Antonio, Texas.

———. 2002a. "Golden Parachutes: Credible Commitments or Evidence of Shirking?" *Journal of Corporate Finance* 8(2): 159–78.

———. 2002b. "Does Partisan Heritage Matter? The Case of the Federal Reserve." *Journal of Law, Economics, and Organization* 18(2): 488–510.

Falaschetti, Dino, and Gary Miller. 2001. "Constraining Leviathan: Moral Hazard and Credible Commitment in Constitutional Design." *Journal of Theoretical Politics* 13(4): 389–411.

Ferejohn, John. 1974. *Pork Barrel Politics*. Stanford, Calif.: Stanford University Press.

Fischer, Stanley. 1980. "Dynamic Inconsistency, Cooperation and the Benevolent Dissembling Government." *Journal of Economic Dynamics and Control* 2(1): 93–107.

Friedman, Jeffrey, ed. 1996. *The Rational Choice Controversy: Economic Models of Politics Reconsidered*. New Haven and London: Yale University Press.

Friedman, Milton. 1962. "Should There Be an Independent Monetary Authority?" In *In Search of a Monetary Constitution*, ed. Leland B. Yeager. Cambridge: Harvard University Press.

Frohlich, Norman, Joe A. Oppenheimer, and Oran R. Young. 1971. *Political Leadership and Collective Goods*. Princeton, N.J.: Princeton University Press.

Gibbard, Alan. 1973. "Manipulation of Voting Schemes." *Econometrica* 41: 587–602.

Green, Donald P., and Ian Shapiro. 1994. *Pathologies of Rational Choice Theory: A Critique of Applications in Political Science*. New Haven and London: Yale University Press.

Groves, Theodore. 1973. "Incentives in Teams." *Econometrica* 41(4): 617–31.

Groves, Theodore, and John Ledyard. 1977. "Optimal Allocation of Public Goods: A Solution to the 'Free Rider' Problem." *Econometrica* 45(4): 783–810.

———. 1987. "Incentive Compatibility Since 1972." In *Information, Incentives, and Economic Mechanisms: Essays in Honor of Leonid Hurwicz*, ed. Theodore Groves, Roy Radner, and Stanley Reiter. Minneapolis: University of Minnesota Press.

Henisz, Witold J. 2000. "The Institutional Environment for Economic Growth." *Economics and Politics* 12(1): 1–31.

Hobbes, Thomas. [1651] 1968. *Leviathan*. London: Penguin Books.

Hogarth, Robin, and Melvin W. Reder, eds. 1987. *Rational Choice: The Contrast Between Economics and Psychology*. Chicago and London: University of Chicago Press.

Holmstrom, Bengt. 1982. "Moral Hazard in Teams." *Bell Journal of Economics* 13: 324–40.

———. 1994. "The Firm as an Incentive System." *American Economics Review* 84: 972–91.

———. 1999. "The Firm as a Subeconomy." *Journal of Law, Economics, and Organization* 15: 74–102.

Hurwicz, Leo. 1979. "On Allocations Attainable Through Nash Equilibria." *Journal of Economic Theory* 21: 140–65.

Ingberman, Dan, and Dennis Yao. 1991. "Presidential Commitment and the Veto." *American Journal of Political Science* 35: 357–89.

Keefer, Philip, and David Stasavage. 1999. "Bureaucratic Delegation and Political Institutions: When Are Independent Central Banks Irrelevant?" Working paper.

Kline, Benjamin, Robert G. Crawford, and Armen A. Alchian. 1978. "Vertical Integration, Appropriable Rents, and the Competitive Contracting Process." *Journal of Law and Economics* 21(2): 297–326.

Kreps, David M. 1990. "Corporate Culture and Economic Theory." In *Perspectives on Positive Political Economy*, ed. James Alt and Kenneth Shepsle. Cambridge: Cambridge University Press.

Kydland, Finn E., and Edward C. Prescott. 1977. "Rules Rather than Discretion: The Inconsistency of Optimal Plans." *Journal of Political Economy* 85(3): 473–92.

Landsburg, Steven. 1993. *The Armchair Economist*. New York: Free Press.

Lazear, Edward. 1981. "Agency, Earnings Profiles, Productivity, and Hours Restrictions." *The American Economic Review* 71(4): 606–20.

MacPherson, C. B. 1968. Introduction to *Leviathan*, by Thomas Hobbes, 9–63. London: Penguin Books.

Mas-Colell, Andreu, Michael D. Whinston, and Jerry R. Green. 1995. *Microeconomic Theory*. New York and Oxford: Oxford University Press.

Mayhew, David. 1974. *Congress: The Electoral Connection*. New Haven: Yale University Press.

Miller, Gary. 1989. "Confiscation, Credible Commitment and Progressive Reform in the United States." *Journal of Institutional and Theoretical Economics* 145: 686–92.

———. 1992. *Managerial Dilemmas: The Political Economy of Hierarchy*. Cambridge, New York, and Melbourne: Cambridge University Press.

———. 1997. "Tying the Owner's Hands: The Moral Hazard of Profit-Maximization." Working paper, Washington University in St. Louis.

Miller, Gary, and Dino Falaschetti. 1999. "Tying the Owner's Hands: The Moral Hazard of Profit-Maximization." Presented to the International Society of New Institutional Economics, Washington, D.C.

Miller, Gary, and Thomas Hammond. 1994. "Why Politics Is More Fundamental Than Economics." *Journal of Theoretical Politics* 6: 5–26.

Niskanen, William A. 1971. *Bureaucracy and Representative Government*. Chicago: Aldine, Atherton.

North, Douglass C. 1981. *Structure and Change in Economic History*. New York: W. W. Norton.

North, Douglass C., and Barry Weingast. 1989. "Constitutions and Commitment: The Evolution of Institutions Governing Public Choice in Seventeenth Century England." *Journal of Economic History* 49(4): 808–32.

Olson, Mancur. 1965. *The Logic of Collective Action*. Cambridge: Harvard University Press.

Oppenheimer, Joe A. 1975. "Some Political Implications of Vote Trading and the Voting Paradox." *American Political Science Review* 69: 963–66.

Ostrom, Elinor. 1990. *Governing the Commons: The Evolution of Institutions for Collective Action*. Cambridge: Cambridge University Press.

Rogoff, Kenneth. 1985. "The Optimal Degree of Commitment to an Intermediate Monetary Target." *Quarterly Journal of Economics* 100 (November): 1169–90.

Root, Hilton. 1989. "Tying the King's Hands: Royal Fiscal Policy During the Old Regime." *Rationality and Society* 1: 240–59.

Rowley, Charles K. 1999. "Constitutional Political Economy and Civil Society." Presented to the Public Choice Society, New Orleans, La.

Samuelson, Paul. 1954. "The Pure Theory of Public Expenditure." *Review of Economics and Statistics* 36: 386–89.

Satterthwaite, Mark A. 1975. "Strategy-Proofness and Arrow's Conditions." *Journal of Economic Theory* 10: 187–217.

Schelling, Thomas. 1960. *The Strategy of Conflict*. London: Oxford University Press.

Sen, Armatya K. 1990. "Rational Fools: A Critique of the Behavioral Foundations of Economic Theory." In *Beyond Self-Interest*, ed. Jane Mansbridge. Chicago: University of Chicago Press.

Shepsle, Kenneth. 1979. "Institutional Arrangements and Equilibrium in Multidimensional Voting Models." *American Journal of Political Science* 23: 27–59.

Shleifer, Andrei, and Lawrence Summers. 1988. "Hostile Takeovers as Breaches of Trust." In *Corporate Takeovers: Causes and Consequences*, ed. Alan Auerbach. Chicago: University of Chicago Press.

Stasavage, David. 2000. "Private Investment and Political Institutions." Working paper, London School of Economics, December.

Tideman, Nicholas. 1977. "Ethical Foundation of the Demand-Revealing Process." Public Choice 29: 71–77.

Tideman, Nicholas, and Gordon Tullock. 1976. "A New and Superior Process for Making Social Choices." Journal of Political Economy 84: 1145–59.

Tideman, Nicholas, and Gordon Tullock. 1977. "Some Limitations of Demand Revealing Processes: Comment." Public Choice 29: 125–28.

Varian, Hal R. 1992. Microeconomic Analysis, 3rd ed. New York and London: W. W. Norton.

Vickers, John. 1985. "Delegation and the Theory of the Firm." Economic Journal 95 (supplement—conference papers): 138–47.

Williamson, Oliver E. 1985. The Economic Institutions of Capitalism. New York: Free Press.

Wittman, Donald. 1989. "Why Democracies Produce Efficient Results." Journal of Political Economy 97(6): 1395–1424.

Can Political Institutions Improve
Citizens' Competence?

MANY CITIZENS base political decisions on limited information about the consequences. If lacking information causes citizens to choose differently than if they knew these consequences, then it is common to say that they are incompetent with respect to the tasks at hand. Many observers are concerned about citizens' competence. While some react by chiding the masses for the apparent qualities of their decisions, others attempt to structure political institutions in ways that increase competence (i.e., they try to help citizens make the same choices they would have made if they were more knowledgeable about the consequences).[1]

As a general matter, it is correct to assert that providing more information to decision makers can increase their competence. It is also correct to assert that political institutions can be designed in ways that increase the amount of information available to decision makers. In what follows, however, I argue that the correspondence between an institutional design that provides more information and the competence of the citizens to whom that information is directed depends on how citizens process the information. In short, institutional designs improve competence only if citizens process information in particular ways.

Consider, for example, the plight of citizens as jurors. Jurors are asked to distill verdicts from competing claims about contentious issues. They hear testimony from many witnesses. Their ability to render a competent verdict—the verdict they would deliver given knowledge of relevant events—depends on which testimony they choose to believe.

When making such decisions, jurors may want to consider witnesses' motives. If jurors know witnesses to be motivated by their desire to tell the truth, they gain an incentive to believe the testimony. But such knowledge is an ideal. In reality, witnesses and jurors often know little about each other, making motives difficult to discern.

Institutional attributes can help jurors overcome their lack of knowledge about witnesses' motives, which, in turn, can help them use testimony more effectively. The ability to cross-examine witnesses and the threat of penalties for perjury, for example, can affect which witnesses jurors believe. When an institutional attribute induces witnesses to tell the truth at the same time that it induces jurors to believe what they hear, then it makes competent verdicts more likely.

More generally, if someone wants to design an institution in order to increase citizens' competence, then they must be reasonably correct about how citizens use information. I have argued elsewhere (Lupia 2002) that mistakes about how citizens use information are why many well-intentioned efforts to improve civic competence—such as public interest Web sites, deliberative schemes, and civic education campaigns—fail to have the effects that their advocates anticipate.[2] Here, I use a formal model and two experiments to reveal a general principle that makes such efforts more effective.

The model, from Lupia and McCubbins 1998, clarifies the conditions under which an instrumentally motivated speaker can persuade an instrumentally motivated receiver to change the latter's beliefs and behaviors. Persuasion—defined as causing a change in beliefs—is critical to the question at hand, as the only way that a speaker's advice can increase a receiver's competence is if it changes the receiver's beliefs. In the model, the receiver must choose one of two alternatives and is uncertain about which one provides higher utility. The speaker advises the receiver about which alternative is better, but the receiver is uncertain about whether his claim is true. If the receiver ignores the signal, she may not have sufficient information to make an optimal choice. But if she believes the speaker, and if the speaker gives false advice, then her choice is also suboptimal.

I use the model to show how variations in a common institutional attribute, *the threat of verification*, affect how citizens process information. In the model, verification comes in the form of subsequent information that allows the receiver to verify whether the speaker's signal is true or false. I show that increasing the verification threat increases the receiver's competence (i.e., causes her to make the utility-maximizing choice) only if

- The receiver perceives the speaker to know more than she does about which alternative is better.
- The increased verification threat is high enough to induce the receiver to follow the speaker's advice.
- The increased verification threat actually induces the speaker to make a truthful statement.

If any of these conditions fails, then the increased verification threat is not sufficient to increase competence.

I then use two experiments to evaluate the model's conclusions. In both experiments, some subjects (receivers) are initially uncertain about which of two alternatives will yield a higher payoff. Other subjects (speakers) send signals about which alternative pays them more. The key experimental variation is a change in the verification threat. The experimental data reinforce the multipart conclusion stated above.

Moreover, it is worth noting that the two experiments are very different. One was conducted in a laboratory; the other was not. In one, I paid people for their choices. In the other, I did not. I conducted one experiment on a self-selected sample of undergraduates; the other was conducted on a randomly selected sample of Americans. In one experiment, I had great control over the subject's environment; in the other, I had little control. That key aspects of the correspondence between verification and competence appear in both experimental contexts reinforces the model's empirical relevance.

In sum, this chapter demonstrates that institutional design can be an important part of efforts to increase citizens' competence, but only if certain conditions are met. To see how the stated conditions can aid future attempts to improve citizens' competence, note that the negation of each condition reveals a reason why such attempts fail. First, information is often provided to people who ignore it. Second, the information is often provided by a source that is not sufficiently credible in the eyes of the intended recipients. Third, people are induced to use information that is not helpful to them. Put another way, to increase citizens' competence it is necessary to get their attention, gain their trust, and then deliver the information that will help them better understand the consequences of their actions. To gain trust, receivers must believe that speakers either have their best interests at heart *or are operating in an institutional context that clarifies speaker motivations and makes truthtelling incentive compatible.*

Theory

Citizens must make decisions about things they cannot experience directly. For voters, the task is to choose candidates whose future actions in office cannot be experienced in advance of the election. For jurors, the task is to determine who is responsible for a crime they did not witness.

Relying on others for information in such circumstances can be an efficient way to acquire knowledge. In political situations, however, the strategy can be fraught with risk. Many people who provide political information (e.g., campaign organizations, lobbyists, courtroom witnesses) do so out of self-interest, which can induce false or misleading presentations.

For citizens who rely on others for information (e.g., witnesses, friends, the media), their competence depends on how they choose whom to believe. If they believe people who provide accurate information, they can make better decisions. *When can institutions help citizens make such choices more effectively?*

In this section, I derive conditions under which a particular kind of institutional design has this desirable attribute. The model integrates and builds from relevant insights in social psychology and economics. Psychology's contributions include Richard Petty and John Cacioppo's (1986) and Alice Eagly and Shelly Chaiken's (1993) work on the ways in which persuasion can occur. From economics I draw insights on how organizational designs affect credible commitment (see, e.g., North 1994) and incentives to convey information (see, e.g., Laffont and Tirole 1993). The model's most direct ancestors, however, are economic signaling and cheap talk models.

The seminal *signaling model* focuses on the plight of an employer who needs to hire a new worker (Spence 1973). While the employer prefers to hire a skilled applicant, she cannot observe skill levels in advance. However, she knows that skilled applicants can purchase a formal education with less effort than can unskilled applicants. Moreover, she can observe whether an applicant has a degree. The model's conclusion is that the degree persuades the employer of the applicant's skill level when unobservable skill levels and observable education levels are highly correlated.

The seminal *cheap talk model* has similar dynamics (Crawford and Sobel 1982).[3] The model features a speaker and a receiver. The receiver's job is to make a choice. Before the receiver chooses, the speaker—who is fully informed—signals the receiver about the consequences of her choice. The model's conclusion is that persuasion requires a speaker and receiver to have *common interests*.[4] The intuition underlying this result is straightforward; if choices that are good for the receiver also benefit the speaker, then the speaker has an incentive to reveal what he knows and the receiver has an incentive to believe what she hears. By contrast, if what is good for a speaker is bad for a receiver, then the speaker has an incentive to reveal nothing and the receiver has an incentive to ignore everything. Collectively, signaling and cheap talk models clarify how the costs of communication (i.e., the purchase of a good in signaling models or opportunity costs in cheap talk models) affect what people say and believe.

The model presented below generates different conclusions about learning in political settings. It does so by relaxing key assumptions about what the speaker and receiver know. In particular, we allow the receiver to be uncertain about what a speaker knows and whether the speaker's interests conflict with her own. In what follows, I describe the part of the model that clarifies when increasing a verification threat boosts the receiver's competence.

MODEL SPECIFICS

In Lupia and McCubbins 1998, communication is modeled as an interaction between two players, a *speaker* and a *receiver*. The *speaker* makes a statement about which of two alternatives, x and y, offers higher utility to the receiver. The receiver then chooses one of these alternatives. Unless stated otherwise, all elements of the game are common knowledge.

The model's key feature is that it contains three distinct sources of uncertainty. The first source of uncertainty pertains to which of the two alternatives is better for (i.e., gives higher utility to) the receiver. The receiver has beliefs about, but need not know, which alternative is better. Lupia and McCubbins 1998 represents these beliefs with the parameter $b \in [0, 1]$, which is the probability that x is better for the receiver.

The second source of uncertainty pertains to the speaker's knowledge. With probability $k \in [0, 1]$, the speaker knows which alternative is better for the receiver. With probability $1 - k$, he knows only b. In other words, *the speaker need not know which alternative is better for the receiver* (i.e., k need not equal 1), and *the receiver can be uncertain about how much the speaker knows* (i.e., the receiver knows k, the probability that the speaker is knowledgeable, but does not know the speaker's actual knowledge).

The third source of uncertainty pertains to interests. The speaker and receiver have *common* interests if the speaker benefits when the receiver makes a utility-maximizing decision. The speaker and receiver have *conflicting* interests if the speaker earns negative utility when the receiver earns positive utility and vice versa. In this model, players have *common* interests with probability $c \in [0, 1]$ and *conflicting* interests with probability $1 - c$. In other words, the receiver can be uncertain about the speaker's interests with $1 - c$ and c being the receiver's prior belief about the probability that she and the speaker have common interests.

Next, the speaker makes one of two statements, "better" or "worse." The statement "better" means "I assert that x is better than y for the receiver." The statement "worse" means "I assert that x is worse than y for the receiver." The speaker selects which statement to make and *need not tell the truth*. Then, the receiver chooses x or y. After she does so, the game ends and both players receive a utility payoff.

The model also features verification threats as one of several institutional attributes that it analyzes. It represents verification as follows—after the speaker speaks, but before the receiver chooses, nature reveals to the receiver whether x is better or worse for her. Verification occurs with probability $0 < v < 1$. For example, when $v = .3$, the speaker believes that there is a 30 percent chance that the receiver will know the truth when she makes her choice and a 70 percent chance that she will have only the speaker's advice and her own prior beliefs to go on.

The direct effect of an increase in the model's verification threat is to reduce the expected return to the speaker of lying to the receiver (Lupia and McCubbins 1998, 56–57). This effect can change the speaker's signal and the receiver's incentive to believe it. For example, if the receiver knows that the increased verification threat dissuades the speaker from lying, then the threat gives her a greater incentive to base her choice on the signal. In cases where an increased threat reduces the receiver's uncertainty about the speaker's willingness to lie, her incentive to believe the speaker can also increase. For a more precise description of the verification effect, see Lupia and McCubbins 1998, 250–51.

The following proposition paraphrases the aspects of theorems 3-1 to 3-3 from Lupia and McCubbins 1998 that are relevant to how verification threats affect competence.[5] Below the proposition, I present an explanation that follows the proposition's sequence of claims.

Proposition:

a. If $v = 0$, perceived common interests ($c > .5$) and perceived speaker knowledge ($k > 0$) are each necessary, but not sufficient, for persuasion.

b. If $v > 0$, the extent to which perceived common interests and perceived speaker knowledge are required decreases when v changes. In other words, with respect to persuasion, the threat of verification can substitute for perceived common interests.

c. Persuasion also requires that the receiver's prior beliefs, b, not be too strong relative to her beliefs about speaker attributes and the verification threat.

d. Increasing the receiver's competence requires persuasion, the receiver initially lacking sufficient information to choose the utility-maximizing alternative, and a correct postverification perception of the statement's veracity.

I begin by explaining the conditions for persuasion, absent a verification threat (part a of the proposition). If the receiver is *certain* that the speaker knows no more than she does about which alternative is better for her ($k = 0$), then persuasion is impossible. This is true even if the receiver is certain that she and the speaker share common interests ($c = 1$). By contrast, if the receiver believes that the speaker *might* possess the knowledge she requires ($k > 0$), then persuasion is possible. Similarly, if the receiver is certain that she and the speaker have conflicting interests ($c = 0$), then persuasion is impossible. By contrast, if the receiver believes that the speaker has common interests (e.g., $c > .5$), then persuasion is possible. A corollary reveals further implications.

Corollary: Actual common interests are neither necessary nor sufficient for persuasion. Actual speaker knowledge is neither necessary nor sufficient for persuasion.

So, if the receiver is uncertain about the speaker's actual knowledge or interests—a plausible assumption for many political contexts—then *perceived* speaker knowledge and *perceived* common interests (as opposed to *actual* speaker knowledge and *actual* common interests) drive persuasion. As a result, a knowledgeable speaker who shares common interests with a receiver will fail to persuade if the receiver does not accurately perceive these speaker attributes. In Vincent Crawford and Joel Sobel's (1982) model, by contrast, "equilibrium signaling is more informative when agents' preferences become more similar" (1431). There are two reasons for this difference. One is that the speaker in our model need not know which alternative is better for the receiver. The other is that the receiver in our model need not know the speaker's actual interests or knowledge.

In sum, part a of the proposition reveals that persuasion in the model requires the receiver to be initially uncertain about which alternative is better for her and to believe that the speaker has such knowledge. Parts b and c state additional requirements. Part b reveals that increasing verification threats reduces the extent to which a receiver must be certain about the commonality of her interests with the speaker. In other words, increased verification threats generally act as a substitute for knowledge of common interests—they give receivers a reason to believe people whom they would not regard as credible absent the threats. Part c reveals that the extent to which perceived common interests or verification threats are needed depends on the strength of the receiver's prior beliefs about which alternative is better. If a receiver initially thinks that alternative x is almost surely better for her than alternative y, the magnitude of interest commonality or verification threat required to induce her to change her mind is much higher than would be the case if she was initially indifferent between x and y. When we combine parts b and c, we find that persuasion requires that the receiver believe that the speaker has an incentive to reveal what he knows—regardless of whether the incentive emanates from perceptions of speaker attributes or the threat of verification—and that the incentives are sufficiently strong to counter her prior beliefs about which alternative is better.

Part d of the proposition reveals that for the verification threat to increase the receiver's competence, it must also be the case that the receiver's new perception of speaker incentives is accurate. For if persuasion occurs with inaccurate perceptions (i.e., the receiver believes that a verification threat, $v = .8$, is sufficient to dissuade many speakers from lying but, in actuality, the speaker with whom she is dealing is one of the rare types not dissuaded), then the receiver has a reason for believing that the statement is true when, in fact, it is false. Put another way, the threat of verification is most helpful to the receiver when—without it—she lacks information sufficient to determine the speaker's interests and—with it—she can correctly infer the speaker's incentive to speak truthfully.

In sum, the model predicts that an increased verification threat increases the receiver's competence only if the following three conditions are true: the receiver lacks so much information about her choice's consequence that she has an incentive to attend to the speaker's advice, the probability of common interests or the verification threat are sufficiently high to induce the receiver to follow the speaker's advice, and the threat and actuality of verification are sufficient to induce truthful advice.

My experiments address two questions about these claims. First, are verification threats sufficient to increase decision makers' competence? Second, are the conditions under which I observe such effects consistent with those derived from the model? In what follows, the answer to both questions is yes.

Experiment 1

In this experiment (from Lupia and McCubbins 1998, 135–39), as in the model described above, the receiver chooses one of two alternatives, while the speaker advises the receiver about his or her choice. Specifically, the receiver predicts whether an unobserved coin toss landed on heads or tails and the speaker advises "heads" or "tails."

We ran these experiments on undergraduates at the University of California, San Diego. We recruited subjects by posting flyers on the campus.[6] When subjects came for their appointments, we paid them a nominal amount (two dollars) for showing up. We then asked subjects to read and sign a standard consent form. The form told them that they would be in an experiment on decision making.

In each trial that followed, we paid the receiver one dollar for a correct prediction and nothing for an incorrect prediction. The key experimental variation lies in how we compensated the speaker. In some cases, the speaker earned one dollar when the receiver predicted correctly (i.e., the speaker and receiver had common interests). In other cases, the speaker earned fifty cents when the receiver made an *incorrect* prediction (i.e., the receiver and speaker had conflicting interests).[7] And, as we describe below, the receivers were often uncertain about which compensation scheme was in place (i.e., they were uncertain about whether or not they and the speaker had common interests).

Most experiments featured one speaker and ten to twelve receivers. The receivers had identical information and payoff schedules. Therefore, to the speaker, their situation was no different than if they were speaking to just one receiver—as is the case in the model.

To isolate the effect of verification, we took steps to limit what the subjects could learn about each other. For example, we used partitions to prevent visual contact. We also asked the speaker to signal "heads" or "tails" by checking an appropriately labeled box on a sheet of paper. A graduate assistant relayed the paper signal to me via hand signal. Then, I, not knowing the outcome of the coin toss or whether the speaker's statement was true or false, announced the speaker's signal. These steps prevented subjects from basing their decisions on information not present in the model. Table 6.1 summarizes our observations.

In our experiments' initial trials, we observed what receivers would choose if fully informed about the coin toss outcomes. In these trials, receivers made correct predictions almost always (97 percent, 376/389). Then we examined what receivers would choose if they were unable to observe the coin tosses and received no further information. In these trials, correct predictions occurred at about the rate of chance (48 percent, 377/780).

In all subsequent trials reported below, receivers did not observe the coin toss outcomes and were uncertain about the speaker's compensation scheme. Specifically, we rolled an eight-sided die once per trial. If the die landed on one or two, then we paid the speaker for each correct prediction a receiver made; otherwise, we paid the speaker for each incorrect prediction. We informed the speaker of the outcome, so the speaker knew whether or not he or she had common or conflicting interests with the receivers. The receivers, by contrast, knew only that for each trial there was a 25 percent chance of common interests with the speaker and a 75 percent chance of conflicting interests.

In the control condition (without verification), the receivers' predictions matched the speaker's advice 56 percent (63/112) of the time and the receivers made correct predictions 46 percent (51/112) of the time. The receivers' behaviors in this variation mimicked the behaviors in incomplete information trials described above. In other words, the receivers made decisions as if they ignored the speakers' advice—even if the speaker did, in fact, share common interests with them and tell the truth. Without verification, the speaker's advice did not improve the receivers' competence (which we measure here in terms of correct predictions).

In the treatment conditions, we introduced the threat of verification. We expect this change to have two related effects. First, it should reduce the value of lying for speakers. That is, speakers who have conflicting interests with receivers and face the threat of verification should expect to gain less from lying than is the case under no such threat. Second, verification gives

TABLE 6.1

Summary of Observations—Laboratory Experiments

Condition	Observe Coin Toss	Message Sent	$V > 0$	Actual Verification	Persuasion	Competence
Full info	Yes	No	No	No	n/a	97%
No info	No	No	No	No	n/a	48%
$V = 0$	No	Yes	Yes	No	56%	46%
$V > 0$	No	Yes	Yes	Yes	86%	86%
$V > 0$	No	Yes	Yes	No	97%	97%
$V > 0$ (total)	No	Yes	Yes	Both	88%	88%

receivers a stronger reason to believe what they hear. In particular, if receivers believe that verification can keep speakers from lying, then verification gives them a greater incentive to base their prediction on the advice they receive.

We instituted the verification threat by rolling a ten-sided die. In the trials reported below, if the die landed on one through seven, then we verified; otherwise, we did not. Put another way, for every trial, there was a 70 percent chance that we would report the true coin toss outcome instead of the speaker's action.[8]

Three aspects of this experimental design were particularly important. First, the speaker did not know before making his or her statement whether or not verification would occur. The speaker and receiver knew only that there was a 70 percent chance of verification in each trial. Second, the receivers had no way to know whether the message they heard came directly from the speaker or was our verification—the receivers merely heard "heads" or "tails." We instituted verification in this manner to replicate the model's incentives for speakers in the experiment without revealing to the experiment's receivers whether the speaker had true or false signals in the past. This procedure allowed us to run multiple trials without reputation effects spoiling the data.

Third, we also told everyone that the speaker would have to pay two dollars for the right to make any statement. We expected speakers to respond by making a statement only if they shared common interests with the receivers. This follows because the 70 percent verification threat made statements unprofitable, in expectation, for speakers with conflicting interests. For example, given ten receivers, a two-dollar fee for making a statement is equivalent to twenty cents per receiver. Given this information, the speaker's expected payoff per receiver, if the receivers base their choice on the signal, is $(.7) \times (-\$.20) + (.3) \times (\$.50 - \$.20) = -\$.05$. This amount is less than the expected payoff of $0 from not making a statement. Therefore, when the speaker had conflicting interests, it was better not to make a statement.

Because we expected the increased verification threat to affect speaker incentives in the manner described above, we expected receivers to base their predictions on the signals they heard and to make more competent choices as a result. Table 6.1 shows that these expectations were realized. In trials where the 70 percent verification threat existed and verification occurred, the receivers followed the advice they heard and made correct predictions approximately 86 percent (187/217) of the time. In trials where the threat existed but *no verification occurred*, and the speaker actually had common interests, we had the same expectations. In these trials, the speaker had an incentive to make a statement and the receivers had an incentive to believe what they heard. In fact, from the receivers' vantage point these trials were observationally equivalent to the trials where verification occurred. In these trials, receivers' predictions matched the signals approximately 97 percent (55/57) of the time, and receivers made correct predictions approximately 97 percent (55/57) of the time. Recall that with no verification threat the percent of correct predictions was less than 50 percent.

Introducing the verification threat into the experiment increases competence. With this competence gain in mind, it is worth noting that in the trials just described three conditions were met:

1. The receivers lacked so much information about the consequences of their choices that they had an incentive to attend to the speaker's advice.
2. The probability of verification was sufficiently high to induce the receiver to follow the speaker's advice.
3. The threat or actuality of verification was sufficiently high that the speaker indeed had an incentive to speak truthfully.

The formal model describes these conditions as sufficient to increase competence—and that they did. Introducing the verification threat in these trials raised the probability of a correct prediction from the level of chance to over 90 percent.

In other trials, we made sure that at least one of these conditions was violated. For example, in trials where there was a verification threat, no verification actually occurred, and the speaker had conflicting interests, we did not expect the speaker to make a statement. In almost all cases he or she did not. On two occasions, however, the speaker did make a statement—contrary to our expectation—and one of the two signals was truthful. The receivers' predictions matched these signals 90 percent (18/20) of the time, which is as we predict given the high verification threat. These receivers, however, made correct predictions only 40 percent (8/20) of the time—they followed bad advice and did not make payoff-maximizing choices. These trials were ones where the verification threat was not high enough to give the speaker an incentive to speak truthfully. These trials, and others like them, clarify when verification threats do and do not increase competence.

Experiment 2

A laboratory experiment is designed to evaluate a causal hypothesis. The control that facilitates causal evaluations, however, can increase the difference between experiments and the substantive settings in which scholarly audiences are interested. Audiences sometimes want to see laboratory findings replicated elsewhere. Such demands motivate my use of general population experiments, which allow researchers to retain some experimental control while interacting with subjects in a setting that differs from the typical lab.

This experiment was part of the *Second Multi-Investigator Study on Political Persuasion and Attitude Change.* The eligible subject population consisted of all English-speaking adults, eighteen years of age or older, residing in households with telephones, within the forty-eight contiguous U.S. states. Professional interviewers conducted all interviews between June 21, 1998, and March 7, 1999. The interviewers randomly contacted 1,913 households using computer-assisted telephone interviewing technology. Of these households, 725 refused to participate, 73 were never at home, and 48 were unable to participate. The remaining 1,067 households constitute the sample.

General population experiments such as this present experimental stimuli to a nationwide sample of randomly selected subjects. As in a phone survey, people are contacted in their homes. In a departure from most such surveys, they are randomly assigned to different experimental groups. I evaluate hypotheses by comparing group reactions.

An advantage of general population experiments is that their subjects are likely to be different from laboratory subjects. Laboratory subjects typically self-select into experiments by taking certain courses or responding to advertisements. They tend to be undergraduates or people who live near universities. If a national sample of subjects need not respond to experimental stimuli in the same way as people who attend or live near universities, then we can use general population experiments to evaluate the extent to which laboratory findings apply more broadly (see, e.g., Sniderman and Grob 1996).

I designed the experiment to evaluate the following null hypothesis: "A statement *is not* more likely to affect subject predictions if it is described as occurring in a context where the verification threat is high and lying is punished." The format of the experiment is depicted in Figure 6.1. The ques-

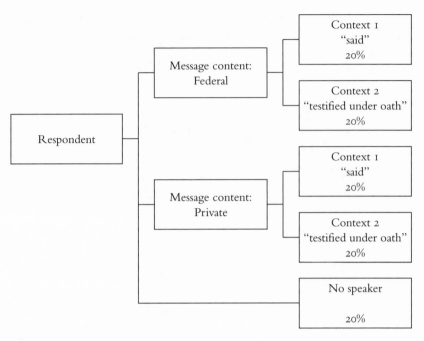

FIGURE 6.1 The random assignment strategy

tions used to conduct this experiment are as follows, with the key experimental variation in *italic*:

Our next questions focus on some issues being discussed in Washington, D.C., these days. One important debate concerns how best to promote airline safety. One proposal is to allow private companies to manage air traffic control stations. The other is to allow the Federal Aviation Administration to continue to manage air traffic control stations.

[No treatment group (20 percent of the sample, randomly selected):]

• Looking ahead to one year from now, who do you think will be managing air traffic control—private companies or the federal government?

[Treatment group (80 percent of the sample; random selection makes all subjects equally likely to hear each version):]

• A safety expert who works for [a private company / the federal government] [*said / testified under oath*] that the government should [remain in charge of / allow private companies to manage] air traffic control. Looking ahead to one year from now, who do you think will be managing air traffic control—private companies or the federal government?

In each case, the variation of interest is the switch between the word "said" and the phrase "testified under oath." This switch is meant to represent a change from a setting in which the verification threat is unstated to one where it is widely known to be high. We draw inferences about the effect of the switch by comparing the responses of those who hear different versions of the question. As in the laboratory experiment, we ask subjects to *predict* what will happen. We do this, rather than ask what government should do, in an attempt to filter people's beliefs about the future from their moral position on the issue. The correct prediction was federal control, an outcome about which there was virtual certainty among experts at the time that this experiment was conducted.[9]

EXPECTATIONS

How we expect subjects to respond to the experimental treatment is tempered by two differences between laboratory experiments and general population experiments. First, subjects in a general population experiment receive no evidence that they are in an experiment. The interview occurs in the subject's home, just like a phone survey, and the questions sound like typical survey questions. Subjects are not aware that others are answering slightly different versions of the same questions. Second, subjects in our general population experiment were not compensated for their participation. Unlike subjects in most economic experiments, who receive behavior-based pay, or subjects in most psychology experiments, who often receive course-relevant credit, our subjects received nothing from us for participating.

These two differences imply that subjects in the general population experiments have less motivation to respond to any particular stimulus than do laboratory subjects. The model described above, however, suggests that a decrease in motivation should affect subject behaviors in a limited fashion. Less motivated subjects are equivalent to receivers whose utility gradients are relatively flat. As a result, we expect to observe an effect of verification in the general population experiments that is smaller in magnitude than that observed in the laboratory.

Caveats aside, if the switch from "said" to "testified under oath" is a sufficient representation of an increased verification threat, then we predict that treatment groups can be rank ordered by the probability that subjects will predict "federal control." The predicted ranking is as follows:

- Subjects who heard someone *testify* that the *federal* government should remain in charge of air traffic control are most likely to predict federal control.
- Subjects who heard someone *say* that the *federal* government should remain in charge of air traffic control are second-most likely to predict federal control.

TABLE 6.2

Raw Data for Key Experimental Groups

	Fraction predicting "federal" control	
Subjects who heard "testified federal"	161/182	88%
Subjects who heard "said federal"	197/227	87%
Subjects who heard "said private"	170/200	85%
Subjects who heard "testified private"	171/217	79%

- Subjects who heard someone *say* that *private* companies should control air traffic control are third-most likely to predict federal control.
- Subjects who heard someone *testify* that *private* companies should control air traffic are least likely to predict federal control.

This is a strong prediction. To see why, consider that there are twenty-four possible orderings of these four groups. As a result, if subjects made predictions independent of what they heard, then the likelihood of realizing any particular ordering is $1/24$, or just under 5 percent (.0417).

Were the institutional variations described within the questions irrelevant to subjects' beliefs or behaviors, we would not expect to see any particular ordering of experimental groups. Observing this particular ordering, by contrast, provides strong support for the notion that institutional variations have systematic and predictable effects on individual behavior—even for subjects with low motivation.

RESULTS

Table 6.2 provides the raw numbers. It shows that the ordering of subjects by treatment groups is precisely as predicted above. Of the four groups, the subjects most likely to predict federal control were the subjects who heard "testimony" to this effect, followed by those who heard the same claim without mention of an oath. The subjects least likely to predict federal control were the subjects who heard contrary testimony, followed by those who heard the same contrary claim without an oath.

The finding in Table 6.2 is not trivial. The likelihood of seeing this ordering if subjects ignore what they hear is less than 5 percent. Moreover, the finding was achieved using a minimal representation of verification threats on subjects who lacked the material incentives given to most subjects in laboratory experiments. Since many political decision makers render judgments in similar low-intensity situations, the finding provides evidence that verification threats affect beliefs in ways that the model predicts even for citizens whose motivation is low.[10]

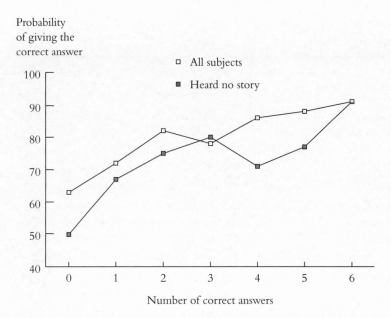

FIGURE 6.2   How awareness corresponds to predicting correctly. The correct answer was "federal control."

While the differences in Table 6.2 are as predicted, they may be the result of a spurious correlation. There is, after all, no a priori reason to expect this very diverse group of subjects to have the same prior beliefs about the future of air traffic control or the same reactions to new information about it. As a result, I looked for other factors that explain the observed variations. I found only one, a measure of political awareness, whose effect is not trivial.

Like respondents on most political surveys, our subjects were asked seven political information questions. While I do not agree with the common interpretation of such questions as a reliable indicator of citizen competence with respect to concrete tasks such as voting (see Lupia n.d. for an elaboration), I do adopt John Zaller's (1992, 21) interpretation of data drawn from these questions as a measure of *political awareness*, "the extent to which an individual pays attention to politics and understands what he or she has encountered." We should expect more aware citizens to have stronger prior beliefs about the likely future of air traffic control (i.e., people who follow news of airline regulation are more likely to know that the federal government has controlled air traffic for decades and that no attempt to change control has advanced far in Congress).

Figure 6.2 reports the relationship between subject predictions and awareness.[11] It shows that as awareness increases, subjects are more likely to

TABLE 6.3

Regressions

	Prediction	Model 1 All Subjects		Model 2 Treatment Only		Model 3 ~ Treatment Only	
		β	p	β	p	β	p
Testified federal	Largest	.88★	3.09	.67★	2.32		
Said federal	Second-largest	.71★	2.76	.50	1.90		
Said private	Second-smallest	.57★	2.20	.36	1.35		
Testified private	Smallest	.21	.09				
Awareness		.26★	5.12	.28★	4.75	.20★	2.05
Constant		.29	.23	.44	1.81	.49	1.35
N		1047		826		221	
Initial LL		-478.91		-354.49		-120.58	
Final LL		-457.56		-338.89		-118.43	
χ^2 (df)		42.68 (5)		31.20 (4)		4.29 (1)	

NOTE: Dependent variable: 1 if subject predicts federal, 0 if subject predicts private.
★ = p-value < .05.

predict federal control. This is true not only for subjects who heard no statement, but also for subjects as a whole.

Given the relative sizes of the effects observed in Figure 6.2, the ordering of treatment groups observed in Table 6.2 may, in fact, be driven by a spurious correlation with awareness. Table 6.3 displays multivariate tests of this hypothesis.

Table 6.3 presents three logistic regressions. In all cases, the dependent variable is the subject's prediction. A prediction of federal control is assigned a value of 1, and a prediction of private control is assigned the value 0. Positive coefficients imply that the named factor corresponds to an increase in the likelihood that a subject predicts federal control. The first regression is for all subjects, the second regression is for subjects who were in one of the four treatment groups, and the third regression is for subjects who were not in a treatment group.

As in Figure 6.2, awareness has a strong effect in all of the regressions. Extracting from analyses of first differences, we can see that each additional awareness question answered correctly corresponds to a five- to nine-percentage-point increase in the likelihood that a subject predicts federal control.

TABLE 6.4

The Effect of Institutions

Message	Aware	Number Predicting Federal Control				Effect of "Testified"	
		"Said"		"Testified"		Predicted	Actual
		Number	%	Number	%		
Federal	Less	20/29	69	19/23	83	+	+14
Private	Less	21/28	75	22/35	63	−	−12
Federal	More	177/198	89	142/159	89	+	0
Private	More	149/172	87	149/182	82	−	−5

Table 6.3 also shows that shifting from "said" to "testified" had a substantial effect. In both regressions where the treatment groups are included, the ordering predicted by the theory and witnessed in Table 6.2 not only survives after accounting for awareness but prospers. After awareness is accounted for, and again extracting from analyses of first differences, subjects hearing testimony advocating federal control were approximately seventeen percentage points more likely to predict federal control than were those who heard testimony to the contrary. By contrast, a shift in the content of the message without the verification threat ("said federal" versus "said private") corresponds to a shift in subject predictions, but the difference is neither as large as that seen "under oath" nor is it significant.

Having demonstrated that subjects respond to the institutional shift in the way the theory predicts, I turn to showing when the shift increases competence. Recall the theoretical result that verification increases competence only if the receiver lacks so much information about the consequence of his choice that he has an incentive to attend to the speaker's advice, the probability of verification is sufficiently high to induce the receiver to follow the speaker's advice, and the verification threat is sufficiently high that the speaker does indeed make a truthful statement. Table 6.4 breaks down the data in a way that helps us evaluate the applicability of this result.

The top half of Table 6.4 shows the effect of the experimental treatment on subjects who could answer no more than one awareness question correctly; the bottom half provides the same data for all other subjects in the treatment groups. A comparison of the top and bottom of Table 6.4 shows that the impact of the verification threat was greater for the least aware. This correspondence is consistent with the idea that those who have less information are more likely to attend to new information.

Table 6.4 also divides subjects by the content of the statement they heard.

Note that half of the subjects in the treatment groups heard advice that turned out to be accurate (statement content = continued federal control), while the other half heard inaccurate advice (statement content = private control). For the least aware among the group hearing accurate advice, the condition "the verification threat is sufficiently high that the speaker does indeed make a truthful statement" is effectively satisfied and, as predicted, institutions increase competence. For the least aware among the group who heard bad advice, however, the condition is not satisfied. As expected, institutions do not increase competence for them.

In sum, this experiment demonstrates three things. First, even subjects with low motivation use a minimal description of the institutional context when choosing what to believe. Indeed, subjects were more likely to follow advice that came from a context that many perceive to have a high verification threat. Second, the effect is largest for the least aware. And third, for the institutional change to increase competence (a correct prediction about the regulation), the perceived attributes of the institution (under oath) must match its actual attributes (an accurate statement). All told, the experiment demonstrates when a verification threat does and does not increase competence.

Conclusion: The New Institutionalism Should Become More Behavioral

Over the last quarter century, institutions reemerged as an explanatory juggernaut in political science. The new institutionalism has made its most important contributions when focusing on elite behavior (see, e.g., North 1994). While its applications have been broad (see, e.g., Levi 1997; Stinchcombe 1997; Thelen 1999), many of its most notable teachings pertain to formal legislative bodies, such as the U.S. House of Representatives (see, e.g., Kiewiet and McCubbins 1991; Aldrich and Shepsle 1997).

This new institutionalism is divisible into rational choice and historical camps. The rational choice camp has demonstrated that institutions matter because they alter individual incentives. Historical institutionalists, by contrast, view institutions as affecting beliefs directly—often through a process of path dependency.

Both camps adopt the idea that institutions provide new information about the future consequences of current actions. For the rational choice camp, the information is about incentives. For the historical camp (also known as the cultural approach), the information is about precedent and norms. As Peter Hall and Rosemary Taylor (1996, 939) report,

Those who adopt a [rational choice] approach focus on those aspects of human behaviour that are instrumental and based on strategic calculation. . . . What do institutions do, according to the calculus approach? Institutions affect behaviour primarily by providing actors with greater or lesser degrees of certainty about the present and future behaviour of other actors. More specifically, institutions provide information relevant to the behaviour of others, enforcement mechanisms for agreements, penalties for defection, and the like. The key point is that they affect individual action by altering the expectations an actor has about the actions that others are likely to take in response to or simultaneously with his own actions. . . . Contrast this with a "cultural approach" to such issues. The latter stresses the degree to which behaviour is not fully strategic but bounded by an individual's worldview. . . . From this perspective, institutions provide moral or cognitive templates for interpretation or action.

Both camps' arguments depend on certain assumptions about how institutions affect beliefs. These assumptions, however, are often unstated or untested, a point on which Guy Peters (1996, 211) has criticized the historical camp:

While valuable in attempting to reunite political science with some of its roots, in theoretical terms the approach may encounter some problems. In particular, knowing how a particular policy has developed over time it may be difficult to imagine any other sequence of development. Thus, refutation of the institutionalist approach may be difficult. In overly simplified terms, the argument appears to be that there was a set institution, there was a policy outcome, and the two must be linked.

The rational choice camp is also vulnerable to this critique. While some work in this tradition examines how structural variations affect people's willingness to convey information to others, the correspondence between institutional design and information processing has not been this camp's primary focus. The rational choice camp focuses on incentives (the effect of external forces on actions), not persuasiveness (the effect of external forces on beliefs)—and the two are not always equivalent.

Simultaneously, research on political behavior focuses on individual attributes as determinants of how people react to information (see Sniderman, Brody, and Tetlock 1991 and Zaller 1992 for leading examples). Together with related work on persuasion in social psychology (Petty and Cacioppo 1986, Eagly and Chaiken 1993), this literature clarifies how individual differences cause variations in how stimuli affect behaviors. For all of its virtues, however, the literature on political behavior has evolved with minimal attention to institutions. As Sniderman (2000, 68) notes,

Initially, we asked how citizens effectively can simplify political choices so as to make them coherently. Putting the question this way led us, like virtually everyone else, to start the explanatory process by focusing on the characteristics of citizens. How much attention do they pay to politics? What do they know about it? . . . Answer these questions, and we should be in a position to figure out how citizens make political choices. Or so it seemed then. Now, I am persuaded, we had the order of things wrong. Citizens do not operate as decision makers in isolation from political institutions. If they are in a position to overcome their informational shortfalls by taking advantage of judgmental shortcuts, it is because public choices have been organized by political institutions in ways that lend themselves to these shortcuts.

The chasm between research on institutions and research on political behavior hampers our discipline's ability to explain when institutions can change beliefs (e.g., about whether a particular affirmative action program is necessary or sufficient to change behaviors toward certain racial groups).[12] As a result, it hinders our ability to inform the decisions of the many well-intentioned public and private interests who seek to build institutions that increase civic competence.

The way forward is, in this regard, for political science to pursue a more *behavioral institutionalism*—research which ignores neither the incentive effects of common political contexts nor the aspects of our physical endowments that lead us to acquire and process information in particular ways. Like behavioral economics, such an effort would strengthen "the accuracy and empirical reach of [institutional] theory by incorporating information from neighboring social science disciplines, especially psychology and sociology" (Russell Sage Foundation 1999). Formal theory should be a critical part of this endeavor, as the logical rigor it requires helps document the complex interactions between cognitive endowments and institutional attributes.

The research described in this chapter takes a small step in the direction of behavioral institutionalism. Using a formal model and two experiments, I find that the extent to which institutions increase competence depends on what information subjects lack, what incentives they have to change their existing behaviors, and the extent to which the context clarifies the credibility of the advice they receive. The key factor in all experiments *is the interaction* between what institutions reveal about the quality of the subjects' information and the behavioral attributes that make subjects differ in the extent that they are willing to seek and accept new information.

Notes

I thank the National Science Foundation for supporting this research (SBR-9422831 for laboratory experiments and SBR-9633743 for general population experiments); Sean A. Cain for research assistance; James N. Druckman, Karen Garrett, Mathew D. McCubbins, and the Survey Research Center at the University of California–Berkeley for advice on experimental design; and Elisabeth R. Gerber, James H. Kuklinski, Jennifer Jerit, Howard Lavine, David P. Myatt, Kenneth A. Shepsle, and seminar participants at the University of California–San Diego, the University of Maryland, the 2000 Annual Meetings of the Midwest and American Political Science

Associations, and the volume's editors for comments on previous versions of this manuscript. I also acknowledge the support of the Center for Advanced Study in the Behavioral Sciences.

1. Following Lupia and McCubbins 1998, 24–25, I define knowledge as the ability to make accurate predictions and information as data. Knowledge requires information because accurate predictions require data—at a minimum you need some data to verbalize the prediction you are making. By contrast, you can know a long list of facts and fail to put them together in a way that allows you to make accurate predictions. Thus, while you cannot have knowledge without having information, you can have information without having knowledge. I define competence as the ability to accomplish a concrete task. The kind of task that motivates the present study is "Can voters make the same decision they would have made if knowledgeable on issue positions *a* through *z*?" If they can, we say they are competent; if they cannot, we say that they are incompetent. Therefore, competence requires sufficient knowledge, which requires sufficient information.

2. Reviews of evidence on the pathologies of deliberation in the context of group or team decision making include National Research Council 1994, chapter 7, and Van Avermaet 1996.

3. A cheap talk model is a signaling model in which speech does not directly affect payoffs. For example, in the seminal signaling model, a speech act was the purchase of a formal education that imposed direct costs on the speaker. In cheap talk models, a speech act does not require the purchase of any such good.

4. Vincent Crawford and Joel Sobel (1982) find that "equilibrium signaling is more informative when agents' preferences are more similar" (1431). In their model, all equilibria are partition equilibria, which means that all equilibria can be stated in terms that describe the accuracy of the speaker's statements (i.e., the message space is partitioned and the more segments a message space contains, the more persuasive the message). They conclude that "the more nearly [the speaker's and receiver's] interests coincide—the finer partition there can be. . . . As [the distance in their interests goes to infinity], [the number of partitions] eventually falls to unity and only the completely uninformative equilibrium remains" (1441).

5. This proposition describes the most informative equilibrium. Like many strategic communication models, this model also yields an equilibrium in which no informative communication occurs (i.e., a babbling equilibrium). Henceforth, I follow convention and describe only the nonbabbling equilibrium. See Lupia and McCubbins 1998, 245–46, for more information.

6. Our flyers gave prospective subjects a number to call for an appointment. Our research assistants fielded these calls, verified the callers' age (eighteen years or older) and undergraduate standing, and assigned experiment appointment times to eligible callers. Typically, we scheduled more subjects than we needed in a given experiment because of an expected 20 percent no-show rate. When extra subjects arrived, we admitted only the number needed for the experiment into the laboratory on a first-come-first-admitted basis. We then paid the extras five dollars and invited them to sign up for another experiment. No person was a subject in our experiments more than once.

7. This design also has the virtue of presenting subjects with simple and familiar situations. To ensure that subjects saw these situations as simple and familiar, we began each experimental session with simple explanations and examples of the experiment's sequence of events, what information subjects would have, and how subjects would earn money. After we gave a set of instructions, we administered a brief quiz on the instructions. Most subjects achieved perfect scores on these quizzes. That subjects understood the instructions so well gives us confidence that they, like the speaker and receiver in our model, understood the situation they were in. As a result, we were confident about our ability to use the results from our experiments to draw meaningful inferences about the theoretical hypotheses.

8. Lupia and McCubbins 1998, 135–39, 145–46, reports other variations of this experiment in which the effects of verification threats are consistent with the model's substantive predictions.

9. Without data on subjects' priors about the relative credibility of private companies and the federal government on the topic of air traffic control, we have no a priori reason to expect that variation in the identity of the speaker would correspond to variations in observed behaviors. We chose not to collect data on subject priors because we did not want to prime subjects about the questions that were to come. However, we allowed variation in the speaker's identity to ensure that the speaker did not have an amorphous identity, which could vary among subjects and affect responses in ways that we would then be unable to explain. My analyses reveal no independent effect of speaker identity.

10. Subjects who heard no statement about the future of air traffic control were the least likely to predict federal control (169 / 221), 76 percent. This pattern of behavior, while not directly relevant to our hypothesis test, is curious. The fact that all treatment groups were higher implies that being primed to such a conversation led people to make more accurate predictions, regardless of what they heard. This conclusion is, however, speculative. In addition, eighteen subjects replied "don't know" and two refused to answer.

11. The six questions used (with percentage responding correctly in parentheses) are: Which party has the most members in the House of Representatives? (79), How much of a majority is required for the U.S. Senate and House of Representatives to override a presidential veto? (59), Would you say Democrats are more conservative than Republicans, or Republicans are more conservative than Democrats? (68), Whose responsibility is it to determine if a law is constitutional or not? (74), How many four-year terms can the president of the United States serve? (92); and How many members of the Supreme Court are there? (64). I also ran analyses using six dummy variables, each of which indicated whether subjects gave a correct response to individual awareness questions. While there was a high correlation between these dummy variables, each had a similar correspondence to subject predictions (i.e., answering any question correctly corresponded to predicting federal control).

12. Such chasms are not unique to political science, as Chip Heath, Richard Larrick, and Joshua Klayman (1998, 3) explain: "On the one side, research in cognitive psychology has largely treated individual learners as 'rugged individuals' who face a

difficult environment alone, equipped only with their own, flawed cognitive strategies. On the other side, organizational research has largely ignored the literature on individual cognition, focusing instead on issues of motivation or incentives."

References

Aldrich, John H., and Kenneth A. Shepsle. 1997. "Explaining Institutional Change: Soaking, Poking, and Modeling in the U.S. Congress." Presented for a conference in honor of Richard F. Fenno at the University of Rochester.

Churchland, Paul M. 1989. *A Neurocomputational Perspective: The Nature of Mind and the Structure of Science*. Cambridge: MIT Press.

Crawford, Vincent P., and Joel Sobel. 1982. "Strategic Information Transmission." *Econometrica* 50: 1431–51.

Eagly, Alice H., and Shelly Chaiken. 1993. *The Psychology of Attitudes*. Fort Worth, Texas: Harcourt Brace Jovanovich.

Hall, Peter, and Rosemary C. R. Taylor. 1996. "Political Science and the Three New Institutionalisms." *Political Studies* 44: 936–57.

Heath, Chip, Richard P. Larrick, and Joshua Klayman. 1998. "Cognitive Repairs: How Organizational Repairs Can Compensate for Individual Shortcomings." *Research in Organizational Behavior* 20: 1–37.

Kiewiet, D. Roderick, and Mathew D. McCubbins. 1991. *The Logic of Delegation: Congressional Parties and the Appropriations Process*. Chicago: University of Chicago Press.

Laffont, Jean-Jacques, and Jean Tirole. 1993. *A Theory of Incentives in Procurement and Regulation*. Cambridge: MIT Press.

Levi, Margaret. 1997. *Consent, Dissent, and Patriotism*. New York: Cambridge University Press.

Lupia, Arthur. 2002. "Deliberation Disconnected: What It Takes to Improve Civic Competence." *Law and Contemporary Problems* 65: 133–50.

———. N.d. "What We Should Know: The Case for Voter Competence." In *Making Big Choices: Individual Opinion Formation and Societal Choice*, ed. Pierre Martin and Richard Nadeau.

Lupia, Arthur, and Mathew D. McCubbins. 1998. *The Democratic Dilemma: Can Citizens Learn What They Need to Know?* New York: Cambridge University Press.

Lupia, Arthur, Mathew D. McCubbins, and Samuel L. Popkin. 2000. "Beyond Rationality: Reason and the Study of Politics." In *Elements of Reason: Cognition, Choice, and the Bounds of Rationality*, ed. Arthur Lupia, Mathew D. McCubbins, and Samuel L. Popkin. New York: Cambridge University Press.

National Research Council. 1994. *Learning, Remembering, Believing: Enhancing Human Performance*. Washington, D.C.: National Academy Press.

North, Douglass C. 1994. "Institutions and Credible Commitment." *Journal of Institutional and Theoretical Economics* 149: 11–23.

Peters, B. Guy. 1996. "Political Institutions: Old and New." In *New Handbook of Political Science*, ed. Robert E. Goodin and Hans-Dieter Klingemann. New York: Oxford University Press.

Petty, Richard E., and John T. Cacioppo. 1986. *Communication and Persuasion: Central and Peripheral Routes to Attitude Change*. New York: Springer-Verlag.

Russell Sage Foundation. 1999. www.russellsage.org/programs/proj_reviews/behavioral.htm.

Sniderman, Paul M. 2000. "Taking Sides: A Fixed Choice Theory of Political Reasoning." In *Elements of Reason: Cognition, Choice and the Bounds of Rationality*, ed. Arthur Lupia, Mathew D. McCubbins, and Samuel L. Popkin, 67–84. New York: Cambridge University Press.

Sniderman, Paul M., Richard A. Brody, and Philip E. Tetlock. 1991. *Reasoning and Choice: Explorations in Political Psychology*. New York: Cambridge University Press

Sniderman, Paul M., and Douglas B. Grob. 1996. "Innovations in Experimental Design in Attitude Surveys." *Annual Review of Sociology* 22: 377–99.

Spence, A. Michael. 1973. "Job Market Signaling." *Quarterly Journal of Economics* 87: 355–74.

Stinchcombe, Arthur L. 1997. "On the Virtues of the Old Institutionalism." *Annual Review of Sociology* 23: 1–18.

Thelen, Kathleen. 1999. "Historical Institutionalism in Comparative Politics." *Annual Review of Political Science* 2: 369–404.

Van Avermaet, Eddy. 1996. "Social Influence in Small Groups." In *Introduction to Social Psychology: A European Perspective*, ed. Miles Hewstone, Wolfgang Stroebe, and Geoffrey Stephenson. Oxford, England: Blackwell.

Zaller, John. 1992. *The Nature and Origins of Mass Opinion*. New York: Cambridge University Press.

PART III

Toward Democracy

THE LAST SEGMENT of this volume is devoted to the special case of democratic states. We realize that *democracy* may be defined in a variety of more or less satisfactory ways, but for our purposes, democracy has two fundamental characteristics: popular rule and limited government (usually through some constitutional mechanisms that protect individual rights and liberties). As will become apparent, this is the perspective that is taken by the writers of the two chapters in this final section. This is a more restrictive view of democracy than we might have taken. One could reasonably argue that democracy implies no more than popular rule and that limitations on government, often through the vehicle of a constitution, are, at least conceptually, an unnecessary add-on. From a definitional standpoint, this is certainly true. You can define democracy in any way that you wish. And there are certainly plenty of examples, both historically and currently, of states identifying themselves as "democratic" without any significant restraints on government authority. But the rational choice literature that deals with democracy—its feasibility, its development, its maintenance—suggests that these two characteristics are theoretically—and, by implication, practically—*inseparable*. It is simply not possible to maintain a government that is fundamentally based on popular support without some set of mechanisms for constraining its power. Likewise, without an effective means of popular control, formal constraints are more or less easily overridden. This is an underlying theme in Chapters 7 and 8.

To understand this perspective, one must understand something of the development of the field of rational choice and its handling of issues of popular rule and limited government. Arguably, rational choice, in an informal sense, is as old as the concept of the individual. It certainly goes back at least to Machiavelli. But Machiavelli was exclusively concerned with the strategic issues and problems faced by rulers. The idea that average people or citizens might face interesting strategic problems is relatively more recent, though it does go back at least to Hobbes's work in the seventeenth century.

But the modern rational choice theorists' study of popular rule flows most obviously from an interesting finding of an eighteenth-century French mathematician named Condorcet. In general terms, Condorcet realized that majority rule does not ensure a definitive choice in situations where more than two alternatives are considered. More specifically, in a set of three or more alternatives, it is possible (and as the number of alternatives grows, it becomes increasingly likely) that no single alternative will, in pairwise competition, defeat all of the other alternatives. This is an important result because it highlights the importance of the mechanism used to select the order in which the choices will be compared and shows that if one has control over the ordering of pairwise elections, one has control over the outcome. The crucial role of alternative structuring is, of course, problematic from the standpoint of popular rule. While one could theoretically vote on the way in which the alternatives would be paired, that choice would, itself, face the same problem—that is, it would also be manipulable—as the final choice. This suggests, then, that popular rule, by itself, has some serious problems.

Arrow's General Possibility Theorem (Arrow 1963) extends this result substantially by proving that *no* decision rule satisfies even a relatively short list of basic normative criteria (e.g., transitivity—the Condorcet criterion, independence of irrelevant alternatives, nondictatorship, etc.). We cannot be sure of the stability or meaningfulness of the outcome of *any* realistic voting—or collective choice—situation. This important result dominated the rational choice literature for at least two decades following its publication. During this time period, the field's primary research program revolved around the examination of formal models in which one or more of Arrow's criteria were relaxed or eliminated. There was also some interest in the extent to which the obstacles to collective choice that Arrow had highlighted were actually posing frequent problems in real-world decision-making situations. By the early 1980s, it had become obvious that this research program had failed to adequately explain one of the primary empirical characteristics of modern industrialized democracies—stability (see Tullock 1981). This scholarly lacuna was particularly troubling because it highlighted the fact that rational choice theory had, as yet, failed to provide explanations to two important questions:

1. How do democracies develop, or how do nations transition to democracy?

2. How are democracies, once constructed, sustained?

Obviously, a basic explanation for the development of democracy is outlined by social contract theorists such as Locke and Rousseau. Nevertheless, the contractarian foundations of democracy provided only limited insight into how nations moved from more or less authoritarian governments to democracies (as opposed to moving from the "state of nature" to a democracy), and there are precious few examples of thriving democracies that actually transitioned straight from the state of nature (or something comparable). Likewise, Arrow's famous result and much of the related literature that followed suggest that politics is inherently unstable—far less stable than the politics of modern industrialized democracies appear to be.

Since the late 1970s and early 1980s, rational choice research on democratic transition and democratic politics has branched out in at least two discernable directions. Research in this area has begun to focus more on *institutions*. Formal institutions, in particular, became increasingly important components of rational choice models of democratic politics, and the role of institutions in fostering stability received increasing attention. Research on democratic politics and democratic transitions more specifically also advanced technically. Multistage, multiactor models became increasingly common as theorists attempted to capture and analyze the *change* in political dynamics that characterizes the transition to democracy. These intellectual advances are manifest in the final two chapters in this volume, "Constructing Self-Enforcing Democracy in Spain," by Barry R. Weingast, and "Institutionalizing Constitutional Democracy: The Role of Courts," by Jack Knight and Lee Epstein. Both are excellent examples of the frontier of rational choice scholarship addressing the questions of how we get to democracy and how we keep it.

The construction of a democratic government in late-twentieth-century Spain is generally regarded as an archetype of democratic consolidation (Linz and Stepan 1996). By focusing on the Spanish case, Weingast shows how his new model of democratic consolidation provides an interesting and original perspective toward the construction of democratic governments. Weingast argues that the primary flaw in the existing literature on the Spanish case—and democratic consolidations more generally—is the failure to adequately account for the role of incentives. Because incentives are so important, according to Weingast, it may be that it is not possible to understand democratic consolidation outside of a rational choice perspective.

While Weingast is interested in the political dynamics revolving around the initial negotiations of governing "pacts," Knight and Epstein focus on the political institution most responsible for the *interpretation* of these pacts (or constitutions). Nations change over time—demographically, economically, culturally, maybe even geographically—and the states that govern these nations must change also. The question is, how does a state implement change (or undergo change) that is consistent both with democratic principles and with constitutional maintenance? Knight and Epstein's rational choice perspective toward judicial policy making—and the development of judicial institutions more generally—provides several important insights into the development of constitutional systems.

Both Weingast and Knight and Epstein provide a provocative view of the frontier of rational choice theorizing about the nature and concept of democracy. They deal with important questions in an interesting way, show what rational choice theory can do, and perhaps most significantly, highlight some of the extant limitations of rational choice theory. In doing so, they provide at least a glimpse of the future of rational choice theorizing on these issues.

References

Arrow, Kenneth J. 1963. *Social Choice and Individual Values*, 2nd ed. New Haven, Conn.: Yale University Press.

Linz, Juan J., and Alfred Stepan. 1996. *Problems of Democratic Transition and Consolidation*. Baltimore: Johns Hopkins University Press.

Tullock, Gordon. 1981. "Why So Much Stability?" *Public Choice*. 37: 189–205.

Constructing Self-Enforcing Democracy in Spain

Introduction

Spain has long been held as the paradigmatic case of a successful transition to democracy. Prior to the transition, Spain had a tumultuous political history. More than a century of political instability culminated in a short-lived Second Republic in the 1930s, which came to a violent end after less than a decade in the Civil War of 1936–39. This was followed by nearly four decades of social peace born of a repressive authoritarian regime under Francisco Franco. Moreover, many of the issues in the 1930s remained fundamental conflicts after Franco died in 1975: would the monarchy remain, what would the institutions of public choice be, would the capitalist system become sacrosanct or a battleground, and would regionalists in the Basque country and Catalonia seek autonomy as a first step toward independence? Despite a history of violent controversy over a wide range of fundamental issues, Spaniards resolved their differences peacefully. Nearly all analysts agree that Spanish democracy was consolidated by the time the Socialists took control over the government in 1982 (Linz and Stepan 1996, chap. 6).

Analysts disagree about what makes the Spanish case paradigmatic. Moreover, the absence of a widely accepted theory of democratic consolidation means that there is no obvious way to answer this question.

The purpose of this chapter is to develop a new approach to democratic stability and consolidation and to apply it to democratization in Spain. Students of democracy provide a clear notion of consolidation. According to Michael Burton, Richard Gunther, and John Higley (1992, 4), "A consolidated democracy is a regime that meets all the procedural criteria of democracy and also in which all politically significant groups accept established political institutions and adhere to democratic rules of the game. . . . Or again, as Bolivar Lamounier puts it, democratic consolidation is a 'process through which democratic forms come to be valued in themselves, even against adverse substantive outcomes.'" Similarly, Larry Diamond (1999a, 66) adds, "For a democracy to be consolidated, elites, organizations, and the mass public must all believe that the political system they actually have in their country is worth obeying and defending." Juan Linz and Alfred Stepan (1996, 5) provide a concise approach. They argue that consolidation occurs when democracy is the "only game in town" in that no significant groups advocate violation of the rules or secession. Further, constitutionally, citizens and politicians "become habituated to the fact that political conflict will be resolved according to the established norms and that violations of these norms are likely to be both ineffective and costly."

I summarize these approaches with a tripartite definition of consolidation: First, no significant group of citizens, organizations, or parties out of power is willing to attempt to subvert power or to secede. Second, those in power follow the constitutional rules (e.g., they eschew transgressing the rights of their opponents or ignoring electoral outcomes). Third, citizens are willing to defend democracy, even when they are the potential beneficiaries of violations.

Defined in this manner, consolidation requires that democracy is self-enforcing; that is, it must be in the interest of all actors to adhere to the constitutional rules. All three parts of the definition are about incentives. First, actors out of power must have incentives to pursue their goals within the system, such as by trying to capture the government or to block the government proposals within means allowed by the system. Second, actors in power must have incentives to honor the rules, including election results and the rights of minorities and the opposition. Third, part of the incentive system of actors in power is that citizens must be willing to defend democracy against transgressions by political leaders. If any of these incentive conditions fails, democracy is not consolidated and will potentially fail.[1]

Because the essence of consolidation is about incentives, studying it implies that the tools of rational choice institutionalism are not only useful but perhaps even necessary. Unfortunately, the traditional literature studying consolidation studies incentives only tangentially. It therefore provides an incomplete understanding of democratic consolidation.

To study the incentive problems surrounding consolidation, I draw on recent work studying the conditions under which democracy is self-enforcing (Fearon 2000; Przeworski 1991, 2001; and Weingast 1997, 2002). The approach provides three principles central to understanding democratic consolidation.

The first principle concerns the rationality of fear; when citizens fear for their sources of livelihood, their wealth, or their lives, they are willing to take steps to defend themselves, including extraconstitutional action (de Figueiredo and Weingast 1997). Stated in terms of risk from the government, the rationality of fear model holds that the larger the stakes, the lower is the risk that will trigger actions to defend themselves, including extraconstitutional action, such as a coup or secession.

The second principle holds that to survive, successful constitutions must forestall the rationality of fear. Constitutions do so by defining structure and process—structural limits on government policies, such as various citizen rights, and procedures about how to decide new policies, such as parliamentary procedures. Limits that protect what people hold most dear forestall the rationality of fear, and thus citizens have less resort to extraconstitutional appeals. This helps explain why, as Adam Przeworski (1991, chap. 2) observes, all successful constitutions limit the stakes of politics.

The third principle of consolidation holds that to sustain democracy, citizens must be willing to defend democracy against possible encroachments by political leaders. Leaders ignore election results or attempt coups in part based on the expectation that a sufficient portion of the population will support them.

Thus a central question for democratic consolidation becomes, under what conditions will citizens act in concert to defend the rules? Reacting in concert is the fundamental coordination dilemma facing democratic citizens (Weingast 1997). Yet reacting in concert is problematic. Because citizens have widely varying preferences over how to coordinate, there are multiple means of coordination. Solving this coordination problem in a decentralized manner is virtually impossible.

Solving the fundamental coordination dilemma requires the construction of focal solutions. These often occur through pacts, agreements among contending groups that resolve disputes, construct new rules, and often help initiate democracy. The literature recognizes the critical importance of pacts (O'Donnell and Schmitter 1986, Higley and Gunther 1992). What is not recognized is that pacts are centrally concerned with incentives (Weingast 1997). I argue that successful pacts must be self-enforcing; that is, pacts must provide the parties with incentives to abide by the pact's provisions. I further provide four conditions for self-enforcing pacts.

Democracy becomes consolidated, then, when pacts and constitutions satisfy principles two and three; they limit the stakes of politics, they create focal solutions to citizens' coordination problem, and thus they forestall the rationality of fear. Satisfying these two principles implies that the third component of the definition of consolidation holds; citizens are willing to defend democracy. The third component, in turn, provides the incentives for the other two parts of the definition. When citizens are willing to defend democracy, leaders cannot expect citizen support for extraconstitutional action, deterring leaders from attempting to violate the rules.

I apply this approach to Spain as follows. First, a host of issues divided Spaniards during the Second Republic, implying the absence of consensus about the limits on government. Spain during this period failed to satisfy principles two and three. Per the first principle, this implies that the rationality of fear mechanism was at play. When many on the right felt sufficiently threatened, they supported Franco's coup (Alexander 2002, chap. 4; Carr and Fusi 1981, 2).

To explain redemocratization in the 1970s, I follow a host of authors and observe the many structural changes in Spanish society (e.g., Alexander 2002, chap. 5; Gunther 1992; Linz and Montero 1999; Maravall 1978, 1982; Tarrow 1995; and Tortella 2000). Yet these changes do not speak for themselves and do not, of themselves, imply successful redemocratization (Linz and Stepan 1996, chap. 6; Gunther, Montero, and Botella 2003, 87).

Spanish democracy was born of a series of pacts, which follow not only principles two and three but also the conditions for self-enforcing pacts. Per principle three, key leaders helped foster the "invention of tradition" (Perez-Diaz 1990) that created new focal solutions to the fundamental citizen coordination problem. Central to this new tradition were the principles of mutual accommodation, toleration, and compromise.

Both the moderate right and left, including the socialists and many communists, had strong and credible incentives to abide by these agreements and thus to maintain their moderation. Neither group was large enough to impose its will on Spain, so both sides needed each other. Moderates on both sides knew that the extreme right would remain marginalized only so long as they could cooperate. Both sides also knew that unilateral defection would make them worse off, so both sets of groups had incentives to adhere to the agreements.

This history of democratization and consolidation closely corresponds to that in the literature. What this chapter adds is a deeper understanding of how consolidation was constructed. Resting on the tripartite definition of consolidation, my argument shows how the various Spanish pacts helped create the necessary incentives to support democracy, qua mutual accommodation, limited government, and reciprocity. In sum, this chapter provides an explanation for how the events of the transition created the conditions for self-enforcing Spanish democracy.

This chapter proceeds as follows. The next section develops the theory of the self-enforcing democratic consolidation. Section 3 discusses the fundamental conflicts pervading Spanish society throughout much of the twentieth century. Section 4 applies the approach to the failure to secure democracy during the Second Republic and Civil War. Section 5 discusses the significant changes in Spanish economy, polity, and society under Franco. Section 6 contains the main application to democratization after the death of Franco.

A Theory of Democratic Consolidation as Self-Enforcing Democracy

This section develops a theory of democratic consolidation based on the notion of self-enforcing rules. To that end, I propose three principles relevant for democratic consolidation. I draw on ideas in Fearon 2000; Przeworski 1991, 2001; and Weingast 1997, 2002.

PRINCIPLE I: THE RATIONALITY OF FEAR

To understand the problem of democratic stability, I begin with one of the problems that must be solved or avoided, which de Figueiredo and I have called the "rationality of fear."[2] This approach is based on the premise that when citizens or groups are threatened, they take steps to defend themselves. The usefulness of the theory derives from its ability to tell us conditions under which this will occur.

I develop the approach in the context of a simple model of democratic stability. The model is intended not as a full model of democratic stability, but to emphasize the rationality of fear principle as one aspect of the larger problem. To that end, I deliberately make the model simple so that the choices faced by the actors are stark binary choices rather than more nuanced ones that reflect a range of possibilities. Similarly, the model has just two players rather than a multitude of relevant actors. The advantage of this modeling strategy is that it reveals a critical mechanism underlying democratic stability—namely, the relationship between citizens' expectations about harmful policy choices by public officials and the decision by these citizens to support democracy or extraconstitutional action.

Consider the decision of a citizen group (CZ) about whether to play by the rules or to support extraconstitutional action, such as a coup or secession. These citizens interact with elected officials (EO), who face a policy choice: whether to respect or abuse the rights of citizens. For the present, I will leave the nature of these rights abstract, but they may be a variety of rights, such as religious freedom, political freedom, or property rights.

What makes the decision problematic for the citizens is that they are unsure about the inclination of public officials to honor or abuse their rights. Game theory represents this form of uncertainty as uncertainty about the player's "type," where types differ according to their preferences. In this model, I assume that the elected officials' type is either good or bad (as

TABLE 7.1

Actor Preferences over Outcomes

	CZ	Good EO	Bad EO
First choice	A	A	B
Second choice	C	B	A
Third choice	B	C	C

A: The citizen group (CZ) chooses to play by the rules and the elected official (EO) chooses to honor CZ's rights.
B: CZ chooses to play by the rules but EO abuses CZ's rights.
C: CZ chooses to support extraconstitutional action.

judged from the perspective of the citizen group). By convention, the citizen group's uncertainty about the elected official is modeled through a choice by a nonstrategic actor called "nature" (N).

The first stage in the game is for nature to choose EO's type, which is bad with probability p and good with probability $(1 - p)$, $0 \leq p \leq 1$ (see Table 7.1). EO knows his type, but CZ only knows the probability distribution over the types. CZ makes the second move of the game and must decide whether to play by the rules or to support extraconstitutional action. If CZ chooses to support extraconstitutional action, the game ends.[3] If CZ decides to play by the rules, then EO must decide whether to honor or abuse CZ's rights.

As Table 7.1 reveals, there are three possible outcomes: Democratic stability prevails (outcome *A*) when CZ chooses to play by the rules and EO chooses to honor CZ's rights. Democracy can fail in one of two ways: first, when CZ chooses to play by the rules but EO abuses CZ's rights (outcome *B*); second, when CZ chooses to support extraconstitutional action (outcome *C*).

The preferences of the players are straightforward (see Table 7.1). CZ prefers democratic stability (*A*) to all other outcomes. If democracy is to fail, it prefers to support extraconstitutional action (*C*); its last choice is to play by the rules but have EO abuse its rights. EO's preferences depend on its type. The good EO prefers democratic stability (*A*) to abusing CZ's rights (*B*) to CZ supporting a coup (*C*). On the other hand, the bad EO prefers first to abuse CZ's rights (*B*), then democratic stability (*A*), and last, that CZ support extraconstitutional action (*C*).

To solve for the perfect Bayesian equilibrium of this game, we work backward through the tree. See Figure 7.1. Consider EO's decision (assuming that CZ has chosen to play by the rules). If EO is a good type, he knows he is at the top terminal node in the game tree; while if the bad type, he

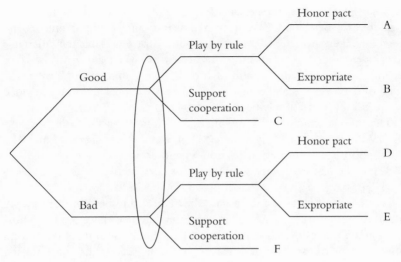

FIGURE 7.1 The rationality of fear and democratic stability

knows he is at the bottom terminal node. At either node, EO has the decision to honor or abuse CZ's rights, yielding A or B respectively. Because the good EO prefers A to B, he will choose to honor CZ's rights; the bad EO prefers B to A, so he will choose to abuse CZ's rights.

Backing up a stage, we consider CZ's decision. If CZ knew EO's type, she should clearly choose to play by the rules only if EO is the good type. But CZ is uncertain about EO's type, knowing only that EO is bad with probability p. If CZ chooses to support extraconstitutional action, she gets outcome C for sure. If she chooses to play by the rules, the outcome is uncertain, yielding A with probability $(1 - p)$ and B with probability p.

CZ will choose to play by the rules if (and only if) the payoff from the risky choice of playing by the rules exceeds that from supporting extraconstitutional action—that is, if

$$(1 - p)A + pB > C \tag{1}$$

Inequality (1) has two important implications. First, it implies that there exists a critical probability threshold, $p^\star$, that EO is the bad type, such that whenever $p < p^\star$, CZ will choose to play by the rules. That is, when the risk (that EO will abuse its rights) is lower than the probability threshold, CZ's expected value from playing by the rules exceeds that of supporting extraconstitutional action. Moreover, we can derive $p^\star$ from the inequality (1), which yields

$$p^\star = (A - C) / (A - B) \tag{2}$$

Equation (2) says that $p^\star$ represents a balance of the stakes; the numerator is the difference between CZ's valuation of its most preferred outcome, A, and its second alternative, C; whereas the denominator represents the difference between its most preferred outcome, A, and its worst alternative, B. Less technically, $p^\star$ represents a ratio of the stakes: the difference between the value of democratic stability (A) and extraconstitutional action (C) divided by the risk or stakes of relying on EO ($A - B$).

The value of equation (2) is twofold. First, it says that CZ will choose to play by the rules if and only if $p < p^\star$. This can also be turned around; CZ will support extraconstitutional action whenever $p \geq p^\star$.

Second, equation (2) yields an important comparative static result. Let $S = (A - B)$ be the risk or stakes of playing by the rules. Then $\delta p^\star / \delta S < 0$. This result says that as the stakes rise the critical threshold probability, $p^\star$, falls. Put another way, as CZ's valuation of the difference between EO's honoring and abusing its rights rises, the $p^\star$ falls. The intuition is that, given a constant value of extraconstitutional action, as the stakes inherent in relying on EO increase, the probability triggering CZ's choice of the latter falls. Another way to interpret this result says that the larger the perceived risk of relying on democracy, the smaller the set of circumstances under which democracy is stable.[4]

The model implies that for very large threats—for example, threats to citizens' livelihoods or even their lives—the critical probability threshold triggering defensive action can be quite low. That is, for very large stakes, $p^\star$ can be much closer to 0 than to 1.

Finally, the model implies discontinuous political change. Suppose that initially $p < p^\star$; then CZ will play by the rules. Suppose, however, that some event occurs that raises CZ's estimate of p so that $p \geq p^\star$. Then CZ will switch from playing by the rules to supporting extraconstitutional action.

The rationality of fear principle has dozens of applications. For example, in Chile during the early 1970s, many on the political right felt their economic rights threatened by President Salvador Allende's government, leading them to support the military coup (Valenzuela 1978). Similarly, during the Second Republic in Spain (1931–39), many agrarian landholders, the church, and industrialists felt threatened by the democratically elected regime, leading them to support General Francisco Franco in the Civil War against the regime (Agüero 1995; Alexander 2002, chap. 4). In the early nineteenth century, large numbers of Southerners in the United States felt their property in slaves threatened by the newly elected Republicans in 1860, leading to secession and Civil War (Weingast 1998). In each case, a sufficiently large group of citizens felt threatened by a legitimately elected regime and supported extraconstitutional action (such as a civil war or coup) to defend themselves.

The rationality of fear model captures only one aspect of the problem of democratic stability, namely, the relationship between CZ's expectations of EO's behavior and its willingness to play by the rules. EO's decisions are mechanical, depending on its type. A more complex and realistic model would add several features, such as some investigation of the determinants of EO's type, elected officials who do not act mechanically, repeated interactions, and collective action problems among the citizenry. This more complex model is beyond the scope of this chapter. For now, I discuss only the first issue, namely, where does EO's type come from and hence where do CZ's beliefs come from?

EO's type depends in part on strategic and structural issues that are not modeled but subsumed in the games structure. For example, Gerard Alexander (2002) argues that an important determinant of elected officials' type concerns the nature of their constituents. Do elected officials' constituents advocate moderate or radical policies? Do elements of these constituents advocate abrogating or abusing the rights of other citizens? In terms of the model, Alexander's logic implies that EO's type is likely to be bad when important elements of its constituents advocate abusing CZ's rights and good if they do not. As discussed below, Alexander's observation has important implications for the rationality of fear and citizen choice of whether to play by the rules or to support extraconstitutional action.

PRINCIPLE 2: LOWERING THE STAKES OF POLITICS

The rationality of fear model has direct implications for constitutional stability. Because one of the principal ways in which democracies fail is when citizens support coups owing to the fear of oppressive action or abuse of their rights, democratic stability requires that the rationality of fear mechanism be short-circuited. The principal means of doing so is constitutional—through the structure and process created through pacts, major political agreements, and explicit constitutions. An important aspect of these agreements is that they create "structure and process"—structural constraints that place direct limits on the government's action, and procedures for government action whose requirements rule out some actions, for example, by empowering various veto players.[5]

The importance of these constraints, as Przeworski (1991, chap. 2) emphasizes, is that constitutions that limit the stakes of politics are more likely to survive. The reason is that when the constitution places credible limits on elected officials in ways valued by citizens, citizens are less likely to destroy democracy through their support of extraconstitutional action.

As Przeworski (1991, chap. 2) also observes, lowering the stakes of politics has another beneficial effect for democratic stability. Consider the decision of elected officials at what I call the "Przeworski moment"—that is, when

elected officials have just lost an election but retain power for some inter-
regnum. When will they give up power? The answer is in part that the more
they have to lose from turning over power, the less likely they are to do so.
Put another way, the larger the stakes of power, the greater the likelihood
that democracy will fail when incumbents who lose elections fail to abide
by these results.

The perspective of self-enforcing democracy thus shows there is a positive (as opposed to normative) link between constitutional and democratic
stability and a liberal constitution that places restrictions on democratic
choices.

PRINCIPLE 3: CITIZEN COORDINATION

The third principle draws on the third part of the definition of consolidation, which holds that sustaining democracy requires that citizens be willing to defend democracy against transgressions by political leaders. Leaders
attempt coups in part based on the expectation that a sufficient portion of
the population will support them.[6] Similarly, elected officials attempt to set
aside constitutional rules when despite doing so they expect sufficient constituency support to retain power.

The third component of the definition provides the incentives for its
other two parts. When citizens are willing to defend democracy, leaders cannot expect citizen support for extraconstitutional action; rather than risk
failure, leaders are deterred from violating the rules by adverse citizen reaction.

Thus the central question for democratic consolidation becomes, what
are the conditions under which citizens act in concert to defend the rules?
Citizen coordination is problematic since citizen disagreement implies that
citizens have no obvious way to coordinate. As noted, differences in citizens'
economic and social situations imply that they disagree about the nature of
their rights and the appropriate form of the state. This implies that they disagree about what constitutes a governmental transgression. These disagreements also imply that citizens have no natural means by which to coordinate
their reactions to government transgressions. Solving this coordination problem in a decentralized manner is virtually impossible for a diverse group of
citizens.

SOLVING THE COORDINATION DILEMMA AND CREATING
CREDIBLE LIMITS ON THE STATE

The three principles of constitutional stability are characteristics of a self-
enforcing constitutional equilibrium. The widespread failure of new constitutions demonstrates that many constitutions are not naturally self-enforcing. In this subsection, I explain how self-enforcing constitutions are

constructed. The following conditions are necessary for constitutional self-enforcement: Citizens must have a means of coordinating their reactions against governmental transgressions, and constitutions must lower the stakes of politics. When these hold, they reduce the likelihood that the rationality of fear mechanism will be invoked, destroying constitutional democracy.

Consider the second principle: appropriately designed constitutional institutions help lower the stakes of politics by creating self-enforcing limits on politics. But how do they do so? In two ways. The first way constitutions place limits on government concerns structure and process (McCubbins, Noll, and Weingast 1989). Procedural limits specify how particular governmental activities take place. For example, in the United States, legislation requires a majority in both legislative chambers and a presidential signature (subject to the qualification about the veto override). Structural limits concern specific powers and prohibitions. The U.S. government has no authority over a range of policies, such as religion. Moreover, its authority is subject to a series of substantive limits, such as the Fifth Amendment's requirement that taking property requires just compensation. Similarly, constitutions that credibly guarantee private property rights limit the ability of governments to confiscate citizen wealth and thus reduce the likelihood of invoking the rationality of fear.

Democratic stability in the United States in the early nineteenth century illustrates this conclusion. Southerners were constantly anxious about the security of their slave property. A necessary condition for them to remain in the Union was that Northerners provide a credible commitment to honor Southern rights in slaves (see Weingast 1998). In the nineteenth century, Southerners required an additional limit not specified in the Constitution. Both North and South agreed to the principle of sectional balance, which granted both sections equal representation in the U.S. Senate, affording each a veto over national policy making. Southerners could thus protect themselves by vetoing Northern attempts to use the national government against slavery. In combination with the Constitution, sectional balance made democracy in the United States self-enforcing, at least until the Kansas-Nebraska Act of 1854, which initiated the crisis leading to the Civil War.

The second way constitutions create credible limits on the national government is by helping citizens solve their coordination problems (Hardin 1989). Recall that disagreements among citizens plague their coordinated reaction against political officials, allowing the latter sometimes to transgress the rights of some citizens.

The critical ingredient in solving coordination problems is the creation of a focal point (Schelling 1960), which creates common expectations among citizens about what others will do in a given situation. In the face of multiple ways to coordinate, the existence of a focal point changes citizen incentives. Although each citizen may prefer to coordinate in one of many particular ways, the fact that citizens value coordination means that when others coordinate around a given focal point, they are better off coordinating using this focal point than following their most preferred way.

In the context of constitutions, focal points define the appropriate bounds on governments and rights of citizens. These in turn define transgressions so that citizens can react in concert. When citizens agree on what constitutes governmental transgressions, they can coordinate their reactions against them. Obviously, citizens may disagree about what rights the constitution ought to include. To ensure that the constitution is self-enforcing, the focal point must (1) create a compromise among those with differing views about rights, (2) create a situation in which citizens believe themselves better off with these rights than without them, and (3) provide citizens with the incentives to defend the rights. Thus the set of rights specified in the constitution cannot be arbitrary, but must be, as a set, valued by citizens.

Constitutional creation of these focal solutions can be seen in the context of pacts, agreements among opposing sides that modify or specify the rules of the political decision making (Higley and Gunther 1992; O'Donnell and Schmitter 1986). To succeed, pacts must be self-enforcing; that is, they must provide the parties to the pact with incentives to abide by the pact's provisions.

I provide four conditions for self-enforcing pacts (Weingast 1997, 2002). First, the pact must create (or be embedded in a context that has already been created) structure and process—citizens' rights and a set of rules governing public decision making—defining a series of limits on the state. Second, the parties agreeing to the pact must believe that they are better off under the pact than without it. If this condition fails for one of the parties, that party will be better off without the pact, so the pact will fail. In particular, they must believe that the structural and procedural limits on average lead the government to make them better off. Third, each party agrees to change its behavior in exchange for the others simultaneously doing so. Fourth, the parties to the pact must be willing to defend it against transgressions by political leaders. In particular, they must be willing to defend the parts of the pact benefiting themselves, but also the parts benefiting the others against transgressions by political leaders. This fourth condition occurs when each party anticipates that its rights will be defended by the others, that each party is better off under the agreement than not, and that if ever one party fails to protect the rights of others, the others will fail to come to its rescue. Put another way, the pact becomes self-enforcing when all parties are better off under the pact and when all realize that unilateral defection implies that the others will also defect, destroying the pact.

Pacts thus accomplish several goals at once. First, they are agreements to adhere to new structure and process, often including elections. Second, they alter the parties' incentives, again in part through structure and process. Third, they help solve the critical citizen coordination problem that plagues nondemocratic states. By creating focal procedural and substantive limits, pacts help citizens react in concert to violations of the rules.

SUMMARY

Because there is no external authority to police constitutional rules, these rules must be self-enforcing. One of the principle mechanisms helping to police governmental adherence to the rules is the threat of a concerted reaction by citizens against a government that violates these rules. Yet massive impediments make this coordination difficult. There is no natural way for citizens to coordinate against adverse government decisions. Hence most societies cannot sustain democracy and constitutions; those in power can violate democratic or constitutional rules by retaining the support of some citizens.

To survive, democratic constitutions require a set of structure and process that creates incentives for political officials to abide by the rules. This structure and process must reduce the stakes of politics, helping to avoid the rationality of fear mechanism. As we have seen, this is accomplished through constitutions and pacts that limit the stakes of power and that create solutions to the citizens' coordination problem, allowing them to react in concert against potential constitutional and democratic violations.

Pervasive Political and Social Divisions in Mid-Twentieth-Century Spain

Throughout the period under consideration, including the Civil War and the transition to democracy, Spanish society exhibited three fundamental dimensions of political conflict: (1) the degree of regional autonomy; (2) basic questions about the state, such as the rules of political representation and public choice, the status of the monarchy, the nature of the economic system, and the rights accorded various groups and citizens ("stateness" in the Linz and Stepan 1996 terminology); and (3) the role of the Catholic Church in Spanish society.

The first dimension of conflict, the degree of decentralization in Spain, held the potential to rip the society apart. An issue for the previous 150 years, it was the cause of three civil wars in the nineteenth century and a major issue in the 1930s (Maravall and Santamaria 1986, 86). Many on the right, particularly in the military, worried that regional nationalists might use regional freedom to develop political strongholds from which to launch stronger bids for autonomy and independence. For these groups, preserving the integrity of Spain was a major issue. Many regional groups—particularly in the Basque region and Catalonia, but also in other regions such as Galicia—deemed obtaining a degree of independence from the central state as critical. Under many regimes, including Franco's, centralized policies discriminated against these regions, creating deep resentment and fanning demands for autonomy.

The second dimension, the nature of the political system and the degree of political and civil rights, reflects a set of deep policy issues about the role of the state. Could the state be used for radical redefinition of rights—for example, restructuring the ownership of the means of production in industry and agriculture? Because several parties of the left in the 1930s advocated radical restructuring of Spanish economy and society, many among moderates and especially among the right were reluctant to support full political representation because it risked opening a range of policy conflicts. In part because of this history, a critical issue in the 1970s concerned the degree of political freedom to organize parties; for example, should the Communist Party be legalized?

Also at stake were the basic rules of representation and public choice. Many favored a monarchy or authoritarian regime without elections. Others favored a republic with full electoral freedom, including all parties. Anarchists sought to use the state for a radical restructuring of society.

The secular-clerical issue also pervaded this era. What was the appropriate role of the Catholic Church in society? Should Catholicism be the official state religion and various privileges accorded the Church, such as a significant role in education?

The first implication of this discussion is that the pervasive political and social divisions implied an absence of a natural consensus on the form of the Spanish state, the rights accorded various groups, and the rules governing political decision making.

Consistent with the lack of consensus, deep political conflict and instability characterized the 150 years prior to the Civil War. Spain often went from one extreme to another, from monarchy to republic, democracy to authoritarianism, striking centralization to regional autonomy (Gunther 1992, 43).

Political Conflict During the Second Republic and Civil War

As noted, many on the left in the 1930s sought to use the state to construct a radically new society. Conflicts among these groups reflected significant differences as to the form of that society. These conflicts also hindered cooperation among leftist groups, both in the Republic and during the Civil War. Moreover, many of these groups proved to be "maximalists" because they would rather risk violence and failure than compromise their vision (Colomer 1995, chap. 1).

The Second Republic's electoral laws created several problems. First, these laws granted those with the most electoral support more than their share of representatives. This implied that small swings in the electorate could have large effects on the government. In practice, the short-lived republic was plagued by three swings following the major elections of 1931, 1933, and 1936. Three elections in the short years of the Republic combined with electoral swings to imply that no coalition held power long enough to sustain a consistent and stable program.[7] Second, the overrepresentation of the plurality winners implied that electoral institutions could give a party majority control of the government even though it gained only a plurality of support in the election. This implies that the government could pursue policies opposed by significant majorities, thus accentuating the political risk of governance to the opposition.

According to the theory, the noncooperation equilibrium should prevail in this setting. This equilibrium manifests all of the characteristics noted above: an absence of limited government, threats to what opposition groups considered their fundamental rights, the operation of the rationality of fear and hence the appeal of extraconstitutional means of defense. I discuss these in turn.

First, the fundamental disagreement implies an absence of agreements about limits on government. The radical programs of the left conflicted with what many on the right believed were their fundamental rights. The lack of consensus about limits on the state implied significant uncertainty about the future policies of the Republic. Although the regime never initiated massive economic restructuring, the rhetoric of radical revolution and significant pressure from below implied that a large range of rights remained up for grabs (Alexander 2002, chap. 4; Linz 1978b, 84–95). For many on the right, workers' demand for control over the means of production raised the specter of the onset of Soviet-style communism. Similarly, the large group of landless rural poor threatened radical action, transforming conservative landholders into reactionaries willing to support Franco.

Alexander (2002, chap. 4) argues that the Republican regime's moderation during this period was tactical. That is, the Republican regime constantly fought important constituency groups, such as labor and the rural poor, to suppress their radical demands. For many on the right, this tactical suppression provided insufficient protection.

The Second Republic's adoption of an anticlerical constitution implied that many conservative groups rejected the regime from the start. As Richard Gunther (1992, 45) suggests, "Adoption of an anticlerical constitution led significant sectors of Spanish society to reject that regime as a partisan imposition on the rest of society of the values of a temporary majority. The legitimacy of the Second Republic was thus challenged from the very moments of its birth."

The absence of limits on government implied the operation of the rationality of fear. Many on the right were threatened by the left's rhetoric during the Second Republic, and the absence of credible limits on the regime implied that these threats could become a reality (Alexander 2002, chap. 4; see also Linz 1978a, 189). Franco played on these fears, arguing that the regime was dominated by godless radicals bent on remaking Spain, including confiscating assets and destroying traditional Spanish society. The risk implied by the absence of limits on the state meant that many found this argument appealing.

As Raymond Carr and Juan Pablo Fusi (1981, 2) conclude, "The fundamental reason for the failure of the democratic experiment of 1931–36 was that politicization raised working-class expectations to a level the Republic could not satisfy. Conversely, conservatives regarded the mere existence of these expectations as a dangerous threat to their way of life." Carr and Fusi also suggest the rationality of fear in operation. The Republic did not undertake massive economic or social policy change, so that those groups dominant in 1931 remained so in 1936. Yet they were threatened and supported the opponents, "convinced nevertheless, that they were faced by an imminent Socialist revolution" (Carr and Fusi 1981, 2). Per the rationality of fear principle, citizens do not always wait for bad acts to take actions to defend themselves.

Alexander (2002, chap. 4) argues that the right bided its time while the Republican government moderated its policies for tactical reasons (1931–33) and also while the right held office (1933–36). Yet when the left returned to power in 1936, "the right's calculus changed dramatically. In the face of a left government, radicalized unions, and accelerating violence and direct action in many regions, even an authoritarian project that imposed some risks of repression and regime/opposition conflict was preferable. In particular, in Spain more than in any other case considered here, rightists' safety was threatened in democracy" (Alexander 2002, 105). Similarly, Carr and Fusi argue,

The maximalist wing of the [socialist] party, under Largo Caballero, without any revolutionary intent or plan, used the rhetoric of the proletarian revolution and the mobilization of its masses to force an advanced social policy on a government manned by bourgeois Republicans. With the government under pressure from the streets, with peasants invading the great estates, with church burnings and bomb outrages, with what they considered a collapse of the political and social order (which the right were themselves both provoking and using as a proof of the generalized collapse), the Catholic right increasingly deserted legalism for the counter-revolution long preached by hard-core monarchists and authoritarians. (Carr and Fusi 1981, 3)

The absence of credible limits on the state combined with the rationality of fear to suggest why a large portion of Spanish society supported the military coup in 1936. Under other circumstances, many of these groups might have supported more moderate compromise. This applies to elements of the Church, agrarian landowners, much of the middle class, and the older businesses. For compromise to have occurred, the regime would have had to establish limits on its exercise of power that protected these groups' interests. Because the regime (and many of its constituents) eschewed those protections, large portions of these groups sought protection against more radical action from the Republican regime.

In sum, the theoretical principles articulated above provide significant insight into the struggles during the Second Republic leading to Civil War. First, the new government proved unable or unwilling to create focal solutions necessary to support the constitution. Large elements of Spanish society considered the government illegitimate. Second, the absence of focal solutions implied the absence of self-enforcing limits on government. Third, the first two principles combined to invoke the rationality of fear mechanism. A large portion of Spanish society proved willing to support extra-constitutional action to defend themselves, their perceived rights, and their way of life. In combination, these conclusions implied social conflict, leading to Civil War.

Changes in Spanish Society Between the 1930s and the 1970s

The Spain of the 1970s was not the Spain of the 1930s. A range of economic, political, and social changes altered the political landscape of the 1970s from that of the 1930s (Alexander 2002, chap. 5; Gunther 1992; Linz and Montero 1999).

Economic growth under Franco implied a range of changes. Ironically, the economic success of the regime in the 1960s served to undermine the regime's support (Maravall 1978, 1982; Tarrow 1995; and Tortella 2000). By the 1960s, Spanish gross domestic product per capita neared that of other western European countries. Economic growth also swelled the ranks of the middle class and those who sought to join them. Spain became much richer, and many more people came to have a stake in social peace.

Demographic effects contributed to these changes. The depopulation of the countryside dramatically reduced the rural poor, whose political demands had proved problematic in the 1930s. As Sidney Tarrow (1995, 224) concludes, "By 1976, only nine percent of the active Spanish population still worked in agriculture, and there were twice as many small proprietors as farm workers." In the 1970s, "there was no equivalent of the class war in the countryside that had turned Spanish conservatives into reactionaries and provided a mass base for General Franco's coup d'etat."

Economic growth also divided much of the elite. Many industrialists came to favor integration with Europe, believing that the authoritarian regime remained an impediment to this goal. A large and growing professional class, as documented by José Maravall (1982), came to view Franco's idea of Spain "outside" of Europe as an anachronism. The clerical issue also changed. Put simply, in the increasingly secular society, the role of the Catholic Church had become less important.[8]

Many scholars emphasize the importance of the growth of the civil society under Franco, including the growth of worker and student organizations and of the press (Gunther 1992; Linz and Stepan 1996; Maravall 1978, 1982; Tarrow 1995; Tortella 2000). This growth created a space for political organization and dissent. All would prove critical during the transition.

Finally, Josep Colomer (1995, chap. 1) proposes an important dimension underanalyzed in the literature. He suggests that the number preferring democratization to the alternatives was no greater in the 1970s than in the 1930s. Instead, the major difference was that there were fewer extreme leftists (i.e., those who would prefer to fight rather than to compromise) in the 1970s. Through a clever analysis of incentives, Colomer shows that this one difference drastically altered the strategic setting.

All of these changes improved the chances of democratization in the 1970s. They imply more support than in the 1930s for liberalization and democratization.

Yet these changes did not speak for themselves. Although they may have made the political environment of the 1970s more propitious for democratization than that of the 1930s, they did not ensure its success. As Richard Gunther, José Ramón Montero, and Joan Botella (2003, 87) conclude, "By the 1970s Spain had emerged as a modern, urbanized, relatively affluent society, with a political culture substantially different from that of the 1930s. While these altered social characteristics were certainly compatible with democratization, however, they were far from determinative of a successful transition to a stable and consolidated democracy."

Deep conflicts on all of the three fundamental issues remained, especially the first two. Conflicts over regionalism and the form of the state may well have blown up rather than resulting in acceptable compromise.

Consolidation of Democracy in Spain, 1975–1982

As noted, two principal dimensions of disagreement about the state con-fronted Spaniards in the 1970s: the "integrity of Spain," which concerned the degree of regional autonomy, and the nature of the political system, includ-ing the degree of political and civil rights.[9]

The theory above suggests that political conflict born of heterogeneity in Spain implied that there was no natural consensus about the constitution, the appropriate role of the state, or the rights of individuals, parties, and re-gions.[10] Per principle 3, the absence of agreement on the fundamental issues implied the potential absence of limits on a new government. This absence, in turn, implied high stakes, the potential for large losses, and hence the pos-sible operation of the rationality of fear principle. Creating a stable demo-cratic environment required constructing focal solutions to various issues of difference and institutional solutions to define the appropriate limits to pro-tect various groups, but also to make these limits credible and thus prevent the rationality of fear.

The Spain of the 1970s was not the Spain of the 1930s. Nonetheless, the theory suggests that none of these trends determined which of the two types of equilibria Spain would end up with. Nothing about the situation *ex ante* impelled a successful transition (Linz and Stepan 1996, chap. 6). No obvious compromise existed on either principal dimension of conflict. The poten-tially irresolvable conflict, in turn, implied that it was not obvious that Spain could sustain mutual security and democracy.

ANALYSIS OF THE TRANSITION

How was the democratic consolidation established in Spain? The theory requires that we explain what prevented the rationality of fear, how citizen coordination and hence consensus about the rules was constructed, and fi-nally, how mutual security was created. The theoretical perspective above re-veals how the various compromises not only helped create the relevant focal points but created a series of credible limits on government tied to fore-stalling the operation of the rationality of fear.

Given the fundamental Spanish disagreements about the appropriate form of the state, the model suggests that the natural political equilibrium is the absence of coordination and hence the inability to support democ-racy.

A useful if simplified way of thinking about the political balance in Spain in the mid-1970s is that there were three sets of political actors. On the right were the continualists, those preferring to continue the Franco regime and, if not feasible, to engineer the minimal amount of reform allowing the regime to remain in power. These groups included the conservative Popular

Alliance (AP), led by Manuel Fraga. Many in the military also favored continuity.

Toward the right-center stood the moderate reformers, represented by Adolfo Suárez, appointed as prime minister in July 1976. As a first step, he sought to reform the system by creating limited representative democracy. Rather than break with the past and create new institutions, he relied on existing Francoist institutions to engineer the reform.

Those on the left sought political rupture—a distinct break with the past to create full representative democracy. Many of these groups called for elections for a new Cortes that would write a constitution. They also sought full amnesty for those persecuted by the Franco regime. Most preferred a republican form of government to a constitutional monarchy. Included among this set of groups were the Spanish Socialist Party (PSOE) and the Spanish Communist Party (PCE). Also included were many regionalists from the Basque country and Catalonia.

Fundamental to the transition was that no group, faction, or party was sufficiently strong that it could dominate politics alone (see, e.g., Colomer 1995; and Maravall and Santamaria 1986). The Francoist regime could be sustained as long as Franco was alive. Once the leader died, however, the ancien régime could not be sustained without far more repression, and most likely not even then. Unable to succeed on their own, continualists were forced to negotiate with others to create some form of acceptable compromise and governing political coalition.

The initial attempt, following Franco's death, at minimal reform failed. Arias Navarro's modest reform proposals were blocked by the right, which fought reform. The result was exploding civil unrest. This showed that to survive, those in power had to construct some type of reform.[11]

Admitting that the Arias Navarro government had been a disaster, the king engineered the appointment of a relative unknown, Aldofo Suárez, as prime minister (Colomer 1995, chap. 3). Suárez proved a dedicated reformer. He began by creating a coalition among many from the right and those in the center for moderate reform. Initially, Suárez sought a limited representative democracy, allowing political parties and universal suffrage. The government would impose the electoral system, with a bias toward itself and away from the left. Many issues were also to be kept off the table, at least initially.

Critical to his success was that Suárez became the leader of the pivotal moderate group that could swing either way to form a governing coalition—toward either the continualists or the rupturist opposition (Colomer 1995, chaps. 4–5). As predicted by standard median voter models, Suárez's pivotal position gave him a degree of negotiating power over the other two sets of factions and their followers. Because a coalition of the continualists and the democratic opposition was unlikely, both of these groups needed to join Suárez and his faction to become part of the governing coalition.

In accord with our theory, constructing focal solutions proved central to Suárez's institutional negotiations. In his masterful analysis of the transition, Victor Perez-Diaz (1990, 2–3) emphasizes the invention of tradition: "the process of 'invention' of a new tradition in our political culture since the mid 1970s: that of a 'democratic Spain,' involving a selective collective memory and an array of political symbolisms (myths and rituals) that imply a new understanding of Spanish history and of Spanish identity."[12] Consider the range of focal solutions. First, Suárez began his reforms by obtaining the continualists' support for moderate reform. Continualists went along in part because moderate reforms might allow them to retain power (Colomer 1995, chap. 4). The reforms included an electoral law (biased toward the right), a prohibition on participation by the Communists and other potentially radical opponents, and an absence of reprisals for policies or repression of the previous regime. Finally, any discussion of the monarchy and state unity was out of bounds (Colomer 1995, chap. 4).

The continualists were willing to support this level of reform for at least two reasons. Failing to do so might force Suárez to negotiate with the opposition. Or worse, deadlock within the government might cause the government to fail, as had the previous Arias Navarro administration, with risks of greater social unrest and uncertainty about political control.

In the fall of 1976, Suárez achieved a remarkable success—the Francoist Cortes passed his Bill for Political Reform, dissolving itself and creating new elections. Suárez also submitted the reform proposal for a referendum. With a turnout of 78 percent, 94 percent of those voting approved the transition to democracy in December 1976. The successful referendum strengthened Suárez's hand, especially given that the democratic opposition failed to convince the electorate not to vote (Maravall and Santamaria 1986, 83). Suárez's success also made him the natural leader of a coalition of moderate parties (e.g., the Christian Democrats, Liberals, and Social Democrats), creating the Union of Democratic Center (UCD).

Having secured a pact with the continualists and popular support for his program, Suárez then sought to expand the inclusion of support by negotiating with the left. The initial reform advantaged the moderate opposition by allowing them legal rights to organize before the potentially more radical opposition, such as the Communists, could participate.

Suárez also began negotiations with Santiago Carrillo, the PCE secretary-general. Both bargaining parties faced a dilemma. Consider Suárez's dilemma: maintaining the prohibition on the Communists risked their boycott and open challenge of the legitimacy of his reform program, while legalizing them risked possible polarization of the electorate and the reemergence of fundamental political conflict. The Communists, in turn, faced the dilemma of remaining true to their traditional principles or accepting participation in a restrictive representative system not of their making. Waiting for an opportunity to foster a more radical rupture risked allowing the moderates and moderate left to organize and gain the upper hand with the electorate, possibly shutting them out.

Suárez helped resolve this problem through reciprocity. In return for legalization (and per the theory), he required that the Communists accept central aspects of the reform program and institutions: the monarchy, the flag, and the rules of the game, biased as they were. Carrillo surprised Suárez by willingly accepting these.[13]

Suárez's decision in early 1977 to legalize the Communist Party illustrates the construction of trust and participation in the democratic regime. In terms of our approach, Suárez's "invention of tradition" created a focal principle of the right of organization, of political participation, in exchange for moderation. Although ideologically opposed to the Communists, Suárez defended their right to organize and participate. Per our theory, this included the right by the opposition to participate, the duty of others to defend that right, and that the legal prohibition could only be maintained by repression and other means inconsistent with the goals of democratization. It is worth quoting at length Suárez's televised speech justifying his action:

> The rejection [of the request of legalization] would not be consistent with the reality that the Communist Party exists and is organized. The struggle against it could only be carried out by repression.
>
> Not only am I not Communist, but I reject strongly its ideology, as it is rejected by the other members of my cabinet. But I am a democrat, and sincerely democratic. Therefore I think that our people are sufficiently mature . . . to assimilate their own pluralism.
>
> I do not think that our people want to find itself fatally obliged to see our jails full of people for ideological reasons. . . . We have to instill the respect for legal minorities. Among the rights and duties of living together is the acceptance of the opponent (adversario). (quoted in Linz and Stepan 1996, 96–97)

The creation of consensus, per principle 3, captures this insight. Suárez negotiated a pact with a reciprocal set of concessions. In doing so, he manufactured a consensus on the appropriateness and importance of democratic rights and rules of participation.

What made the Communists' promises self-enforcing? That is, once gaining the right to participate, why did they not renege on their promise? Several reasons can be adduced. Euro-communism of the post-Prague 1970s differed considerably from its embodiment in the 1930s. But Suárez may have acted on a greater strength than this. A more radical program presented two risks for the Communists (Colomer 1995, chap. 5). First, it risked lack of suc-

TABLE 7.2

Vote and Seat Proportions for the Four Largest Parties in the 1977 Spanish Elections

	Votes (%)	Seats (%)	Ratio of Votes to Seats
Spanish Communist Party (PCE)	9.4	5.7	.61
Spanish Socialist Party (PSOE)	29.3	33.7	1.15
Union of the Democratic Center (UCD)	34.6	47.4	1.37
Popular Alliance (AP)	8.8	4.6	.52

SOURCE: José Ramón Montero, "Stabilising the Democratic Order: Electoral Behavior in Spain," in *Politics and Policy in Democratic Spain: No Longer Different?* ed. Paul Heyword (London: Frank Cass, 1999), table 1.

cess with the electorate (see Gunther 1992; and Alexander 2002, chap. 5), and second, it risked the threat from the right that would either force Suárez to alter his decision, or worse, provoke a reaction from the military.

Suárez's move was nonetheless controversial. Many on the right viewed Suárez's legalization of the Communists as a violation of their pact initiating moderate reform (Colomer 1995, 74). Reflecting this judgment, the threat from the right would remain for several years.

Another example of inventing tradition occurred prior to the transition—the transformation of the meaning of the Civil War. For the first two decades following the Civil War, the right and the left both had "opposing yet very similar and simple Manichaean interpretations . . . portraying the war as a contest between good and evil" (Perez-Diaz 1990, 23). In the newly constructed view, the Civil War became a tragedy of shared guilt; both sides had their share of blame. The old views pitted two irreconcilable interpretations against one another. The new views included a component of the reciprocal process of accommodation, tolerance, and mutual acceptance; each side viewed the other as legitimate and as having grievances about the past and claims on the future.

After the reform law, the next step in the transition was an election to produce a new Cortes. Held in June 1977, the election confirmed the moderation of the electorate; the most extreme parties on right and left received too few votes to gain parliamentary representation. Table 7.2 shows the biases of the electoral law for the four largest parties. The two largest—the moderate right (UCD) and the moderate left (PSOE)—received 34.6 and 29.3 percent of the votes and 47.4 and 33.7 percent of the representatives. In combination, they held over 80 percent of the seats, reflecting an overrepresentation owing to the electoral law of nearly one-third. The other two main parties—the AP on the right and the PCE on the left—received only 8.8 and 9.4 percent of the vote, affording them only 4.6 and 5.7 percent of the representatives. The predominance of the moderates on both right and left was clearly established (Maravall and Santamaria 1986, 85).

Following the elections, Suárez sought to have the new Cortes write a constitution. In doing so, he exploited his centrist political location. Suárez's ability to play off each side against the other helped moderate their demands (Colomer 1995, chap. 6). This effort resulted in a series of pacts. The first, known as the Pact of Moncloa in September 1977, focused on the economic problems. Various reforms were promised in exchange for support of an austerity program necessary to avoid deepening economic crisis. According to Gunther (1992, 55), these pacts

> pledged the government to a continuing program of reforms of political institutions, the social security system, and the regressive taxation system inherited from the Francoist regime; to government controls on price increases; to democratization of the education system; and to certain other policy changes. . . . In exchange, the Socialist and Communist parties promised to induce those trade unions over which they had influence to refrain from excessive strike activity, to limit demands for pay increases to 22 percent, and to accept more restrictive monetary and expenditure policies.

This moderation illustrates the structural point emphasized by Alexander (2002, chap. 5). He argues that leftist constituents moderated their demands during the transition, reducing the perceived risk to those on the right. In terms of this chapter's theory, the bargaining parties' mutual acceptance of goals and limits through pacts helped to reduce the rationality of fear.

Next followed the institutional pacts, which dealt with the regional and constitutional issues. Colomer (1995, chap. 6) provides an insightful analysis of the strategic incentives facing Suárez and the parties represented in the Cortes. As in the initial phase of the transition, the centrist UCD was pivotal, yet it needed the support of either the right or the left to form a solid majority in writing the constitution. Colomer (1995, table 6.1) shows that this balance held not only in the Cortes but in the various constitutional drafting and reviewing committees.

This setting afforded two types of coalitions and hence different constitutions. The UCD could ally with the AP and form a right-center coalition leaning to continualism and moderate reform; it could ally with the various parties on the left, leaning toward a sharp break with the past (rupture); and it could attempt an inclusive compromise coalition of support from both the right and the left. A right-left coalition against Suárez was virtually unthinkable.

From Suárez's perspective, all three potential coalitions held dangers. A coalition with the right risked continued social challenge from the left and regionalists, including strikes, terrorism, and the lack of legitimacy. A coalition with the left risked the active resistance from the right, including terrorism and possible military coup. An inclusive coalition risked failure owing to the inability to shape a feasible compromise acceptable to all or most of the participants.

Paralleling William Riker's (1986, chap. 8) analysis of the U.S. constitutional convention, Colomer's analysis of the constitution writing suggests that compromise was achieved through vote trading in which the various parties gave ground on issues of lesser importance to gain on issues of greater importance (Colomer 1995, chap. 6). The remarkable achievement is that it worked.

The right wanted a short constitution specifying few rights and institutionalizing the monarchy with an amendment procedure making it difficult to change. The left acceded to a monarchy, but only one with strict limits on its power. The left also agreed to recognize a "free market economy" in exchange for agreement that the government could intervene in the economy. It accepted a strong and stable cabinet with clear supremacy over parliament in exchange for a proportional election law. The left also wanted the strict amendment procedure to cover "all possible revisions of a progressive and detailed bill of rights that was to preface the constitution" (Maravall and Santamaria 1986, 88).

For the right, there were guarantees to two of the main corporate groups privileged under Franco, the military and the Catholic Church. The military was charged with ensuring the "sovereignty, independence, and territorial integrity of Spain" and was given "an explicit role as defenders of the constitutional order" (Maravall and Santamaria 1986, 88). In addition, there was to be no wholesale ousting of the Francoist bureaucracy.

A compromise also occurred on the regional issue. The main regionalist parties sought special recognition for the Basque country and Catalonia along the lines granted during the Second Republic. This was opposed by the right, including the military. Moreover, many other regions did not want special recognition for those two regions. The compromise was a general decentralization. Although the compromise did not contain special recognition of the two most historically active nationalist regions, the decentralization was sufficient to satisfy most voters in these regions (Linz and Stepan 1996, 101–8).

Similarly, although the constitution granted the majority the right to govern, "consensualism applies to the staffing of certain government bodies which are regarded as above partisan politics due to their fundamental roles as guarantors of fair-play, basic civil or political rights, and/or the universalism of key state institutions" (Gunther, Montero, and Botella 2003, 160).

Suárez's strategy of consensus, compromise, pacts, and mutual accommodation put Spain on the path toward consolidated democracy. The theory
helps us understand how it works. To be self-enforcing, pacts have to make
all parties to the pact better off; and further, each party must know that unilateral defection implies the pact's failure. Both conditions held for the pacts
negotiated by Suárez.[14] Here too the balance of perspectives reduced the rationality of fear by making it difficult for narrow interests to capture these
critical bodies.

The success of the referendum on the constitution was the final capstone
for the constitutional process. Only the most extreme on the right, including the "Bunker," failed to support the constitution. A potential problem
therefore remained with the military. Their acceptance of the regime was
"cautious and conditional, limited in any case by their loyalty to the king as
commander of the armed forces. . . . Hence during the early years, the consolidation was overshadowed by a permanent threat of impending coup d'e-
tat" (Maravall and Santamaria 1986, 90).

We now know that elements on the right, including many in the military,
bided their time, waiting for a propitious moment to act. This came in February 1981, when a group of military leaders attempted a coup. Part of the
coup leaders' bet involved the acquiescence of the king, who had yet to
prove himself both a staunch proponent of democratization and a man with
backbone (Agüero 1995, chap. 7; Boyd and Boyden 1985; Colomer 1995,
chap. 7; Podolny 1993). In a dramatic move, the coup proponents took over
the Cortes at gunpoint on February 23. Yet the king proved implacable.

In the face of the king's active resistance and the absence of widespread
support for a coup, the coup failed (Alexander 2002, chap. 5). The king became a hero, while the coup proponents were prosecuted. The new socialist
government undertook a military reform, replacing many of those loyal to
the Franco regime with leaders more favorable to democracy. The prospects
for a second attempt were greatly diminished.

IMPLICATIONS

The theory provides insights into why Suárez's steps worked. First, the
balance of political forces implied that no party could write the constitution
without the support of at least some of the others.

Second, the political conflicts plaguing mid-century Spain implied that
no natural solution existed to the fundamental conflicts over the state or the
rights accorded to various individuals, groups, parties, and regions. Two very
different equilibria were possible: a noncooperative one failing to sustain a
democratic constitution, with those in power potentially taking advantage of
or discriminating against those out of power; and a cooperative equilibrium
sustaining a democratic constitution in which those in power respected an

agreed-upon set of limits on government. Obtaining the cooperative equilibrium required the construction of focal solutions to the problem of limits on government, and this implied the need to obtain concessions from both sides.

Third, Suárez sought to create the cooperative equilibrium by inventing a new tradition of inclusion, moderation, negotiation, and compromise. The result was the construction of trust and reciprocity. Nearly all the major parties to the negotiations compromised their ideals, but with the important exception of elements on the right which supported the military coup of 1981 and factions in the Basque country, nearly all judged themselves better off under the compromise than the alternatives.

Fourth, the parties created a range of structure and process limits on the government that protect what most individuals and groups considered most dear. These limits helped mitigate the rationality of fear mechanism and hence provide the basis for mutual security. First, consider the features benefiting the right. The right obtained protections for the capitalist system, an absence of reprisals for action under Franco, and a constitutional monarchy instead of a republic. The military obtained a specific charge to protect the constitution and the integrity of Spain. The Catholic Church retained a privileged role, though not one as extensive as that under the Franco regime. The electoral law institutionalized a bias toward the rural areas, inducing a conservative element into political representation. Next, consider the features benefiting the left and the regionalists. Although the nationalists did not get regional freedom in the form they originally advocated, they did obtain considerable decentralization (only minority elements among the Basques were dissatisfied with not receiving special privileges). The left received a range of important rights, including rights of full political participation, a proportional electoral system, a general amnesty, and the promise of social legislation. Indeed, the Socialists captured the government in 1982, initiating a series of social and economic reforms and restoring the era of economic growth (Tortella 2000).

Fifth, the creation of the constitution, including a range of limits on government, provided the means for various parties to coordinate to defend it. The incentives making the limits on government credible provided the basis for mutual security. In short, the creation of the constitution was in part about creating incentives for the parties to follow it—the definition of consolidation.

The institutions of Spanish democracy, reflecting a series of pacts, had all four characteristics required by the theory to support the cooperative equilibrium: (1) the pacts defined a set of structure and process, group rights, and other limits on government; (2) virtually all parties to the agreement judged themselves better off under the pact; (3) all parties simultaneously agreed to accommodation, moderation, reciprocity, and tolerance; (4) all understood that unilateral defection could destroy the agreement, so all restrained their behavior. Moreover, per Alexander's (2002) theoretical point about the sources of moderation, the incentives for various parties to moderate their demands were not just tactical or ephemeral. Because of the self-enforcing agreements, each party could rely on the others, thus preventing the rationality of fear principle from operating. Put simply, the new institutions implied that Spanish democracy had become self-enforcing and therefore consolidated.[15]

Sixth, the creation of mutual gains helped the underlying consensus supporting the new rules. The many public votes supporting the various stages made this widespread support apparent to all. For example, not only did the constitution go through many different review stages, but the two houses of the legislature favored it by votes of 326 to 6 (with 14 abstentions) and 226 to 5 (with 8 abstentions); and in the voter referendum, 87.8 percent voted yes, 7.9 percent voted no, and 4.3 percent submitted blank or void votes (Newton and Donaghy 1997, 16).

The theory helps explain the contrast between the failed 1981 coup attempt and the successful 1936 coup. First, the absence of limits on government in the 1930s implied that the rationality of fear mechanism was at work. In the 1930s, Franco could count on large-scale support because the Republican regime genuinely scared large segments of Spanish society. Second, these fears were reinforced by the absence of reciprocity and mutual security.

Finally, let me end with some comments on the role of *fortuna*. Although the circumstances in Spain were propitious for the transition to democracy in the 1970s, nothing about the arguments here suggests that success was inevitable. As Linz and Stepan (1996) observe, there is a tendency to consider the outcome of the Spanish transition "overdetermined" and bound to succeed. But at many points during the seven-year transition, the process seemed touch and go. The sequence of events necessary for successful transition was hardly inevitable, and the absence of some may well have doomed the transition. For example, nothing about the process ensured that Suárez, an unknown on whom the king "bet the kingdom," would prove as talented, committed, or as skilled a negotiator as he turned out in practice. Nothing about the king's position ensured that he had the courage to risk confrontation with the old regime, especially during the 1981 coup; a weaker monarch (such as the previous Spanish king in 1923 or the more recent Greek king) might have acquiesced. Franco's Cortes, which passed the critical Law for Political Reform writing itself out of business, could have resisted reform, attempting instead to retain its hold on power.[16]

Several of these differences could have implied failure for the attempt to create the appropriate focal solution to Spain's conflicts. That failure, in turn, implied a strong risk of the emergence of the noncooperative equilibrium in Spain. In short, the analysis does not imply that success was inevitable. It instead emphasizes that incentives were the key to the transition and to democratic consolidation.

Conclusion

This chapter presents a new approach to democratic consolidation based on incentives. It began with a three-part definition: that no one out of power attempt to subvert democracy, that those in power follow the constitutional rules, and that citizens be willing to defend against potential violations of the rules by withdrawing their support from leaders who attempt to violate the rules. Each part of the definition is about incentives, and thus a theory of democratic consolidation must explain how these incentives arise. Put another way, democratic consolidation must explain how democracy becomes self-enforcing; that is, it must be in the interest of all actors to adhere to the rules. Although a rich literature exists on democratic consolidation (see, e.g., Higley and Gunther 1992; Diamond 1999a; Linz and Stepan 1996), these scholars study incentives only tangentially and therefore fail to provide a complete theory of consolidation.

Drawing on recent work on the theme of self-enforcing democracy (Fearon 2000; Przeworski 1991, 2001; and Weingast 1997), this chapter seeks to provide a piece of the missing link. The main theoretical logic is based on three principles. First, the rationality of fear holds that citizens are willing to support extraconstitutional action when they believe what they hold most dear is at risk by democratic governments. Second, successful constitutions must, therefore, impose limits on democratically elected governments in order to forestall the rationality of fear. Third, to survive, citizens must be willing to defend democracy, that is, to punish leaders who seek transgressions. Yet this type of coordination by citizens is problematic since people naturally disagree about the nature of their rights and about government transgression. The issue of rights and transgressions creates a complex coordination problem that citizens are unlikely to solve in a decentralized manner. Appropriately constructed constitutions can create such coordination by establishing focal solutions to the citizen coordination problem. They do so through creating structure and process, such as citizens' rights and the procedures of governmental decision making.

I apply this framework to democratization in Spain. All the elements of the story exist in the literature. Yet the literature's lack of attention to incentives implies that existing portraits of democratic consolidation in Spain remain incomplete.

The chapter shows how the main events during the democratization follow the theory. They created various forms of limits on the state that forestalled the rationality of fear, and they helped create new focal solutions to citizen coordination dilemmas. Per the theory, much of the negotiations during the critical years, 1976–78, helped create new focal solutions to citizen coordination problems through the invention of a new tradition of moderation, mutual accommodation, and reciprocity (Perez-Diaz 1990; Linz and Stepan 1996).

The process began with a series of fundamental economic, political, and social changes under the Franco regime. For example, Spain became richer, and with their new wealth, many had changed expectations. Workers became organized and demonstrated the ability to strike effectively for political reasons (Fishman 1990; Maravall 1978; Tarrow 1995). This made continuing the old regime virtually impossible. Some sort of reform was necessary for the old guard to have a hope of remaining in power. Still, democratization was not inevitable.

Serious reform began when King Juan Carlos appointed Adolfo Suárez as prime minister in July 1976. Over the next three years, Suárez negotiated a series of agreements that initiated full constitutional democracy. I show that these agreements fit the theory. In each agreement, the parties to the agreement gave up something to get something. This encouraged moderation and accommodation.

The critical pacts creating the new constitution resolved two of the most fundamental conflicts over the prior hundred years, both central issues during the ill-fated Second Republic and its demise in the Civil War of 1936–39. The first concerned the integrity of Spain, the degree of rights accorded to the Basques, Catalonia, and possibly other regions. The second concerned the form of the state—would Spain be a republic or a monarchy, what would be the institutions of public choice, what rights would citizens have, and would the state be an instrument of radical economic restructuring?

The pacts creating the new Spanish democracy satisfied the four characteristics identified by the theory as necessary to make them self-enforcing. They set up a new set of procedures to govern and place limits on the new government; they made nearly all parties better off; the parties agreed to change their behavior simultaneously; and the parties all had incentives to help defend the pacts against violations.

The one notable exception concerned elements on the right, which supported the failed coup in February 1981. This removed the last source of significant resistance to the new constitution and hence the last source willing and able to use force to subvert the system. Sometime in the year after the coup's failure, democracy in Spain became consolidated. Put in the terms of this chapter, Spanish democracy had become self-enforcing.

Notes

The author is Senior Fellow, Hoover Institution, and Ward C. Krebs Family Professor, Department of Political Science, Stanford University. The author gratefully acknowledges helpful conversations with Gerard Alexander, Robert Barros, Maite Careaga, Rui de Figueiredo, James Fearon, David Laitin, Irwin Morris, Joe Oppenheimer, and Konrad Siewierski. He also gratefully acknowledges the research assistance of Juliana Bambaci.

1. As Larry Diamond (1999a,70) suggests, "Only when this commitment to police the behavior of the state is powerfully credible (because it is broadly shared among key alternative power groups) does a ruling party, president, or sovereign develop a self-interest in adhering to the rules of the game, which makes those constitutional rules self-enforcing."

2. de Figueiredo and Weingast 1997; see also North, Summerhill, and Weingast 2000 and Weingast 2002.

3. More realistically, one might model the uncertainty about the success of this move, but I suppress this complication and assign the expected value of this choice to the players.

4. This result also shows that citizens' decisions do not depend on a simple assessment of whether the risk of abuse is more likely than not. The reason is that they must weight the risks by how they value the outcomes. For large threats, they may rationally react to threats with very low probability.

5. The concepts of structure and process are developed in McCubbins, Noll, and Weingast 1989 and elaborated with respect to the constitution in Weingast 2002.

6. A host of authors note that coups take place in democracies only when coup leaders expect considerable support. See, for example, Alexander 2002, chap. 1; Linz 1978b, 85–86; and O'Donnell and Schmitter 1986, 27.

7. Further, Linz (1978a, 170) emphasizes "the enormous discontinuity and inexperience of the political personnel of the regime." As he shows, there was very little continuity among members of the legislature after each election.

8. Moreover, over the years of the Franco regime, the younger priests held views different from those of the Civil War generation (see Perez-Diaz 1993, chap. 3). Indeed, in 1973 the church renounced its having chosen sides in the Civil War, and many in the church actively worked for democracy.

9. The third issue, the role of the church, was substantially diminished, although Gunther, Montero, and Botella (2003, 129–30) observe that differences on this issue could still exert "a harmful influence on Spanish society."

10. Linz and Stepan (1996, 98–99) summarize the import of these differences:"If Spain had been a relatively homogeneous nation-state, like Portugal, Greece, and the Latin American cases we will discuss, the Spanish transition to democracy would probably have been completed with the approval of the constitution. However, the

strong nationalist feelings in Catalonia and the Basque Country raised problems of stateness."

11. Alexander (2002, chap. 5) is the one scholar disagreeing with this claim. He argues that the costs of maintaining the regime were falling, not rising. His main evidence for this claim is that many in the Francoist regime and its supporters believed that the regime could be continued and could continue to contain civil unrest.

12. See also Gunther, Montero, and Botella 2003, 14–15.

13. Indeed, Colomer (1995, 73) reports that Communist Party documents at this time, "far from reproducing the traditional principles of Marxism-Leninism, proletarian internationalism, and the programme for 'toppling the regime of capitalists and land-owners,' claimed that the 'essential aim' of the PCE was 'to contribute democratically to the determination of Spanish politics.'"

14. Marvarall and Santamaria (1986, 91) explain the logic noted above for the case of Spain: the new pragmatism and consolidation, "together with the common dangers experienced by most parties as a consequence of the double threat represented by terrorism or coup, clearly contributed to setting up both an encompassing network of political communication among parties, leaders, government, and opposition, and to reducing any temptation to resort to a pattern of adversarial politics with the debilitating effects it would have produced during the early stages of consolidation."

15. There exists a minor debate in the literature about whether to date consolidation of the new regime at the coup's failure or the following year with the election of the Socialists to power. Regardless of the resolution of that debate, most analysts agree that by the time the Socialists took power, Spain had successfully completed the consolidation process. Although elements of the Basques continued to oppose the regime, no group with the power to disrupt the regime had the incentive to do so. Democracy had become self-enforcing and hence consolidated.

16. Indeed, Linz and Stepan (1996, 95) report that "on the day before the vote, many close observers were not certain that the Law of Political Reform would be passed."

References

Agüero, Felipe. 1995. *Soldiers, Civilians, and Democracy: Post-Franco Spain in Comparative Perspective*. Baltimore: Johns Hopkins University Press.

Alexander, Gerard. 2002. *The Sources of Democratic Consolidation*. Ithaca, N.Y.: Cornell University Press.

Almond, Gabriel A., and Sidney Verba. 1963. *The Civic Culture: Political Attitudes and Democracy in Five Nations*. Reprinted, Newbury Park, Calif.: Sage Publications, 1989.

Boyd, Carolyn P., and James M. Boyden. 1985. "The Armed Forces and the Transition to Democracy in Spain." In *Politics and Change in Spain*, ed. Thomas D. Lancaster and Gary Prevost. New York: Praeger.

Burton, Michael, Richard Gunther, and John Higley. 1992. "Introduction: Elite

Transformations and Democratic Regimes." In *Elites and Democratic Consolidation in Latin America and Southern Europe*, ed. John Higley and Richard Gunther. Cambridge: Cambridge University Press.

Calvert, Randall L. 1989. "Reciprocity Among Self-Interested Actors: Uncertainty, Asymmetry, and Distribution." In *Models of Strategic Choice in Politics*, ed. Peter C. Ordeshook. Ann Arbor: University of Michigan Press.

Carr, Raymond, and Juan Pablo Fusi. 1981. *Spain: Dictatorship to Democracy*, 2nd ed. London: George Allen and Unwin.

Chavez, Rebecca Bill. 2000. "The Rule of Law in Processes of Democratization: The Construction of Judicial Autonomy in Latin America." Unpublished Ph.D. dissertation, Stanford University.

Colomer, Josep M. 1995. *Game Theory and the Transition to Democracy*. Aldershot Hants, U.K.: Edward Elgar.

Dahl, Robert A. 1971. *Polyarchy: Participation and Opposition*. New Haven, Conn.: Yale University Press.

de Figueiredo, Rui, and Barry R. Weingast. 1997. "Rationality of Fear: Political Opportunism and Ethnic Conflict." *Military Intervention in Civil Wars*, ed. Jack Snyder and Barbara Walter. New York: Columbia University Press.

Diamond, Larry. 1999a. "Consolidating Democracy." In *Developing Democracy*. Baltimore: Johns Hopkins University Press.

———. 1999b. *Developing Democracy*. Baltimore: Johns Hopkins University Press.

Fearon, James. 2000. "Why Use Elections to Allocate Power?" Working paper, Stanford University.

Fishman, Robert M. 1990. *Working-Class Organization and the Return to Democracy in Spain*. Ithaca, N.Y.: Cornell University Press.

Gunther, Richard. 1992. "Spain: The Very Model of the Modern Elite Settlement." *Elites and Democratic Consolidation in Latin America and Southern Europe*, ed. John Higley and Richard Gunther. New York: Cambridge University Press.

———. 1996. "Spanish Public Policy: From Dictatorship to Democracy." Working paper 1996/84, Juan March Institute, Madrid, Spain.

———, ed. 1993. *Politics, Society, and Democracy: The Case of Spain*. Boulder, Colo.: Westview Press.

Gunther, Richard, José Ramón Montero, and Joan Botella. 2003. *Democracy in Modern Spain*. New Haven, Conn.: Yale University Press.

Gunther, Richard, Giacomo Sani, and Goldie Shabad. 1986. *Spain After Franco: The Making of a Competitive Party System*. Berkeley: University of California Press.

Gunther, Richard, P. Nikiforos Diamandouros, and Hans-Jurgen Puhle. 1995. *The Politics of Democratic Consolidation: Southern Europe in Comparative Perspective*. Baltimore: Johns Hopkins University Press.

Hardin, Russell. 1989. "Why a Constitution?" In *The Federalist Papers and the New Institutionalism*, ed. Bernard Grofman and Donald Wittman. New York: Agathon Press.

———. 2002. *Trust and Trustworthiness*. New York: Russell Sage Foundation.

Heyword, Paul, ed. 1999. *Politics and Policy in Democratic Spain: No Longer Different?* London: Frank Cass.

Higley, John, and Richard Gunther, ed. 1992. *Elites and Democratic Consolidation in Latin America and Southern Europe*. Cambridge: Cambridge University Press.

Huntington, Samuel P. 1990. *The Third Wave*. Norman: University of Oklahoma Press.

Karl, Terry Lynn. 1990. "Dilemmas of Democratization in Latin America." *Comparative Politics* 23 (October): 1–21.

Linz, Juan J. 1978a. "From Great Hopes to Civil War: The Breakdown of Democracy in Spain." In *The Breakdown of Democratic Regimes*, ed. Juan J. Linz and Alfred Stepan. Baltimore: Johns Hopkins University Press.

———. 1978b. *Crisis, Breakdown, and Reequilibrium*. Baltimore: Johns Hopkins University Press.

Linz, Juan J., and José Ramón Montero. 1999. "The Party Systems of Spain: Old Cleavages and New Challenges," Working paper 1999/138, Juan March Institute, Madrid, Spain.

Linz, Juan J., and Alfred Stepan. 1996. *Problems of Democratic Transition and Consolidation*. Baltimore: Johns Hopkins University Press.

Lipset, Seymour Martin. 1963. *Political Man: The Social Bases of Politics*. Garden City, N.Y.: Anchor Books.

Maravall, José. 1978. *Dictatorship and Political Dissent: Workers and Students in Franco's Spain*. London: Tavistock.

———. 1982. *The Transition to Democracy in Spain*. London: Croom Helm.

———. 1990. "Economic Reforms in New Democracies: The Southern European Experience." *East South System Transformations*, working paper #3, Department of Political Science, University of Chicago.

Maravall, José María, and Julian Santamaria. 1986. "Political Change in Spain and the Prospects for Democracy." In *Transition from Authoritarian Rule: Southern Europe*, ed. Guillermo O'Donnell, Philippe C. Schmitter, and Laurence Whitehead. Baltimore: Johns Hopkins University Press.

McCubbins, Matthew, Roger Noll, and Barry Weingast, 1989. "Structure and Process, Politics and Policy: Administrative Arrangements and the Political Control of Agencies." *Virginia Law Review* 75: 431–82.

Milgrom, Paul, Douglass C. North, and Barry R. Weingast. 1990. "The Role of Institutions in the Revival of Trade: The Medieval Law Merchant, Private Judges, and the Champagne Fairs." *Economics and Politics* 2 (March): 1–23.

Montero, José Ramón. 1999. "Stabilising the Democratic Order: Electoral Behavior in Spain." In *Politics and Policy in Democratic Spain: No Longer Different?* ed. Paul Heyword. London: Frank Cass.

Newton, Michael, and Peter Donaghy. 1997. *Institutions of Modern Spain. A Political and Economic Guide*. Cambridge: Cambridge University Press,

North, Douglass C., William Summerhill, and Barry R. Weingast. 2000. "Order, Disorder, and Economic Change: Latin America vs. North America." In *Governing for Prosperity*, ed. Bruce Bueno de Mesquita and Hilton Root. New Haven, Conn.: Yale University Press.

O'Donnell, Guillermo, and Philippe C. Schmitter. 1986. *Transitions from Authoritarian*

Rule: Tentative Conclusion About Uncertain Democracies. Baltimore: Johns Hopkins University Press.

Perez-Diaz, Victor. 1990. "The Emergence of Democratic Spain and the 'Invention' of a Democratic Tradition." Working paper 1990/1, Juan March Institute, Madrid, Spain.

———. 1993. *Return of Civil Society: The Emergence of Democratic Spain*. Cambridge: Harvard University Press.

———. 1999. *Spain at the Crossroads: Civil Society, Politics, and the Rule of Law*. Cambridge: Harvard University Press.

Podolny, Joel. 1993. "The Role of Juan Carlos I in the Consolidation of the Parliamentary Monarchy." In *Politics, Society, and Democracy: The Case of Spain*, ed. Richard Gunther. Boulder, Colo.: Westview Press.

Przeworski, Adam. 1991. *Democracy and the Market*. New York: Cambridge University Press.

———. 2001. "Democracy as an Equilibrium." Working paper, New York University.

Putnam, Robert. 1993. *Making Democracy Work: Civic Traditions in Modern Italy*. Princeton, N.J.: Princeton University Press.

Riker, William H. 1986. "Vote Trading at the Constitutional Convention." In *The Art of Political Manipulation*. New Haven, Conn.: Yale University Press.

Rustow, Dankwart A. 1970. "Transitions to Democracy." *Comparative Politics* 2: 337–63.

Schelling, Thomas. 1960. *Strategy of Conflict*. Cambridge, Mass.: Harvard University Press.

Tarrow, Sidney. 1995. "Mass Mobilization and Regime Change: Pacts, Reform, and Popular Power in Italy (1918–1922) and Spain (1975–1978)." In *The Politics of Democratic Consolidation: Southern Europe in Comparative Perspective*, ed. Richard Gunther, P. Nikiforos Diamandouros, and Hans-Jurgen Puhle. Baltimore: Johns Hopkins University Press.

Tortella, Gabriel. 2000. *The Development of Modern Spain: An Economic History of the Nineteenth and Twentieth Centuries*. Cambridge: Harvard University Press.

Valenzuela, Arturo. 1978. *The Breakdown of Democratic Regimes: Chile*. Baltimore, Md.: Johns Hopkins University Press.

Weingast, Barry R. 1995. "A Rational Choice Perspective on the Role of Ideas: Shared Belief Systems and State Sovereignty in International Cooperation." *Politics and Society* 23 (December): 449–64.

———. 1997. "The Political Foundations of Democracy and the Rule of Law." *American Political Science Review* 91 (June): 245–63.

———. 1998. "Political Stability and Civil War: Institutions, Commitment, and American Democracy." In *Analytic Narratives*, ed. Robert Bates, Avner Greif, Margaret Levi, Jean-Laurent Rosenthal, and Barry R. Weingast. Princeton, N.J.: Princeton University Press.

———. 2002. "Self-Enforcing Constitutions: With an Application to American Democratic Stability." Working paper, Hoover Institution, Stanford University.

Institutionalizing Constitutional Democracy
The Role of Courts

TRANSITIONS TO constitutional democracies are, as scholars have long recognized, ongoing and complex processes. While the basic framework of the democratic system is established by the enactment of a formal constitution, the fine-grained institutional structure evolves over time as the product of the legal and political interactions among various political actors. In principle, constitutional courts play an important role in this evolution, primarily through their authority to resolve constitutional disputes by interpreting the constitution's basic provisions.

In this chapter we investigate the role of constitutional courts in the development of constitutional democracies over time. More specifically, we demonstrate how strategic models of judicial decision making help us to build explanations of the role of courts in this historical process. The intuition that judges act strategically is an old one, traced back to the early work of Glendon Schubert (1958) and, most especially, Walter Murphy (1964). The recent revival of interest in the strategic behavior of judges is part of a broader emphasis on strategic analysis in the study of social and political institutions. It has taken many forms (game theory, spatial models, statistical analysis, historical research), but it rests on the basic proposition that judges often act strategically in the pursuit of various personal, policy, institutional, and jurisprudential goals (Epstein and Knight 1998.)

We proceed as follows. First, we briefly explain the logic of a strategic approach to judicial decision making. Second, we offer two examples of how such an approach helps to explain how constitutional courts can directly affect the development of constitutional democracies. Third, we discuss the implications of these analyses and the strengths and weaknesses of the approach.

The Strategic Approach to Judicial Decision Making

On the strategic account, (1) social actors make choices in order to achieve certain goals, (2) social actors act strategically in the sense that their choices depend on their expectations about the choices of other actors, and (3) these choices are structured by the institutional setting in which they are made (see, generally, Elster 1986).

GOALS

The strategic approach assumes that judges are goal-oriented. What it does not assume is that judges have any particular goal that they pursue. Under the strategic account, it is up to the researcher to specify a priori the actor's goals; the researcher may select any motivation she believes that the particular judge holds. Most of the existing research on the strategic behavior of judges posits that justices pursue policy, that is, their goal is to see law and public policy reflect their preferences. But this need not be the case (Baum 1997). Judges may pursue an array of possible goals. They may, for example, be motivated by a concern for institutional legitimacy, causing them to either select or avoid cases based on their potential to influence the long-term legitimacy of the courts. Or they may be motivated by a concern for adhering to particular jurisprudential principles, such as original intent or plain meaning. The only relevant constraint placed on judicial motivations by the strategic approach is that judges desire to be efficacious, in the sense that they want their goals instantiated in the nature and content of the law over time.

INTERDEPENDENCE

A judge faces an interdependent choice whenever the outcome that follows from that choice depends on the choices of other legal and political actors. While varying with the particular type of court on which the judge sits, the number of actors on which the outcome depends may be substantial. Consider the justices on the U.S. Supreme Court. For an individual justice on the Court, there are three sets of actors whom she must consider in assessing the implications of her own choice for the ultimate legal outcome: the other justices on the Court, the relevant actors in the other branches of government, and the American people. For each of these groups, the choices of the other actors affect the ability of the individual justice to achieve her goals. In regard to the other justices, the interdependence is straightforward; the Supreme Court's decision is a product of the choices of the nine justices. In regard to the other branches of government, the interdependence is a function of the checks and balances established in the constitutional scheme of separation of powers. In regard to the American people, if the Court is going to be effective in establishing its decision as the law which the public will accept and comply with, it must take account of the potential responses of the public to its decisions.

A simple example will demonstrate the implications of interdependence for the nature of a strategic judge's choice. In offering the example we want to clarify the difference between the strategic decision-making model and an alternative account, the attitudinal decision-making model, to which it is often mistakenly compared.[1] The attitudinal model predicts that judges base their decisions on their normative and policy-based attitudes, without attention to the implications of the choices of the other justices. The fact that the attitudinal approach does not acknowledge a strategic component to decision making leads to very different predictions about judicial behavior.

Consider the following example. Suppose a justice must choose one of three alternative standards of review to apply in abortion cases. Further suppose that she sincerely prefers "compelling interest" (least restrictive standard) to "undue burden" (moderately restrictive standard) to "rational basis" (most restrictive standard). Theoretically speaking, if she is motivated in the way assumed by, say, those attitudinal models that suggest a direct connection between personal attitudes and voting, the prediction is simple enough. She would always choose "compelling," regardless of the positions of her colleagues. That is because she makes decisions that are in accord with the background characteristics that produce her attitudes—characteristics that do not change after she has ascended to the bench. The strategic account, on the other hand, supposes that the justice might choose "undue burden" if, depending on the preferences of the other players (e.g., her colleagues), that would allow her to avoid "rational basis," her least preferred outcome.

INSTITUTIONAL CONTEXT

The interdependent decisions that judges face are structured by the institutional setting in which they are made. Goal-oriented judges face complex strategic decisions in their efforts to affect the law. In the case of the U.S. Supreme Court, the justices must take account of three different strategic relationships: the relationships among the justices, of the Court to the other branches of government, and of the Court to the public (Epstein and Knight 1998). Their success in crafting particular laws depends on their ability to anticipate the reactions of the other actors in their decisions. That is, the effectiveness of an individual justice depends on how skillful she is in developing reliable expectations of the actions of others. It is in this task of expectation formation that social, legal, and political institutions play a crucial role.

On this strategic account, institutions are treated as rules, rules that structure the various relationships involving judges. Rules help strategic actors by providing information about how people are expected to act in particular situations (Knight 1992). For example, certain expectations are established by the rules of the road; we cannot drive safely unless we know what to expect from others at lights and stop signs. Court rules perform the same kind of function.

For institutions to play this role, however, two conditions must hold. First, only those rules that are widely known and generally accepted by members of the community will be effective. When knowledge of the rules is socially shared, people have a common basis for anticipating the choices of other actors. This is not to say that rules determine exactly what people are going to do—a driver may not stop at a red light—but rules establish the constraints on the range of acceptable behavior. Second, before an individual can confidently rely on institutional rules as a basis for expectation formation, she must have good reason to believe that other actors will comply with them. If she is confident that others will comply, then she can use the rule to establish expectations about how others will act and respond to her actions. The most common situation in which these two conditions are satisfied is the case of pure coordination. In such a case, the information alone is enough to ensure compliance because the information gives the actors an incentive to comply with the rules. This is the logic of self-enforcing institutions and the primary mechanism of compliance for informal conventions and norms.

But in situations where the interaction is more complicated than the case of pure coordination, information alone may not ensure compliance. In this type of situation, sanctions become important. Two types of sanctions, formal and informal, are relevant to our analysis. Formal sanctions are attached to a state's legal rules; if an actor does not comply with the law, public officials may punish him. In the case of Supreme Court justices, impeachment is an extremely severe form of sanction for noncompliance with the law. Informal sanctions are attached to the various conventions and norms that evolve over time to structure social relations. If an actor does not comply with these social norms, it is likely that the other actors will apply informal sanctions, which can range from ostracism to a refusal to interact cooperatively with the offending party. Such norms and the accompanying sanctions are the primary sources of institutional constraint on Supreme Court justices. If a justice occasionally violates a norm, the other justices can invoke simple forms of informal sanctioning as a way of reinforcing the validity of the norm. For example, when a chief justice violates the opinion assignment norm by selecting a writer from among the members of the minority, justices in the majority may temporarily challenge his authority. But if a justice (or a group of justices) consistently fails to conform to prevalent legal norms, the informal sanction might be outright rejection of her decisions, resulting in her loss of legitimacy and, ultimately, her efficacy. In either case the pri-

mary effect of sanctions is to increase the costs and diminish the benefits of
noncompliance with institutional rules.

In developing an analytical framework for studying the strategic behavior
of judges, the institutional context in which the judges act is a fundamental
feature of that framework. We must take account of the internal rules relevant to collegial courts, where applicable, as well as the external rules, both
laws and norms, that structure the relationship between courts and other social actors.

Constructing Explanations of How Constitutional
Democracies Develop Over Time

In order to effectively use the strategic approach to develop explanations of
how constitutional democracies develop over time, it is necessary to identify
the following features of the process or outcome to be explained: (1) the
goals and beliefs of the judges, (2) the goals and beliefs of the other relevant
actors, and (3) the institutional context in which the judges make their decisions. If these factors can be properly identified, then the strategic approach
can be employed for a wide range of explanations about the court's role in a
constitutional democracy. In this section we offer two sketches of how the
strategic approach can explain how courts affect the institutionalization of
constitutional democracies. They differ in the level of generality sought in
the explanation. The first example is an effort to develop a general framework for analyzing how courts interact with the other branches of government to establish the basic institutional structure of the democratic system.
The second example is more specific, an effort to construct an explanation
of a particular historical event in the more general institutional process. In
the two examples we employ different analytical tools, demonstrating some
of the variety of methods available for developing strategic explanations.

A GENERAL FRAMEWORK

Epstein, Knight, and Shvetsova 2001 proposes a general approach for assessing the role of constitutional courts in the establishment and maintenance of constitutional democracies. It is intended to generate testable
propositions about judicial decision making in emerging democratic societies. As we noted in the introduction, the process of institutionalizing a
constitutional democracy is a complex one, and courts can have a significant
effect on that process through their authority to resolve constitutional conflicts. But the court's capacity to effectively use this authority is, in important
ways, a function of its legitimacy. It is to the question of the effects of the legitimacy of the constitutional court that this approach is specifically addressed.

The basic idea underlying this approach is that the legitimacy of any constitutional court is in significant part a product of the ongoing strategic interactions between the court and the other branches of government. These interactions can be modeled as a strategic game among the three branches. For this particular analysis, we constructed a model of the Russian constitutional system, but the model could be adapted to take account of the specific characteristics of any constitutional democracy. This model takes the form of a strategic interaction between a constitutional court (CC) and three elected actors: a president (P); an upper chamber (UC) of parliament, with representatives from each region within the society; and a lower chamber of parliament (LC), which is drawn nationwide. The interaction between the court and these other actors begins with CC deciding whether to take a case involving a particular policy issue and, if it accepts the case, where to place the policy. After CC makes this decision, the other actors must decide (1) whether to modify, override, evade, or otherwise disregard CC's decision and (2) whether to directly affect CC in some other way. These sorts of "attacks," we assume, may have short- and long-term effects on the court. In the short term, they may nullify or render inefficacious particular decisions (Eskridge 1991a, 1991b; Vanberg 1999). In the longer term, they may chip away at the court's legitimacy; that is, their impact may accumulate over time such that CC itself becomes an ineffective political institution (Ahdieh 1997; Gibson, Caldeira, and Baird 1998; Knight and Epstein 1996).

We further assume that all actors involved in this interaction have positions, what we call "most preferred positions," over a given policy space, that is, the position where they would ideally like to see government policy placed. Figure 8.1 depicts these points over a two-dimensional space in an environment in which the actors' preferences are separable and utility functions are linear. Each dimension represents a range of solutions to a constitutional question potentially facing the court. The general framework is applicable, in principle, to any such question. For purposes of this example, we have chosen two general institutional dimensions which are likely to face any constitutional court in an emerging democracy: separation of powers and federalism. As illustrated, the president (P) and the upper chamber (UC) and lower chamber (LC) hold distinct positions on the separation-of-powers dimension, with P favoring a strong executive system and the chambers preferring one that endows significant authority to the parliament. CC is between the two on this dimension; it also takes a middle position, somewhat between P and the LC on the one side and UC on the other, on the federalism dimension, which taps the extent to which actors desire a government that is centralized (at one extreme) or decentralized (at the other).

All actors prefer policy that is as close as possible to their ideal points, but they are not unfettered in their ability to achieve that goal. Beginning with

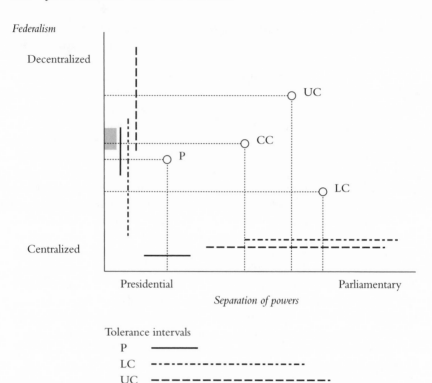

FIGURE 8.1 Hypothetical set of preferences and tolerance intervals of key governmental actors

the elected actors, because they may incur costs associated with challenging a decision produced by the court (Eskridge 1991b; Rodriguez 1994), they may be willing to tolerate policy that is not on their ideal points. Specifically, an interval—what we called a tolerance interval—exists around each of their ideal points such that they would be unwilling to challenge a court decision placed within that interval.

Those intervals, which the figure depicts for the president and the upper and lower chambers and which are common knowledge among them and the constitutional court, represent the elected actors' *ex ante* assessment of the relative costs and benefits of attempting an "attack" on the court. To make that assessment, as previous literature suggests, these actors take into account four factors, some of which speak to the particular case at hand and others, to the court itself: (1) case salience—the degree to which the case under consideration by the court is especially relevant or important to them (e.g., Canon and Johnson 1998; Epstein and Knight 1998; Vanberg 1999); (2)

case authoritativeness—the ability of the justices to produce a clear, consensual ruling in the general legal area at issue in the dispute (e.g., Eskridge 1991a; Kluger 1976; Murphy 1964); (3) public (specific) policy preferences—the position of the public, in policy space, with regard to particular matter under review (e.g., Barzilai and Sened 1997; Vanberg 1999); and (4) public (diffuse) support for the court—the confidence the public has in the court (e.g., Caldeira 1987; Gibson 1989, 1991; Holland 1991; Vanberg 1999). Each, in turn, serves to define the breadth of tolerance intervals over a particular court decision, such that (1) the less salient the case, (2) the more authoritative past decisions within the general issue area, (3) the closer the court's policy is to the public's preferences, and (4) the more confidence the public has in the court, the longer the tolerance interval (and vice versa).

For policies falling within their tolerance interval, the actors have calculated that the benefits of acquiescing to the court's decision override the cost of an attack; for policies falling outside the interval, they have determined that the benefits of an attack outweigh the costs of acquiescence; and for policies at the extreme ends of the interval, they are indifferent between attacking and not so doing. Note, though, that the inclusion of the confidence dimension ensures that the judges on the court can contribute to the court's own well-being. If the judges are attentive to the preferences of relevant actors, then their institution's legitimacy should increase over time, assuming that they reach decisions that other actors accept and with which they comply. In our model, this requires the court to either reach decisions that are within the intersection of tolerance intervals or avoid disputes for which no intersection exists. What this, in turn, suggests is that tolerance intervals can increase (or decrease) over time, quite apart from the particulars of a dispute (Ahdieh 1997; Caldeira 1987).

Finally, given that attacks on the court may have both short- and long-term effects on its ability to establish efficacious decisions and, more generally, its legitimacy in society, the court itself is constrained by the existing tolerance intervals of the elected actors. If, for example, CC places a case on its agenda and decides that dispute outside a range acceptable to these actors, it runs the risk of producing a decision that the president, lower chamber, and upper chamber will attempt to overturn or ignore; if such decisions accumulate, they may work to undermine CC in the eyes of, say, the public, thereby shortening the elected actors' tolerance intervals over the long term. That is because, to reiterate, the elected actors construct their tolerance intervals with some attention to the public's overall (or diffuse) support for the court, and not just on the basis of those factors relevant to a particular dispute (Caldeira 1987; Smith 1996). On the other hand, if the court over time accepts and decides cases within the overlap of the tolerance ranges, not only will the elected actors implement those decisions but there also will be a cumulative effect on the court's legitimacy and its ability to maximize its policy preferences; in the long run, the tolerance intervals will expand, thereby giving CC a good deal more leeway, both in terms of case selection and decision making (Epp 1998; Caldeira 1987; Volcansek 1991).

Figure 8.1 enables us to explore these conditions. Consider, first, the separation-of-powers dimension. In this example, the intersection of the tolerance ranges is empty, meaning that the court is maximally constrained. Any decision may be subject to attack by one or more elected actors. Because, under such circumstances, CC cannot safely issue any ruling on the merits, we would expect to see it avoiding such disputes—that is, not accepting them for review, much less resolving them on their merits. Federalism presents a different story. On this dimension, the intersection of the tolerance ranges is nonempty (represented by the gray area in the figure), suggesting that the CC could place policy anywhere in this set. Even more to the point, since the court's ideal point falls within the intersection, it is able to act as if it were an unconstrained actor—not only accepting federalism cases but deciding them as it desires.

From this relatively simple model emerge several rather intriguing conceptual predictions about the ability of constitutional courts to establish legitimacy and credibility within their societies. The first set of predictions centers on the short term. If courts wish to issue efficacious decisions, then they will not accept petitions for review that involve policy dimensions for which an intersection of tolerance ranges does not exist; so doing would lead elected actors to challenge them or their decisions. Rather they will accept cases involving policies for which the tolerance set is nonempty and will reach decisions, within that set, that are as close as possible to their ideal points.

The second set of predictions focuses on the longer term. If courts agree to resolve disputes that involve policy dimensions for which an intersection of tolerance ranges does not exist and do so repeatedly over time, then they shorten those tolerance ranges. This, in turn, makes it more difficult for them to exercise discretion over case selection (as well as to issue decisions in line with their policy preferences) and to establish their legitimacy. Alternatively, if courts accept cases involving policies for which the tolerance set is nonempty and reach decisions within that set, then they lengthen the tolerance intervals. Such has the effect of making it easier for them to exercise discretion over case selection and, in turn, to issue decisions in line with their policy preferences and establish their legitimacy.

Taken collectively, these hypotheses have direct bearing not only on case-level decisions but also on the aggregate level. We should see particular kinds of disputes dominating courts' agendas (in our example, federalism), with others (in our example, separation of powers) remaining unresolved—at least until the actors' preferences change or the tolerance intervals alter in length. While some portion of these changes may be beyond the control of the justices (such as, turnovers in the parliament or presidency), they can affect the other by taking into account the preferences of the relevant actors.

There are three compelling features of the predictions generated by our model. First, we can assess them in various contexts. That is because the predictions (1) are not, in the main, bound to any particular society—be it an established democracy or democratizing society—and (2) seek to capture the process by which judicial tribunals establish and maintain legitimacy—a process with which all courts grapple (Goebel 1971; Knight and Epstein 1996). Second, the predictions sit comfortably with existing literature, that is, they square with the insights generated by a range of studies—from those that focus on public opinion (Gibson, Caldeira, and Baird 1998) to formal (Barzilai and Sened 1997; Eskridge 1991a, 1991b; Knight and Epstein 1996; Vanberg 1999), statistical (Spiller and Gely 1992; Vanberg 1999), and jurisprudential (Ahdieh 1997; Smithey 1999) treatments of judicial decision making.

Third and related, a good deal of anecdotal evidence exists to support the predictions our model generates. Some of this comes from the U.S. context, specifically from studies of the early Supreme Court, which show that the justices would have been unable to establish efficacious policy had they failed to take into account the desires of other key actors and the nature of the political environment under which they were operating (Alfange 1994; Epstein and Walker 1995; Graber 1998; Knight and Epstein 1996). In the next section of this chapter, we illustrate this dynamic with a game-theoretic treatment of a seminal case in the development of the Supreme Court—*Marbury v. Madison*. We show how the establishment of the prerogative of judicial review depended upon a constellation of preferences among key political actors that was conducive to the extension of judicial authority.

Evidence for the significance of the preferences of key political actors for the extension of judicial authority also emanates from the comments of various contemporary constitutional court justices, both in emerging and established democracies, which lend credence to the notion that they do, in fact, take into account external political actors when they set their agendas and reach their decisions, as well as acknowledge the importance of cultivating the public's confidence (e.g., Ahdieh 1997; Attanasio 1994; Nikitinsky 1997; Reid 1995; Vanberg 1999). There also is scattered support for the idea that elected officials may be willing to tolerate court decisions that do not fall on their ideal points. Georg Vanberg's (1999) interviews with members of the *Bundestag* provide some, as does commentary offered by observers of the Eastern European political scene (e.g., Savitsky 1995; Waggoner 1997). Finally, in an effort to assess the research potential of the model, we did a preliminary analysis of the decisions of the Russian constitutional court in the 1990s. While the analysis was very tentative, it did show that the trajectory of decisions of the Russian court during this period was quite consistent with the predictions of the model.

More generally, this analysis has important substantive implications for questions about the role of constitutional courts in a democratic society. In the initial stages of the transition to a constitutional democracy, if the legitimacy of the constitutional court is low, as will commonly be the case, the court is caught in an uncomfortable dilemma. At a time when the emerging democracy is most in need of a way of resolving basic constitutional questions, such as the distribution of authority among the branches of government, the court is least able to do so effectively. That is, for courts that are concerned about establishing their own long-term authority and power in their constitutional systems, they will be least willing to consider basic questions about the authority and power of the other branches of government.

And this suggests a potentially fundamental point about the role of these courts in the early stages of transition to a constitutional democracy. Their primary role will be to reinforce those features of the constitutional system about which there is already substantial agreement. As for those issues about which there is greater disagreement, new constitutional courts will leave those for another day, either for the day when these issues have been resolved through political agreement by the other branches or when the courts themselves have solidified their own place in the constitutional system.

A SPECIFIC HISTORICAL CASE

In Knight and Epstein 1996, we use game theory to analyze a critical event in American history: the struggle between President Thomas Jefferson and Chief Justice John Marshall in the early 1800s that led to the enunciation in *Marbury v. Madison* (1803) of the Supreme Court's power of judicial review. The sequence of interactions between Jefferson and Marshall is characterized by many of the conditions that prove fundamental in the general framework discussed above.

At issue in *Marbury* were several judicial appointments that President John Adams had made but that the incoming president, Jefferson, refused to deliver. When William Marbury, who was denied his commission, brought suit, the Supreme Court, led by Chief Justice Marshall, had to decide whether to force the new administration to deliver the commission. Certainly Marshall, himself an Adams appointee, wanted to give Marbury his appointment. But at the same time, Marshall was well aware of the serious repercussions of ordering the administration to do so. Jefferson made no secret of his disdain for Marshall; he had threatened to impeach some of the justices or weaken the Court in other ways. Marshall was confronted with a dilemma: vote his sincere political preferences and risk the institutional integrity of the Court and possibly his own job, or act in a sophisticated fashion with regard to his political preferences and elevate judicial supremacy in a way that Jefferson could accept.

As this set of events is taught in American government, judicial politics, and constitutional law courses and as it is treated in scholarly accounts and textbooks, Chief Justice Marshall generally emerges the victor because the dispute over the commissions was resolved without injury to the Court and, more important, the principle of judicial review was established. Yet scholars posit a range of reasons for Marshall's success; they also disagree over why both Marshall and Jefferson took the strategic paths they did (see, e.g., Alfange 1994; Boyd 1971; Dewey 1970; Stites 1981). Our use of a game-theoretic framework permits us to disentangle competing claims and explanations in a highly systematic way. Our analysis allows us to assess factors fundamental to most explanations of the Jefferson-Marshall conflict: the political and institutional preferences of the actors, the strategic structure of the political interaction in which the constitutional dispute arose, and the larger political environment in which the conflict took place.

In Knight and Epstein 1996 we modeled the Jefferson-Marshall conflict as an extensive-form game. In the course of the analysis we constructed two versions of the game, the difference being in the assumption we made about Jefferson's preferences about judicial review. A detailed analysis of the two versions of the game is beyond the scope of this chapter.[2] But for our purposes here, the primary reason for discussing the game is to demonstrate how strategic analysis can be used to enhance our explanations of historical events.

Historians disagree over whether Jefferson supported or opposed the practice of judicial review, so we analyzed the game under both assumptions. We posited two classes of motivations, the political and the institutional. By political, we meant that the actors cared about the advancement of their partisan causes and their parties. In this context, there were two relevant political factors. The first involved the resolution of the problem of the appointments and presented two alternatives: appointments going to the Democratic-Republicans (as desired by Jefferson) or to the Federalists (as desired by Marshall). The second—involving the consequence of Jefferson's use of the impeachment strategy—also presents two alternatives: success or failure on Jefferson's part if he tried to invoke it.

By institutional, we meant that the actors were concerned with the relative power and authority of the political branches of government. In this context, two aspects of the judiciary were at issue: its structure (the Repeal and Amendatory Acts, which attempted to restructure the federal judiciary in ways closer to the interests of the Democratic-Republicans) and its supremacy (judicial review). On the structural dimension, the alternatives were successful establishment of the Repeal Act, the status quo, and the unsuccessful attempt to establish the Repeal Act. On the judicial review dimension, the alternatives were establishment of judicial review, the status quo, and failure to establish judicial review.

The historical record suggests that Marshall and Jefferson were differentially concerned about these various dimensions (see, e.g., Beveridge 1919; Haskins and Johnson 1981; Malone 1970; Warren 1926). Given our extensive review of the historical sources, we ranked the dimensions as follows for the two actors: Marshall (judicial supremacy > judicial structure > political) and Jefferson (judicial structure > politics > judicial supremacy). With these assumptions we constructed utility functions for both actors.

In addition, we needed to incorporate the fact that the Jefferson-Marshall conflict took place in a political context in which the actions of Congress affected the likelihood that either actor would successfully achieve his goals. More specifically, Jefferson's success in any effort to impeach Marshall was a function of the political actions of members of Congress, and neither Jefferson nor Marshall knew with certainty what Congress would do if Jefferson attempted impeachment. Rather, they had at best a belief that there was a particular probability that Jefferson would be successful. To capture these probabilities, we distinguished two states of the world at each node at which Jefferson attempted impeachment: a political environment in which Jefferson would be successful in his impeachment effort and one in which he would fail. In assessing the relative merits of the various strategies available to them, both Jefferson and Marshall had to base their decisions on assessments of these probabilities.

Through the use of the two game-theoretic models, we sought to test the plausibility of different historical claims about why the Marshall-Jefferson conflict produced the outcome that it did. But, it is worth stressing, we used the idea of testing loosely. What our study attempted to do was to take advantage of the fact that game theory involves counterfactual analysis.[3] That is, the solutions to these models entail claims about what actors will do under certain conditions and what they would have done differently if the conditions were different. By varying the relevant conditions in the game, we could assess the relative merits of the historical counterfactuals that underlie the different explanations of this period.

In making such assessments, our primary focus was on those conditions inducing equilibrium behavior that replicated historical events. If a model induces behavior similar to the historical choices we observe, then it highlights the importance of the conditions that produced the behavior. If a model fails to reconstruct previously observed events, then it calls into question explanations based on the conditions embedded in it. While replication alone does not definitively answer the question of why an event occurred, it can lend strong support to the explanation at hand.

The solutions to the two games identified several equilibria that were characterized by different sets of assumptions about the actors' preferences and about their beliefs about the political environment in which the conflict took place.[4] These assumptions can be associated with various explanations offered by historians of the period. The equilibria that most closely replicated the actual historical pattern of events—Marshall denies Marbury the commission, the Repeal Act is established by Congress and affirmed by the Court, Jefferson chooses not to act against Marshall, and the Court successfully asserts the power of judicial review—is supported by the following important assumptions: Jefferson was not opposed to judicial review, and both Jefferson and Marshall believed that the political environment of the day favored Jefferson's interests.

This leads us to the following conclusion. The political conflict between Jefferson and Marshall exemplifies the dynamic and incremental nature of the process of institutionalizing democracy. At the time of the framing of the U.S. Constitution, the role of the judiciary in the three-branch structure of American democracy was underdeveloped. The major long-term consequence of the Jefferson-Marshall interaction was a restructuring of the institutional division of labor among the branches. And this was, in large part, a result of the short-term political interests of the two major political parties. The Supreme Court's authority for judicial review emerged, not because of some complex intentional design and not because of some brilliant strategic move by Marshall in the face of overwhelming political opposition, but merely because it was politically viable in the existing environment. Put simply, Marshall took the actions that he did because it was the best he could do at the time.

Discussion

Constitutional democracies are not so much designed and planned as they are the product of a complex web of legal and political interactions. And these interactions are characterized by mixed motives on the part of the relevant actors; while they seek to establish an institutional solution that can be accepted by all of the parties, they prefer an outcome that favors their own institutional and policy interests. The task of explaining the development of constitutional democracies over time is primarily a task of understanding how these various interactions affect the evolution of democratic institutions.

The analyses that we have discussed here identify an important role for constitutional courts in that historical process. But they also identify a set of significant political constraints on the efficacy of these courts' efforts. The resulting picture is of a set of justices who act in a strategic and often highly political manner in their effort to interpret the constitution and to resolve constitutional disputes. While it might seem obvious to many that law is politics and courts are political actors, these analyses do more than reinforce this view. The strategic approach helps us to identify the particular causal mechanisms that are a necessary part of any adequate explanation of how and why the courts may or may not affect the evolution of democratic institutions at any specific historical moment.

In the theoretical analysis of the separation-of-powers scheme in an emerging democracy, the formal model was used to generate testable propositions about the short- and long-term choices of courts and about the interactive effects of the separation-of-powers system on the development of legal institutions. In the historical analysis of *Marbury v. Madison*, the game-theoretic model was used to assess counterfactual claims about the legal and political interactions that resulted in the norm of judicial review. The primary contribution of the strategic approach in both of these cases is to identify and analyze in a systematic way the interdependent dimension of the interplay of goal-oriented actors.

At the same time, these analyses illustrate the importance of combining rational choice models with other methods and approaches in order to provide complete and adequate explanations of these historical processes. Fundamental to the development of such explanations is an account of the preferences and beliefs of the actors and the institutional context in which the decisions are made. The plausibility of the explanation depends in large part on the relationship between the assumptions made about the factors in the models and the actual circumstances that we seek to explain. For explanations of particular historical events such as the Jefferson-Marshall conflict, the relationship between assumptions and actual circumstances is of paramount importance. The requirement in such cases that the preferences and beliefs posited by the model be empirically accurate is obviously a stringent one. For example, the plausibility of the explanation of the emergence of the norm of judicial review is contingent on the plausibility of the claims about preferences and beliefs.

On the other hand, for theoretical analyses such as the model of the separation-of-powers system, the relationship between the assumptions of the model and actual circumstances is more complicated. The purpose of models like the separation-of-powers model discussed in the previous section is to provide a framework for a general analysis of legal and political institutions and for broader analyses of legal and political processes. Such analyses produce a variety of claims that can be differentiated in terms of potential sets of preferences and beliefs. At the theoretical level, concern about the empirical accuracy of the assumptions is of less immediate relevance, as the primary focus is on the logic of social and institutional processes. The relationship between assumptions and actual circumstances becomes increasingly relevant when we want to assess the empirical plausibility of these claims. Then the relevant question becomes, for what sets of actual circumstances are the general theoretical claims appropriate? If there are important sets of actual circumstances that match the assumptions on which the claims are based, then the propositions generated by the model are relevant for explanations of actual legal processes.

Now, what this suggests is that in the construction of explanations of law and judicial decision making, the strategic approach will be to a greater or lesser extent dependent on other approaches for the provision of relevant evidence of the nature of preferences, beliefs, and institutional context. This fact seems to form the basis of a common criticism of rational choice approaches to law, that rational choice approaches may be appropriate but for rather limited and unimportant factors. In this form the criticism implies that explaining and providing evidence of the nature and content of preferences and beliefs is the hard work and the most important part of an explanation of judicial decision making. But this view underestimates the fundamental importance of the social interactions that affect how preferences and beliefs lead to legal and political outcomes. The two cases of legal and political decision making discussed in the previous section provide but two examples of the crucial effects of interactive choice on legal outcomes. Knowledge of the content of preferences and beliefs alone would not, in and of itself, lead to adequate and plausible answers to the questions under consideration in these examples.

The central role of social interdependence in law in general and the courts in particular provides the primary justification for the strategic approach to law and judicial decision making. In our efforts to understand the role of courts in the development of constitutional democracies over time, the importance of understanding the legal and political interactions that produce change in the system cannot be underestimated. Such a focus serves to highlight the central role of constitutional courts in this historical process.

Notes

1. For a comprehensive analysis of the differences between attitudinal and strategic approaches in the social sciences, see Barry 1978.

2. See Knight and Epstein 1996 for a presentation of the formal model of the two games.

3. For an excellent and informative discussion of the role of counterfactual reasoning in game-theoretic analysis, see McCloskey 1987.

4. It is important to note that when we use game theory to assess the merits of historical explanations, the key to the analysis is the way in which we define the conditions of the game (including the definition of the actors' preferences). From the very logic of this form of analysis, it follows that the solutions to games will be sensitive to changes in the conditions that are posited in the particular model. Thus a valid criticism of the kind of analysis we presented in this paper would not rest on the fact that the solution of any model is sensitive to changes in the parameters. Rather, an appropriate criticism would focus on weaknesses in the historical claims that we incorporate in the definitions of the conditions of the game.

References

Ahdieh, Robert B. 1997. *Russia's Constitutional Revolution: Legal Consciousness and the Transition to Democracy, 1985–1995.* University Park: Pennsylvania State University Press.

Alfange, Dean, Jr. 1994. "Marbury v. Madison and Original Understandings of Judicial Review: In Defense of Traditional Wisdom." *Supreme Court Review* 1993: 329.

Attanasio, John B. 1994. "The Russian Constitutional Court and the State of Constitutionalism." *St. Louis Law Journal* 38: 889.

Barry, Brian. 1978. *Sociologists, Economists, and Democracy.* Chicago: University of Chicago Press.

Barzilai, Gad, and Itai Sened. 1997. "How Do Courts Establish Political Status, and How Do They Lose It? An Institutional Perspective of Judicial Strategies." Presented at the annual meeting of the American Political Science Association, Washington, D.C.

Baum, Larry. 1997. *The Puzzle of Judicial Behavior.* Ann Arbor: University of Michigan Press.

Beveridge, Albert J. 1919. *The Life of John Marshall.* Boston: Houghton Mifflin.

Boyd, Julian P. 1971. "The Chasm That Separated Thomas Jefferson and John Marshall." In *Jefferson*, ed. A. Koch. Englewood Cliffs, N.J.: Prentice-Hall.

Caldeira, Gregory A. 1987. "Public Opinion and the U.S. Supreme Court: FDR's Court-Packing Plan." *American Political Science Review* 81: 1139.

Canon, Bradley C., and Charles A. Johnson. 1998. *Judicial Policies: Implementation and Impact*, 2nd ed. Washington, D.C.: CQ Press.

Dewey, Donald O. 1970. *Marshall Versus Jefferson: The Political Bacjground of Marbury v. Madison.* New York: Knopf.

Elster, Jon. 1986. *Rational Choice.* New York: New York University Press.

Epp, Charles R. 1998. *The Rights Revolution.* Chicago: University of Chicago Press.

Epstein, Lee, and Thomas G. Walker. 1995. "The Role of the Court in American Society: Playing the Reconstruction Game." In *Contemplating Courts*, ed. L. Epstein. Washington, D.C.: CQ Press.

Epstein, Lee, and Jack Knight. 1998. *The Choices Justices Make.* Washington, D.C.: CQ Press.

Epstein, Lee, Jack Knight, and Olga Shvetsova. 2001. "The Role of Constitutional

Courts in the Establishment and Maintenance of Democratic Systems of Government." *Law and Society Review* 35: 117–64.

Eskridge, William N., Jr. 1991a. "Overriding Supreme Court Statutory Interpretation Decisions." *Yale Law Journal* 101: 331.

———. 1991b. "Reneging on History? Playing the Court/Congress/President Civil Rights Game." *California Law Review* 79: 613.

Gibson, James L. 1989. "Understandings of Justice: Institutional Legitimacy, Procedural Justice and Political Tolerance." *Law and Society Review* 23: 469.

———. 1991. "Institutional Legitimacy, Procedural Justice, and Compliance with Supreme Court Decisions: A Question of Causality." *Law and Society Review* 25: 631.

Gibson, James L., Gregory A. Caldeira, and Vanessa A. Baird. 1998. "On the Legitimacy of High Courts." *American Political Science Review* 92: 343.

Goebel, Julius. 1971. *Antecedents and Beginnings to 1801.* Vol. 1, *History of the Supreme Court of the United States.* New York: Macmillan.

Graber, Mark A. 1998. "Establishing Judicial Review? *Schooner Peggy* and the Early Marshall Court." *Political Research Quarterly* 51: 221.

Haskins, George L., and Herbert A. Johnson. 1981. *Foundations of Power: John Marshall, 1801–1815.* Vol. 2, *History of the Supreme Court of the United States.* New York: Macmillan.

Holland, Kenneth M., ed. 1991. *Judicial Activism in Comparative Perspective.* New York: St. Martins.

Kluger, Richard. 1976. *Simple Justice.* New York: Random House.

Knight, Jack. 1992. *Institutions and Social Conflict.* Cambridge: Cambridge University Press.

Knight, Jack, and Lee Epstein. 1996. "On the Struggle for Judicial Supremacy." *Law and Society Review* 30: 87.

Malone, Dumas. 1970. *Jefferson the President: First Term, 1801–1805.* Boston: Little, Brown.

McCloskey, Donald. 1987. "Counterfactuals." *The New Palgrave: A Dictionary of Economics,* ed. J. Eatwell, M. Milgate, and P. Newman. New York: Stockton.

Murphy, Walter F. 1964. *Elements of Judicial Strategy.* Chicago: University of Chicago Press.

Nikitinsky, Leonid. 1997. "Interview with Boris Ebzeev, Justice of the Constitutional Court of the Russian Federation." *Eastern European Constitutional Review* 83 (winter).

Reid, Fispeth. 1995. "The Russian Constitutional Court, October 1991–October 1993." *Co-existence* 32: 277.

Rodriguez, Daniel B. 1994. "The Positive Political Dimensions of Regulatory Reform." *Washington University Law Quarterly* 72: 1.

Savitsky, Valery. 1995. "Judicial Protection of Personal Rights in Russia." In *Legal Reform in Post-Communist Europe: The View from Within,* ed. S. Frankowski and Paul B. Stephan II. Dordrecht, Holland: Martinus Nijhoff.

Schubert, Glendon. 1958. "The Study of Judicial Decision Making as an Aspect of Political Behavior." *American Political Science Review* 52: 1007–25.

Smith, Gordon B. 1996. *Reforming the Russian Legal System.* Cambridge: Cambridge University Press.

Smithey, Shannon. 1999. "Strategic Assertions of Judicial Authority." Presented at the annual meeting of the Midwest Political Science Association, Chicago, Ill.

Spiller, Pablo T., and Rafael Gely. 1992. "Congressional Control or Judicial Independence: The Determinants of U.S. Supreme Court Labor-Relation Decisions." *RAND Journal of Economics* 23: 463.

Stites, Francis N. 1981. *John Marshall: Defender of the Constitution.* Boston: Little, Brown.

Vanberg, Georg Stephan. 1999. "The Politics of Constitutional Review: Constitutional Court and Parliament in Germany." Ph.D. diss., Political Science, University of Rochester, Rochester, New York.

Volcansek, Mary L. 1991. "Judicial Activism in Italy." In *Judicial Activism in a Comparative Perspective*, ed. K. M. Holland. New York: St. Martin's.

Waggoner, Jeffrey. 1997. "Discretion and Valor at the Russian Constitutional Court: Adjudicating the Russian Constitutions in the Civil Law Tradition." *Indiana International and Comparative Law Review* 8: 189.

Warren, Charles. 1926. *The Supreme Court in United States History.* Boston: Little, Brown.

Conclusion

Rational Choice and Theoretical History

THE INTRODUCTORY CHAPTER by Irwin Morris and Joe Oppen-heimer gives a picture of the basic principles of the rational choice tradition, its method, its psychological and institutional starting points, and its norma-tive theory. It brings out the value and interest of rational choice models. The rest of the volume reinforces the argument in favor of rational choice by providing a broad range of examples showing what it can do. A puzzle still remains, it seems to me: why has this tradition become so deeply con-troversial? In this chapter I begin by considering those controversies and then paint a picture of the rational choice tradition, which seems to me less vulnerable to some of the more passionate attacks.

Some critiques of rational choice are fairly easy to handle. If some of it is empirically sloppy, as Ian Shapiro and Donald Green (1994) have charged in a famous critique, we will need to make it less so. But we can certainly rely on a broad consensus in favor of good empirical tests, both within rational choice and outside it. This should be a matter for routine scientific contro-versies about individual research projects, not the sort of Big Battle that has emerged over rational choice as a whole. Something else must be going on.

To deal with the deeper controversies (which are more likely to be the real sources of anti-rational-choice passions), it is useful to note that rational choice is not what many people think it is. And it is evolving in new and unexpected directions. In this chapter I want to emphasize especially the growing role of what I call "theoretical history" in rational choice. This is an important theme in most of the chapters of this book and in many ways its chief organizing principle. It seems that rational choice is becoming increas-ingly historical, and it is time to make this intellectual evolution both more explicit and more emphatic.

Rational choice theory has provoked very strong and passionate opposition, in political science and sociology especially. Its proponents have been puzzled by this; why is so much passion brought to bear? What is really at stake? On the surface the debate may be, say, about the empirical adequacy of rational choice claims, or the flimsiness of the empirical tests used (Shapiro and Green 1994). But if that is in fact what the debate is about, then there is much room for agreement between the proponents and opponents of rational choice. Not many people on either side of this debate oppose solid empirical grounding of theories. So that hardly explains the heated rhetoric.

One can only speculate about the source of the passion, but there are two very plausible candidates. Rational choice is seen as "hyper-positivist," so preoccupied with being a science in some strong sense (with special emphasis on mathematical rigor and deductive logic) that it forgets the distinctive qualities of the subject it studies and even the need for proper empirical grounding. And it is also seen as cynical, unable to see in human beings anything more than simpletons who either manipulate or are manipulated. But rational choice theories and models need not be either.

The rational choice tradition has developed so far a deep understanding of one aspect of human decisions and interactions: instrumental rationality. This aspect is especially prominent in market interactions, where it has been made more visible by the measuring rod of money. Hence rational choice theory, however far back we can trace its origins (to Hobbes, say), clearly made its first significant strides within economics. And now many of its proponents, as well as its critics, identify the rational choice tradition with the study of instrumental rationality, or even with the (cynical) view that instrumental rationality is all there is. And it is true that some of the most implausible claims and models produced by rational choice theory are the product of a too dogmatic commitment to the view that all human choice is a product of instrumental rationality, that we only manipulate the world and each other.

But while rational choice attracts its share of cynics, it is hardly committed to cynicism. In fact a great deal of interesting work has been put into the development of models and theories that accommodate cognitive limits, selves with a complex structure, various altruistic and moral motivations, noninstrumental forms of rationality, and nonrational forms of commitment. Among the most famous and interesting have been Thomas Schelling's (1960) analysis of the strategic uses of irrational commitments; Amartya Sen's (1977) discussion of rational fools; Howard Margolis's (1982) model of altruism; various works of Jon Elster, especially his *Ulysses and the Sirens* (1979) and *Sour Grapes* (1983); George Ainslie's (1992) pico-economics; Ronald Heiner's (1983) model of rule following; and Serge Christophe Kolm's (1985) rational choice Buddhism.[1]

And rational choice is hardly "hyper-positivist" either, even if often presented in positivist garb. It certainly includes those who would deny serious cognitive status to normative theory, and to history, but it also includes important contributions to normative theory, political philosophy, and theories of institutional design as well as what I will call "theoretical history." The rational choice tradition is a developing project. Its simplest form concerns the principles governing the choice of individuals acting alone (these are sometimes called games against nature). It develops a far greater power and complexity when applied to principles of choice in situations of strategic interaction, where what one person should do depends on what others do. This is the subject of game theory. And it has now added in a number of different ways the dimension of time. This is clearest in games in extended form, in which players take decision-making turns, and in various models which study choices in *sequences* of games. It is now moving also to study the large-scale transitions of macro history, the development of social order, of the state and of democracy prominent among them. A number of chapters in this book are excellent examples of this trend: Jonathan Bendor and Piotr Swistak on the development of social order (Chapter 2), Robert Bates, Avner Greif, and Smita Singh on the dynamics of kinship societies (Chapter 3), Barry Weingast on the consolidation of democracy (Chapter 7), or Jack Knight and Lee Epstein on the role of constitutional courts in the development of constitutional democracies (Chapter 8).

Rational Choice and the Battle over Positivism

A commonly accepted map of intellectual terrain in the social sciences centers around the battle between positivists, committed to unity of science, and hence to the natural sciences as a methodological and theoretical model for the social sciences, and their opponents. For some of the opponents, the study of social phenomena should rely more on a methodological rapprochement with the humanities, developing narrative histories and the interpretation of the social world as text. For others it should aim to perform an emancipatory function that is largely out of place in the natural sciences or the humanities (Habermas 1971, 1973), or it should be normative in the manner of political philosophy and theories of institutional design more broadly.

There is no place in this picture for the rational choice tradition. In some ways it belongs in the avant-garde of scientific principles in the social sciences, more strict in its methodology and more precise in its logic. The style of thought of rational choice is more deductive (and less inductive) as well as more precise and analytical than the available alternatives in the social sciences. It is persistent, in a manner quite reminiscent of the natural sciences, in its search for the microstructure of social phenomena. In this way rational choice belongs on the positivist side.

But positivist social science has also developed in opposition to the mixing of normative and explanatory theory, and in opposition to history. On these matters the rational choice tradition is distinctly unpositivist. Normative theory has been an element of rational choice in at least two ways. The theory of instrumental rationality, which is at the heart of this tradition, is a normative theory (it tells us what we ought to do), even if it is limited to instrumental norms and principles (which guide us only in the choice of means, not of ends). Normative social choice and the theory of constitutional and institutional design have also been a part of this tradition from its beginnings. We include among the "classics" of rational choice Kenneth Arrow's *Social Choice and Individual Values* (1963) and James Buchanan and Gordon Tullock's *The Calculus of Consent* (1962), for example. This tradition is continued in a variety of ways, as we see in the chapters of Part 2 of this volume, on institutional design.

Even more strikingly, an increasing amount of work in rational choice has become historical. Some of it is obviously so, in a manner any historian will recognize (a clear recent example is Bates et al. 1998). But much of the recent rational choice work is more subtly historical. It proposes accounts of sequences of events (as a history would) but does so in the form of models, unrelated to any explicit narrative. So an important new theme in rational choice is its development of various forms of theoretical history. Some of it is micro history, history in the small—sequences of decisions in a game, or sequences of games. But increasingly the rational choice tradition tackles the great transitions of history: the transition from anarchy to institutional order and to the state, or transitions to democracy. These grand transitions of macro history are the organizing topics of our volume. Rational choice theorists tackle these transitions in a very distinctive way, continuous with the distinctive qualities of their tradition. The reader will find here some of the *questions* of the great masters of theoretical macro history from the past. But the answers will be of a different order.

Deductive and Analytical Style

So what is distinctive about the rational choice tradition? What does it bring to bear on these macro-historical questions? We will probably find no agreement on this issue among the authors and editors of the present volume, let alone in any larger group. Some people think that the idea of rational choice itself is central. Others emphasize methodological individualism or reliance on mathematical models. Some people even think that the assumption of human self-interest is central. But if we want to disentangle rational choice tradition from the battle between positivists and antipositivists and help along the new forms of theoretical history which we present in this volume, a different emphasis may be more useful.

It will be good to begin with what is most obvious. Among the main characteristics of the rational choice tradition is its deductive and analytical style of thought, which it shares with many natural sciences. The deductive style of thought takes basic principles and pushes them as far as they will go. Its main instrument is deductive logic, which allows the deductive derivation of conclusions from those principles. And the perfect example is a deductively constructed axiomatic system. In empirical sciences the main alternative to it, or its principal complement, is the inductive style, which concentrates on establishing facts ("What is really going on?" is its central question) and adapts our picture of the world to fit the facts that it establishes. Any empirical science, it seems to me, must contain at least some elements of the inductive style (though some philosophers of science come close to denying this, most famously Karl Popper [1962]). But different sciences and different traditions within the sciences can differ quite substantially in the balance of styles within them. Certainly a notable feature of the rational choice tradition is the dominance of the deductive style and the weakness of the inductive style.

The analytical style is also strong in rational choice, with its attempts to identify and distinguish different component parts of complex situations and to reconstruct the microstructure of the social world. The analytical style applies in the world of ideas the same art of separation that Michael Walzer (1984) identified as a fundamental practical art of the liberal democratic tradition (separating state and church, state and dynasty, state and property, separating the different powers of the state, and so on). In the practical sphere the key idea is the division of labor or of tasks. This allows people to develop specialized skills and distinct incentives. In the intellectual sphere we follow a similar logic; we separate components and elements to better understand social life, but also to improve it and manipulate it more effectively. We develop precise and reliable pictures of its microstructure—how it works in the small, what are its component parts and how they interact.

There are two effective instruments for doing so, both first more fully developed and articulated during the scientific revolution in the sixteenth and seventeenth century. The first is an intellectual strategy which relies on precise abstractions; the second is experiment (and various approximations of experiment). What are precise abstractions? Consider some examples from law. A law requiring everyone to pay a tax of precisely 15 percent on all their income is about as precise as a law can be. And it is abstract and general; it refers to only one general property of the people subject to it (their income), and it treats all income the same, no matter whose income it is. A law

220 KAROL EDWARD SOLTAN

that is specific, by contrast, will single out some individual or small group for special treatment. Joe McDonald's company shall be able to deduct the losses it incurred in the search for oil (say). This is not good law, and it is not an abstract proposition.

There is another kind of law, also bad law, which is in some sense quite general but also fails the precise abstraction test. Let us say that, out of concern with fairness, we write a law which simply requires that the tax on each individual be as equitable as possible, taking into account all relevant considerations. And we set up a special agency of experts in tax equity to determine in each individual case what would be the appropriate tax. Here the problem is not the absence of generality or abstractness, but the extraordinary vagueness of the law. Both science and the rule of law favor precise abstraction over these other styles. In science the specific and telling case can be used as evidence but does not substitute for general principles. And the vague generalizations are entirely condemned.

Abstractions allow us to think about one element of a situation at a time, ignoring—for the moment at least—all other elements. We think of the world one component at a time. Experiments allow us to go one step further. We don't simply think about the world one aspect at a time; we systematically study the effects of one element or factor in the situation, also ignoring all other factors. In an experiment we don't passively observe the world; we manipulate the world. We change it one aspect at a time, allowing us to separate the effects of different aspects of the world. It is no accident, it seems to me, that the rational choice tradition is committed to precise abstractions in its theoretical formulations *and* contains one of the most active programs of experimental research in the social sciences (Plott 1979; Ledyard 1995). Both are instruments for the discovery of the microstructure of the social world, including the microstructure of politics.

When we search for microstructures, we necessarily look at the world in the small. Among the rational choice theorists, this search has often led to the adoption of methodological individualism, the principle that only properties of individuals matter in decisions. But this is not the only possibility. Institutions, cultures, ideas understood as something standing independently of individuals can be seen to matter as well. And this is increasingly recognized by many rational choice theorists. But we won't know how they matter in any useful way unless we have a picture of the microstructure of their possible influences. So methodological individualism is not required by the search for the microstructure, but a rejection of vague notions of institutional and cultural influence is required.

Rational Choice

There is little doubt about the deductive and analytical style of the rational choice tradition, a style it shares with many of the "hard" sciences. But beyond this, the distinctive qualities of rational choice are quite unlike what we find in physics or chemistry. The notion of rational choice itself identifies a key strategy, which is quite unorthodox if measured by the usual scientific standards and "positivist" criteria. It incorporates normative theory into explanatory models, mixing the normative and the positive. The axioms and principles of rational choice are normative; they identify what decision makers ought to do, given the ends they have and the constraints of the situation they encounter.

Mixing normative and positive principles is often seen as an old-fashioned, prescientific practice familiar in political philosophy, or in prescientific political and social commentary, but long since abandoned by serious social science (and promoted by its "anti-positivist" critics). And many rational choice theorists are at best ambivalent about this unorthodox feature of their models. Some minimize its significance or even deny its existence. And some do in fact avoid it by substituting alternative behavioral assumptions. But they are a minority. Most rational choice models happily incorporate a normative component.

Early pioneers, William Riker and Peter Ordeshook (1973) prominent among them, used the term *positive political theory* to identify the then new rational choice approach in political science. But that name was misleading then, and it is even more misleading now. Normative theory has a significant place in the rational choice tradition, even in models designed only to explain, and more obviously so in the numerous theories with an explicit normative purpose. Despite its frequent positivist rhetoric, and the frequent anti-positivist rhetoric of its critics, the rational choice tradition does not fall in line here with positivist practice; it mixes the normative and the positive.

What is the source of this peculiarity? It is illuminating to see it in a larger intellectual context (see Johnson 1991). The key step, I believe, is to see the microstructure of human decisions as a joint product of various skills (competence) and of errors, so we can distinguish between competence and performance. The strategy is to see human action as a product of two types of factors: competence, which can be formulated in normative terms, as various forms of rationality, and accidents and errors (including systematic accident and error). Instrumental rationality of the kind incorporated in the standard models of rational choice is one example of the sort of normative theory that is in question here. What is the microstructure of a choice then? It is a combination of the operation of some set of normative principles (e.g., those of instrumental rationality) combined with errors and accidents.

In some applications it is enough to consider one set of normative principles (instrumental rationality) and to neglect our propensity to error and accident. This might be taken as the standard case in rational choice theory. But it is hardly a necessary assumption.

Seen in this way the intellectual strategy of rational choice theory is partly shared with generative grammar in linguistics (to take a prominent example), though the details are of course entirely different. Generative grammar had its origins in Noam Chomsky's (1965) critique of the then dominant behavioral approach in linguistics (see also Lyons 1970). Instead of trying to predict and explain actual linguistic behavior or "performance," Chomsky proposed to give a fully rigorous description of the rules language speakers and hearers use in distinguishing grammatical from ungrammatical sentences. This is what Chomsky called linguistic (or, more precisely, grammatical) competence. The goal of generative grammar is to give a mathematical reconstruction of those rules. What people actually say would then be seen as a product of these rules combined with various forms of error. In rational choice theory, we do something similar. To understand what people actually do, we develop accounts of competence as well as accounts of departures from competence. Rational choice theory centers on an account of one kind of competence, the choice of best means when the ends (or preferences, or utility functions) are given.

This strategy of disaggregating the microstructure of choice into competence and error seems to me the best response to the growing experimental evidence that human beings do not in fact choose in a manner consistent with the normative theory of rational choice. This was of course well known for many years (see Simon 1957; Lindblom 1959, 1965; Braybrooke and Lindblom 1963), but the research program of Daniel Kahneman and Amos Tversky (1979) really drove the point home. Kahneman and Tversky themselves famously conclude that the mistake in rational choice theory is precisely to combine the normative and positive function. They want to preserve the rational choice account of choice as an exclusively normative theory. But they develop a quite different account, which they call prospect theory, for how people actually choose. And that account has no normative component. In short, they explicitly reject the competence plus error strategy.

Kahneman and Tversky's experiments (and those by others, in what is now a large literature: Grether and Plott 1979; Machina 1987; Quattrone and Tversky 1988; Cook and Levi 1990; Moser 1990; Tversky, Slovic, and Kahneman 1990; Rabin 1998) reveal significant features of human decision making. But their prospect theory has encountered much skepticism. Resistance to Kahneman and Tversky's prospect theory within rational choice and elsewhere is not driven (as unfriendly critics might presume) by some sort of dogmatic rejection of what are undeniably important experimental results. The complaints are rather mainly about the ad hoc, curve-fitting quality of prospect theory and its overwhelmingly inductive style. There is no fundamental principle in prospect theory, and hence no deeper explanation of the way people make decisions. Choice is simply seen as a product of a series of distorting and editing moves. And when new evidence of irrationality is found, we can simply add to the distortions prospect theory allows. We can fit the curve to new data without any limit. This sort of curve-fitting exercise turns theory into nothing more than a list. A more systematic alternative is called for, and a number have been developed, many following in some way the competence plus error strategy.[2]

What then, to conclude, does rational choice bring to the topics it studies? It brings a preference for deductive theorizing and a commitment to discover the microstructure of social phenomena, and to see the microstructure of decisions as a combined product of competence and accident. And this describes well the intellectual style of the new theoretical history, which emerges from rational choice.

Theory, History, and Social Science

One of the great debates in the development of the social sciences has centered on the proper role of history in the study of social phenomena. One camp has favored narrative nontheoretical history, the history of "traditional" historians. The more "positivistically" inclined social scientists, by contrast, favored the identification of universal laws of human behavior, which hold independent of time and place. Or they specified universal functions which must be performed for any society to survive, again without regard for time and place. They wanted to exclude history from the social sciences. Sociological and anthropological functionalism (Malinowski 1926; Merton 1957; Parsons 1964) as well as early versions of rational choice theory were prominent examples of this attitude. Nonhistorical forms of explanation were eagerly embraced in economics, sociology, and political science.

It is especially interesting to see, therefore, the transformation of large research areas of the rational choice tradition into increasingly historical forms, not into narrative history (the kind of history that focuses on telling the story of what happened), but into history nonetheless. It is striking how historical rational choice has become. Only a few decades ago one could still write of it as an alternative to historical approaches. Now a great deal of rational choice is better seen as a form of *theoretical history*, which has been the third camp in the perennial battles over the role of history, a camp that does not reject history but also promotes theory. This is both a deep transformation and a very promising one. Much research and model development now assumes that social phenomena are best understood as products of *sequences of events* (hence historically), but develops abstract theories of those sequences (rather than presenting them in a narrative form). This new kind of theoretical history occupies much of this volume.

Theoretical history has a long and distinguished past (see generally Lowith 1949; Brun 1990; Galtung and Inayatullah 1997). It began as a branch of theology, attempting to discern the work of God through time, as in the works of St. Augustine or Joachim of Fiore. It then transmuted into the philosophy of history, in the works of Giambattista Vico (1948 [1744]), Georg Hegel (1956, 1975), and others. And finally, it has become social theory in the works of Alexis de Tocqueville, Auguste Comte, Karl Marx, and Max Weber, and in more recent forms of Marxism, Weberian theories of rationalization, and the broad range of theories of modernity and modernization, now complemented by theories of postmodernization (see Janos 1986; Bell 1973; Inkeles and Smith 1974; Giddens 1990; on postmodernization, see Inglehart 1997). All these theories, and many others, are efforts to identify large trends in macro history, stages in the development of humanity as a whole. They identify some large-scale direction in history toward greater rationality, or the development of productive forces, toward greater liberty, or toward a communist society. In some cases they identify an inevitable cycle, such as the rise and decline of civilizations. These works have typically paid little attention to the microstructure of history. And those concerned with microstructure of social life have returned the favor, for the most part ignoring history. Contemporary rational choice theory is now posed to correct this deficiency, as we hope this volume demonstrates.

Today the field of theoretical history in its traditional form as macro history has lost much of its former intellectual splendor. There are some remnants of it in accounts of modernization and postmodernization, and perhaps a halfhearted attempt at revival in Francis Fukuyama's work *The End of History and the Last Man* (1992). The rational choice tradition will not revive this kind of theoretical history. The work we see in the pages of this volume requires two very substantial modifications of how we think about theoretical history. First, the idea of theoretical history must be separated from the idea of the laws of history, which make the future in some way inevitable and hence predictable. The future is in part a product of unpredictable human creativity, including the development of new ideas, unknowable in advance. It is also decisively influenced by accidents, coincidences, sheer luck or its absence. Machiavelli and the Italians of the Renaissance called this "fortuna," as does Weingast in Chapter 7 of the present volume. Fortuna undermines all inevitability in history. Second, the new kind of theoretical history is more deductive and analytical and is grounded in the microstructures of history. It reflects, in short, the intellectual style of rational choice thinkers.

It is based on models of the microstructure of politics and human interaction, and it mixes positive and normative theory in a quite distinctive way. And, for the moment anyway, it centers on models of instrumental rationality (it need not; see Soltan 1998).

Theoretical History

Works in theoretical history aim to be both stories and theories. A story is an account of a sequence of events, linked in some fashion by logic or causality. It can take the form of a narrative, an account that mixes the abstract with the particular, aiming to present the sequence in a vivid and memorable way. Its chief goals (Aristotle says) are to instruct (to teach the lessons of history, for example) and to entertain. The more analytical and deductive alternative, which the new kind of theoretical history proposes, aims to make clear instead the general features of the sequence. Its chief goal is precision, even at the price of sacrificing the vivid and the memorable. And it abandons (I regret to report) the goal of entertaining. Above all, it defines more precisely the kind of "instruction" it aims for; it either explains or it guides our conduct.

No story can ever convey everything that happened (nor would any audience want this). This is true of the narratives of storytelling, journalism, and history. It is also true of the more abstract models of theoretical history. In all these cases we give an account of what was most important to us, or to our audience, or most important in light of a theory. We communicate only what is in our judgment the "essence of the situation." Or, as Robert Bates and his coauthors put it, "by modeling the processes that produced the outcomes, we seek to capture the essence of stories" (Bates et al. 1998, 12). There is nonetheless a clear difference between a game theoretical model identifying a sequence of decision points and a story about the sequence. We see a gain in precision and a loss in entertainment value. We really do pay attention to only one type of thing at a time. The picture is spare; we add no telling detail to give it life or to make it more vivid.

Still, like all narratives, theoretical history is a construction which must contain three elements: a starting point, a sequence of events or transitions, and an end point. This defines a path, and there is much talk of paths and path dependence in rational choice–based theoretical history (North 1981, 1990).

A great deal depends on the choice of the starting point and the end point. One possibility is that we take both to be real events or real situations. Then our story is likely to be an effort to explain how we actually got from the starting point to the end point. And we can describe these points both in a fairly abstract way and with more detail—since these were events and situations that actually happened. "Analytic narratives" are an example. In a volume under that title, Bates and coauthors (1998) propose them as an approach that mixes narrative and models, historical detail and abstract theory. Analytic narratives concern themselves with real sequences and attempt to provide a simplified explanation of how these sequences happened.

Theoretical history takes quite a different form in the models of Bendor and Swistak (see Chapter 2). Here the start and the end are not real situations in real history. Rather the start is an abstractly defined situation in which an important feature of the real world is missing. All agents are only interested in maximizing their own income. There is no altruism, no love or envy, and no concern with justice. The end is a similar situation but now including these more social features of human motivation. The models, then, are an attempt to explain why those features exist, by showing how one must necessarily get from the starting point to the end point, from an asocial to a social world. The sequences involved do not consist of real historical events; we do not turn to historians for information about when or where they happened. But the explanation involved is based on an abstract account of a sequence of events. It is a highly general and abstract form of theoretical history.

In normative models the path is constructed differently. The start is a situation we should move away from; the end is the situation we should move toward. The model does not tell us that we will witness inevitable progress from start to end. But it might tell us how to move in that direction and what to expect along the way. The starting point is some specification of an undesirable, bad, or wrong state; let us call it hell. The end point is some specification of the desirable, good, or perfect state. We could call it heaven. Among examples of heaven we will find wealth, democracy, or peace. Among examples of hell we have the war of all against all, a world of pure selfishness, or anarchy, or the realm of necessity, in which change occurs only through Darwinian and other biological mechanisms, without any role for choice, decision, or design. From poverty to wealth we have a theory of economic development. From tyranny to democracy we have a theory of democratic development. And from war of all against all to peace we have another example of a path from a hell to a heaven. We identify conditions or strategies favorable (or unfavorable) to change in one or the other direction on the specified path from start to end, or from end to start. Or in a more deductive model, such as that of Bendor and Swistak, we specify the necessary and sufficient conditions for the movement from the start to the end. Generally speaking, normative models ought to tell us two things: what hell and heaven look like in detail and what we ought to do in order to get from hell to heaven as they see them.

In between the starting point and the end point in our theoretically reconstructed path of history, we will find whatever basic units of the microstructure of history we propose. These may be moves in a game consisting of many moves. Or they may be games played in sequence. Or they may be transitions in issue space. Or the basic units of history may be more varied. We may want to consider separately the political logic that allows an issue to enter the agenda of a system, the logic that maintains it on the agenda (allowing movement in the relevant issue space), and the logic that removes it. The issue may be quite narrow and specific, such as a particular provision of the tax code. Or it may concern the nature of the political regime. So, for example, a democratic regime is unsettled when its democratic nature gets on the agenda of the political system, as it becomes a subject of political strategies, threats, and promises of some significant political actors. And a democratic regime is consolidated when its democratic nature ceases to be a significant issue for any of the players who matter. As Weingast emphasizes in Chapter 7, this does not require a consensus of any significant kind. We only need circumstances in which no important actor has an incentive to make an issue of democracy (no matter how much the actors might dislike it).

We thus have transitions from and to democracy and different degrees of consolidation of democracy. In rational choice we look at these transitions as products of interactions among purposive agents, each facing distinctive incentives. We don't see them as causal products of some set of variables in the back of politics, so to speak, such as modernity, economic development, or economic inequality. Politics and strategic interaction is the fundamental causal process through which, and only through which, these other factors can work.

Whether in a narrative or in a mathematical model, our account of the sequence of events must have unity and coherence. We often obtain such unity because the sequence of events has the same players and a continuing setting. For that to happen we must have both agents and various objects that have a continuing existence throughout those events. These continuing agents and objects will typically be of four types: people and other decision-making agents (organizations or states, for example), institutions (rules and ideals), ideas and systems of ideas, and (finally) physical objects. When thinking about all of them, and when attempting to model the way they enter politics (and human interaction more generally), we can often apply many of the ideas and models originally developed for capital in economics. And so in addition to modeling physical capital, we also speak of people as human capital, of organizations, rules, and networks as institutional or social capital, and of systems of ideas as cultural capital. In all those cases human agents will often face similar choices: should we use the capital we control or have access to for immediate gain, or should we rather make sacrifices to improve it, or to maintain and protect it, or in some cases to destroy it (gaining immediate military advantage perhaps, but also improving the credibility of threats for the future)? So we can think of history as a sequence of events which involve the improvement, destruction, maintenance, or use of these various forms of capital (see Soltan 1998). But we also keep in mind that these different object types are in some ways entirely not like physical capital, so we are also ready to develop alternative models of agents, institutions, ideas, and physical objects, and of the role they play in sequences of political interactions. The state, democracy, and courts are all forms of social capital, but this fact does not in itself add a great deal to our understanding of the development of the state, or democratic consolidation, or the institutionalization of the role of the courts, to take three examples from chapters of this volume.

The recent turn toward new institutionalism is commonly presented as a recognition that institutions matter, coupled with a continued commitment to a serious theoretical account of their nature and role (Langlois 1986). But this is misleading. New institutionalism does not limit itself to the recognition of the importance of institutions; it adds that ideas and cultures matter as well. The significant innovation is rather the turn toward a more historical style. Institutions, ideas, and cultures develop over time, and they constrain events today based on their evolution through events of the past. New institutionalism is less about institutions and more about recognizing the importance of political battles of the past (which established those institutions) as constraints on the political battles of the present. The real message is not that institutions matter but that the *past* matters.

Does this sound too obvious to be worth such emphasis? It cannot be *that* obvious, given the widespread popularity of a-historical models and explanations. But it is also in some ways counterintuitive and tends to undermine widely held assumptions about politics and the structures of power. Power structures, on this more historical view, turn out to have a time dimension in a way we are reluctant to recognize. The dead actually have significant amounts of power. And many of our contemporaries who appear to have power, because they get their way, are actually only lucky, since their preferences happen to coincide with those who really do have the power (even though they may be dead), those who have established the institutions which now constrain choice.

If history matters, then agents from the past have power today, and our models of power structures should reflect this. Current outcomes are in part determined by institutions and ideas which have been established and modified over time and reflect the power structures of the earlier times. Thus the simple agent-centered picture of power structures criticized by Eric Nordlinger (among others, see his work of 1981) as involving only different balances among current players (a power elite, or a pluralism of interest groups, or a hierarchy of classes) is actually doubly wrong. Institutions and ideas have power today, and the past has power over the present. Power structures must be seen as having a dimension of time; such is one lesson of theoretical history.

Notes

1. See more generally Elster 1988 and Mansbridge 1990.
2. One example is regret theory (see Loomes and Sugden 1982). We have also seen various attempts to formalize earlier models of "imperfect rationality," such as Herbert Simon's satisficing (1957) or Braybrooke and Lindblom's incrementalism (Lindblom 1959, 1965; Braybrooke and Lindblom 1963), formalized by Jonathan Bendor (1995). The connection between error-proneness and rule following is developed by Ronald Heiner (1983).

References

Ainslie, George. 1992. *Pico-Economics: The Interaction of Successive Motivational States Within the Individual*. Cambridge: Cambridge University Press.

Arrow, Kenneth. 1963. *Social Choice and Individual Values*. New York: Wiley.

Axelrod, Robert. 1984. *The Evolution of Cooperation*. New York: Basic.

Bates, Robert, Avner Greif, Margaret Levi, Jean-Laurent Rosenthal, and Barry Weingast. 1998. *Analytic Narratives*. Princeton, N.J.: Princeton University Press.

Bell, Daniel. 1973. *The Coming of Post-Industrial Society*. New York: Basic.

Bendor, Jonathan. 1995. "A Model of Muddling Through." *American Political Science Review* 89: 819–40.

Braybrooke, David, and Charles Lindblom. 1963. *A Strategy of Decision*. New York: Free Press.

Brun, Jean. 1990. *Philosophie de l'Histoire*. Paris: Stock.

Buchanan, James, and Gordon Tullock. 1962. *The Calculus of Consent: Logical Foundations of Constitutional Democracy*. Ann Arbor: University of Michigan Press.

Chomsky, Noam. 1965. *Aspects of the Theory of Syntax*. Cambridge: MIT Press.

Cook, Karen, and Margaret Levi, eds. 1990. *The Limits of Rationality*. Chicago: University of Chicago Press.

Elster, Jon. 1979. *Ulysses and the Sirens: Studies in Rationality and Irrationality*. Cambridge: Cambridge University Press.

———. 1983. *Sour Grapes*. Cambridge: Cambridge University Press.

———, ed. 1988. *The Multiple Self*. Cambridge: Cambridge University Press.

Fukuyama, Francis. 1992. *The End of History and the Last Man*. New York: Free Press.

Galtung, Johan, and Sohail Inayatullah, eds. 1997. *Macrohistory and Macrohistorians*. Westport, Conn.: Praeger.

Giddens, Anthony. 1990. *The Consequences of Modernity*. Stanford, Calif.: Stanford University Press.

Grether, David, and Charles Plott. 1979. "Economic Theory of Choice and the Preference Reversal Phenomenon." *American Economic Review* 69: 623–38.

Habermas, Juergen. 1971. *Knowledge and Human Interests*. Boston: Beacon Press.

———. 1973. "A Postscript to *Knowledge and Human Interests*." *Philosophy and the Social Sciences* 3: 157–89.

Hegel, Georg Wilhelm Friedrich. 1956. *Philosophy of History*. New York: Dover.

———. 1975. *Lectures on the Philosophy of World History*. Cambridge: Cambridge University Press.

Heiner, Ronald. 1983. "The Origins of Predictable Behavior." *American Economic Review* 73: 560–95.

Inglehart, Ronald. 1997. *Modernization and Postmodernization*. Princeton, N.J.: Princeton University Press.

Inkeles, Alex, and David Smith. 1974. *Becoming Modern*. Cambridge: Harvard University Press.

Janos, Andrew. 1986. *Politics and Paradigms*. Stanford, Calif.: Stanford University Press.

Johnson, James. 1991. "Rational Choice as a Reconstructive Theory." In *The Economic Approach to Politics*, ed. Kristen Monroe. New York: HarperCollins.

Kahneman, Daniel, and Amos Tversky. 1979. "Prospect Theory: An Analysis of Decision Under Risk." *Econometrica* 47: 263–91.

Kolm, Serge Christophe. 1985. "The Buddhist Theory of No-Self." In *The Multiple Self*, ed. Jon Elster. Cambridge: Cambridge University Press.

Langlois, Richard. 1986. "The New Institutional Economics: An Introductory Essay." In *Economics as a Process: Essays in the New Institutional Economics*, ed. Richard Langlois. Cambridge: Cambridge University Press.

Ledyard, John. 1995. "Public Goods: A Survey of Experimental Research." *The Handbook of Experimental Economics*, ed. John Kagel and Alvin Roth. Princeton, N.J.: Princeton University Press.

Lindblom, Charles. 1959. "The Science of 'Muddling Through.'" *Public Administration Review* 19: 79–88.

———. 1965. *The Intelligence of Democracy*. New York: Free Press.

Loomes, Graham, and Robert Sugden. 1982. "Regret Theory: An Alternative Theory of Rational Choice Under Uncertainty." *Economic Journal*, 92: 805–24.

Lowith, Karl. 1949. *Meaning in History*. Chicago: University of Chicago Press.

Lyons, John. 1970. *Noam Chomsky*. New York: Viking.

Machina, Mark. 1987. "Choice Under Uncertainty: Problems Solved and Unsolved." *Journal of Economic Perspectives* 1: 121–54.

Malinowski, Bronislaw. 1926. "Anthropology." In *Encyclopedia Britannica*, supplementary volume 1.

Mansbridge, Jane, ed. 1990. *Beyond Self-Interest*. Chicago: University of Chicago Press.

Margolis, Howard. 1982. *Selfishness, Altruism, and Rationality*. Chicago: University of Chicago Press.

Merton, Robert. 1957. *Social Theory and Social Structure*. Glencoe, Ill.: Free Press.

Moser, Paul, ed. 1990. *Rationality in Action: Contemporary Approaches*. Cambridge: Cambridge University Press.

Nordlinger, Eric A. 1981. *On the Autonomy of the Democratic State*. Cambridge: Harvard University Press.

North, Douglass. 1981. *Structure and Change in Economic History*. New York: Norton.

———. 1990. *Institutions, Institutional Change, and Economic Performance*. Cambridge: Cambridge University Press.

Parsons, Talcott. 1964. *The Social System*. New York: Free Press.

Plott, Charles. 1979. "The Application of Laboratory Experimental Methods to Public Choice." In *Collective Decision Making*, ed. Clifford Russell. Baltimore: Johns Hopkins University Press.

Popper, Karl. 1962. *Conjectures and Refutations*. New York: Basic.

Quattrone, George, and Amos Tversky. 1988. "Contrasting Rational and Psychological Analyses of Political Choice." *American Political Science Review* 82: 719–36.

Rabin, Matthew. 1998. "Psychology and Economics." *Journal of Economic Literature* 36: 11–46.

Riker, William, and Peter Ordeshook. 1973. *An Introduction to Positive Political Theory*. Englewood Cliffs, N.J.: Prentice Hall.

Schelling, Thomas. 1960. *The Strategy of Conflict*. Cambridge: Harvard University Press.

Sen, Amartya. 1977. "Rational Fools: A Critique of the Behavioral Foundations of Economic Theory." *Philosophy and Public Affairs* 6: 317–44.

Shapiro, Ian, and Donald Green. 1994. *Pathologies of Rational Choice Theory*. New Haven, Conn.: Yale University Press.

Simon, Herbert. 1957. *Models of Man: Social and Rational*. New York: Wiley.

Soltan, Karol Edward. 1998. "Institutions as Products of Politics." In *Institutions and Social Order*, ed. Karol Edward Soltan, Eric Uslaner, and Virginia Haufler. Ann Arbor: University of Michigan Press.

Tversky, Amos, P. Slovic, and Daniel Kahneman. 1990. "The Causes of Preference Reversal." *American Economic Review* 80: 204–17.

Vico, Giambattista. 1948 [1744]. *The New Science*. Ithaca, N.Y.: Cornell University Press.

Walzer, Michael. 1984. "Liberalism and the Art of Separation." *Political Theory* 12: 315–30.

Contributors

Robert H. Bates is Eaton Professor of the Science of Government at Harvard University and a Faculty Associate of the Center for International Development. His most recent book is *Prosperity and Violence* (W.W. Norton, 2001), and his most recent articles focus on political violence.

Jonathan Bendor is Professor of Political Economy at the Graduate School of Business, Stanford University. His research largely focuses on models of bounded rationality, evolutionary analyses of political institutions, and theories of bureaucracy.

Lee Epstein is the Edward Malinckrodt Distinguished Professor of Political Science and Professor of Law at Washington University in St. Louis. Her publications include *Constitutional Law for a Changing America* and *The Choices Justices Make*.

Dino Falaschetti writes on political economy and corporate governance as an Assistant Professor of Economics at Montana State University and a Robert Wood Johnson Foundation Scholar in Health Policy Research at the University of California at Berkeley.

Avner Greif is the Bowman Family Endowed Professor of Humanities and Sciences, Professor of Economics, and Faculty Fellow at CREDPR, Stanford University. His research concentrates on the theoretical and empirical relationships between institutions and economic, political, and social outcomes.

Russell Hardin is Professor of Politics at New York University and of Political Science at Stanford University. He is the author of *Collective Action* (1982), *Morality Within the Limits of Reason* (1988), *One for All* (1995), *Liberalism, Constitutionalism, and Democracy* (1999), *Trust and Trustworthiness* (2002), and *Indeterminacy and Society* (2003). He has long been a member of the Board of Trustees of the Carnegie Council on Ethics and International Affairs.

Jack Knight is the Sidney W. Souers Professor of Government at Washington University in St. Louis. His publications include *Institutions and Social Conflict, Explaining Social Institutions*, and *The Choices Justices Make*.

Arthur Lupia is Professor in the Department of Political Science and Senior Research Scientist at the Institute for Social Research at the University of Michigan. He uses surveys, models, and experiments to study relations between information and competence in voters, legislators, and the media.

Gary Miller is a professor of political science at Washington University in St. Louis. He is the author of *Managerial Dilemmas* and several experimental papers that attempt to explore the power and limitations of rational choice models in explaining behavior in hierarchies and other institutions.

Irwin L. Morris is associate professor and director of graduate studies in the Department of Government and Politics at the University of Maryland. His most recent book, *Votes, Money, and the Clinton Impeachment* (Westview, 2002) deals with the political economy of legislative policy making and elections. His other research interests include monetary policy making, public opinion and voting, and Southern politics.

Joe Oppenheimer is Professor of Government and Politics at Maryland and director of its Collective Choice Center. His research focuses on the micro assumptions underlying rational choice modeling. Specifically, he is modeling non-self-interested behavior and developing its implications for the attainment of justice and legitimacy in liberal democracies. His publications include such volumes as *Choosing Justice* (University of California Press). He is working on the implications of such models for the design of democratic institutions so as to ensure better outcomes.

Smita Singh is a Research Scholar at the Institute for International Studies at Stanford University.

Karol Edward Soltan teaches in the Department of Government and Politics at the University of Maryland in College Park. His recent publications include *Institutions and Social Order* and *Citizen Competence and Democratic Institutions*.

Piotr Swistak is an associate professor in the Department of Government and Politics and in the Applied Mathematics and Computation Program of the Department of Mathematics at the University of Maryland at College Park. A large part of his current research focuses on understanding how social and political institutions can be derived as necessary elements of robust equilibria.

Barry R. Weingast is a Senior Fellow, Hoover Institution, and the Ward C. Krebs Family Professor, Department of Political Science, Stanford University. He was elected to the American Academy of Arts and Sciences in 1996. His research focuses on the political foundations of markets, economic reforms, and regulation in American, comparative, and historical perspectives.

Index

242   Index